"GO TO SCHOOL,
YOU'RE A LITTLE BLACK BOY"

∽

"GO TO SCHOOL, YOU'RE A LITTLE BLACK BOY"

The Honourable Lincoln M. Alexander:
A Memoir

DUNDURN PRESS
TORONTO

Writer and editor: Herb Shoveller
Copy-editor: Andrea Waters
Design: Jennifer Scott
Printer: Tri-Graphic Printing Limited

Library and Archives Canada Cataloguing in Publication

Alexander, Lincoln M. (Lincoln MacCauley), 1922-
    "Go to school, you're a little black boy" : the honourable Lincoln M. Alexander : a memoir / Lincoln M. Alexander.

ISBN-10: 1-55002-663-1
ISBN-13: 978-1-55002-663-4

    1. Alexander, Lincoln M. (Lincoln MacCauley), 1922-. 2. Black Canadians--Biography. 3. Lieutenant governors--Ontario--Biography. 4. Legislators--Canada--Biography. I. Title.

FC3077.1.A44A3 2006   971.3'04092   C2006-904264-0

    2   3   4   5   10   09   08   07   06

Conseil des Arts
du Canada

Canada Council
for the Arts

Canadä

ONTARIO ARTS COUNCIL
CONSEIL DES ARTS DE L'ONTARIO

We acknowledge the support of the **Canada Council for the Arts** and the **Ontario Arts Council** for our publishing program. We also acknowledge the financial support of the **Government of Canada** through the **Book Publishing Industry Development Program** and **The Association for the Export of Canadian Books**, and the **Government of Ontario** through the **Ontario Book Publishers Tax Credit program**, and the **Ontario Media Development Corporation**.

Care has been taken to trace the ownership of copyright material used in this book. The author and the publisher welcome any information enabling them to rectify any references or credits in subsequent editions.

J. Kirk Howard, President

Printed and bound in Canada.
Printed on recycled paper.

www.dundurn.com

Photos used in this book, unless otherwise noted, are from Lincoln Alexander's personal collection or were borrowed from Marge Millar and Dr. Alan Lane.

Dundurn Press
3 Church Street, Suite 500
Toronto, Ontario, Canada
M5E 1M2

Gazelle Book Services Limited
White Cross Mills
High Town, Lancaster, England
LA1 4XS

Dundurn Press
2250 Military Road
Tonawanda, NY
U.S.A. 14150

"GO TO SCHOOL,
YOU'RE A LITTLE BLACK BOY"

～

TABLE OF CONTENTS

ACKNOWLEDGEMENTS

～

For years, numerous people have prodded and encouraged me to write my autobiography, but I always found it awkward thinking about such a project. Perhaps it was modesty, combined with my suspicion of my own writing and a reluctance to take on such a large project at this time in my life. I know my former law partner, Jack Millar, had planned to write my biography, but his untimely death in 1992 prevented it. Thus it was unlikely this project would ever get done. Yet among those encouraging me was Alastair Summerlee, president of the University of Guelph, of which I am chancellor. What differentiated Alastair from the others is that he would not take no for an answer; finally, in the summer of 2005, he convinced me to move forward with this book. Consequently, I have him and the University of Guelph heading the list of those I must acknowledge and thank for their boundless support in this undertaking.

I must say that, even as we moved through what seemed like an endless series of interviews and voluminous research, I was moderately enthused at best. Perhaps that was from being immersed in so much detail that it was difficult to see beyond. Then, however, as I began to go through the first drafts of the manuscript with Herb Shoveller, who guided me through the writing and research, the proverbial light, as it were, flashed on with a vengeance. I thought, *You know, that's not a bad story*. On top of that, I was able to advocate on issues I have addressed all my life, such as racism. Thus I was energized by the experience of reading my story in print, and what was once complacency regarding the book was transformed dramatically into impatience. Now I had to wait several long months for the book to come out. Nevertheless, while I could have done without the wait, I am thrilled at how revitalizing this experience has been, and I have many others to thank for that.

In the course of writing this book we have conducted about fifty interviews with friends, family, former colleagues, and acquaintances who graciously helped flesh out my recollections of events and, in some cases, triggered some great memories I'd long since dispatched to the dustbin. From the political sphere, there were the likes of former prime minister Brian Mulroney, former MP and cabinet minister Perrin Beatty, former Ontario premier David Peterson, and many others who gave of their time and thoughts. From the business world, assistance was provided by individuals and friends such as Ed and Anne Mirvish, Greg Aziz of National Steel Car, and Richard Peddie of Maple Leaf Sports and Entertainment. From the educational, cultural, and social services fields, Mort Rozanski, former president of the University of Guelph, Catherine Axford of Ontario Heritage Trust, and columnist George Gross, the champion of Variety Village, are among many who stepped forward. Similarly, an endless roster of friends, too many to mention here, provided not only comments but pictures and mementoes as well to help illustrate this story. Marge Millar, my former law partner's widow, was exceptional in helping with memories and materials, while Drs. Alan Lane and Bill Lockington, friends to this day, provided valuable insights and memories from my trip to Africa in 1960.

Beyond directly contributing to this enterprise, there are many to thank simply for their support and encouragement over the years, such as former Ontario premier Bill Davis, former lieutenant-governors Hal Jackman and Hilary Weston, Hilary's husband Galen Weston, and my dear, departed friend Steve Stavro.

Many others pitched in for the roll-up-your-sleeves elements of producing this book. *London Free Press* writer Burt Dowsett and retired *Free Press* copy editor Mike Smith of St. Marys added their expertise. Researcher Peter McKinley of London delivered extensive materials, with support from Maureen Ryan, government documents librarian at University of Western Ontario's Weldon Library. Chief information officer Michael Ridley and archivist Lorne Bruce of the University of Guelph helped us sift through my seemingly infinite archives. The sports information staff at McMaster University helped us sort out my brief and not particularly brilliant university football career. Among the media sources we relied on for this book, none surpass the *Hamilton Spectator* for its generous assistance and access to the newspaper's archives. In particular, Tammie Danciu and Marilyn McGrory of the *Spectator* library guided us expertly through mountains of material, while Howard Elliott, executive editor, ensured we would have unfettered support from the newspaper. That support was invaluable.

Closer to home — and this might seem a little over the top to some — I absolutely must thank the city of Hamilton and all its wonderful people. My decision to move here after the Second World War not only delivered my dear wife, Yvonne, it also provided a community that permitted me to pursue my dreams. As well, my dear friend and long-time neighbour Ines Freitag kept me focused on the project as necessary and shared with me arts and entertainment distractions as required. And my immediate family — son Keith, daughter-in-law Joyce, and granddaughters Erika and Marissa — not only contributed to making my memories fresh, but Joyce and the girls also assisted me in reviewing one of the final drafts of this manuscript on a spring vacation in Jamaica.

No doubt there have been stories and people missed, but in the end I am satisfied and pleased that I have completed what so many people had been asking for — my story. I owe a debt to Hamilton, Ontario, and Canada, which are glorious in enabling people to be themselves, to be free, and to do good things. That's certainly the case with me. I'd like to hope this book can repay that debt somewhat by encouraging others to never give up pursuing the honourable goals that will continue to make this country great.

Lincoln M. Alexander
June 2006

INTRODUCTION

"Being first means you have to do more ... you can't be ordinary."

If we are fortunate, there will be a series of memorable, critical, and invaluable experiences and events in our lives that will positively shape our outlooks, reinforce our beliefs, give us life goals, and guide us through our life journeys. I have been fortunate in that regard, as my experiences left me determined to be as good as I can be, to not be afraid to break ground or be intimidated by that overwhelming responsibility, and to not accept that my colour should inhibit my opportunities.

When my wife, Yvonne, and I travelled to Africa in 1960, the impact of that trip was overpowering, and even today it continues to resonate with me and define who I am. Race, colonialism, poverty, political turmoil, and the simplest of life's goals for so many wonderful cultures were among the boundless issues and experiences that confronted us every day on that adventure. The trip gave me a great sense of pride in who I am as a human being and in my race, and, in so doing, it shaped and refined many of my goals in life.

It was around the time of this trip, not surprisingly, and in the ensuing years that it became clear to me that blacks could and should be national leaders, university professors, professionals of all sorts — part of the intellectual leadership. The idea of politics was never on my radar, as they say, in my university years and in my early law career. Fortuitous exposure to certain friends and colleagues changed that, leading me to become the first black member of Parliament in Canada and, eventually, the first black cabinet minister, albeit in a short-lived Joe Clark government. Cynics might contend such a first was inconsequential in the scheme of things, but I know differently. I know that from my colleagues at the time, from my constituents, and from members of the black community. It demonstrated what we are all capable of accomplishing and also what this country stands for. As well, I want to believe it served as a beacon of hope for the black community.

Fortunately, I had learned early not to fear being ahead of the pack. My determination was fuelled by my recognition from a very early age that education was the path to limitless possibility, and it has been, I think, fitting and well-suited that I was made chancellor of the University of Guelph in 1991. For a record five terms in that esteemed post, I have seen constant reinforcement of my belief in the grandness of education, from bright and enthusiastic students — the future — to committed educators and administrators who deliver that greatest gift.

Belief in that gift was the legacy that my mother, Mae Rose, gave me. The title of this book, the quote "Go to school, you're a little black boy," is hers, and I use it to honour her insight, beauty, and wisdom. Those words, her words, have been at the core of what I have accomplished in this life. She was a mere maid, but her knowledge and foresight transcended her station in life; she knew that accepting defeat was easy, but success was possible, and education was the vehicle to take you there. She was right, and it has.

CHAPTER 1

The Early Years

Three unidentifiable people, shrouded in hoods and mystery, would regularly come walking up the street toward our home in Toronto when I was a child. I didn't know if they were men or women, but they would come up from Queen Street, just below Dundas. They would proceed slowly and eventually come to a stop outside our apartment building on Simcoe Street. After a pause, they would come up the walkway, frightening and unknown to me. They would enter the house in complete silence, without ever exchanging a word between them. My parents never seemed to be around or to notice. And then, slowly, they would start climbing the stairs toward my bedroom as my mind raced, my little heart pounded, and my fears exploded. Then I'd awaken with a start from that persistent dream, and they would be gone.

From time to time when I wake up in the middle of the night, even today at age eighty-four — eight decades later — I still revisit that chilling scene in my sleep, and it leaves me with a sense of fear and uncertainty. In many ways, those three figures have never been gone. I'm sure psychologists would have a field day trying to sort out the symbolism of that dream. I have spent a good amount of time engaged in my own analysis of it. The one constant is that this vision has remained with me throughout my life, and I've wondered if it can be interpreted as an unconscious motivating force, something always lurking deep in my psyche, reminding me that I was under a surveillance of sorts and so I was required to behave a certain way. I had to set and strive for high goals, and all the while I couldn't allow my colour to restrain me or give me excuses for not pursuing excellence. Otherwise, I could expect one of those night visits.

I wonder if that dream is the sort of imagery we all share. Some of us suppress it. Some of us can't shake it. You've got your family, your colleagues, your union, your place of worship, and any number of support systems. But the message, the bottom-line truth, is that deep in our consciousness we all know we are accountable to ourselves, and within us the motivating force — our own versions of the three hooded figures in black, with their gowns swaying as they walk — will be there to remind us of that.

In truth, if that interpretation is accurate, then the messages are really the ones my mother drilled into my head from the earliest age. For it was she, Mae Rose Royale, a maid born in Jamaica, who really imparted to me those core lessons that endure to this day. When I look back at her circumstances, I am filled with wonder at her courage in advocating and encouraging the pursuit of such noble and lofty goals.

While my family was living at 29 Draper Street in Toronto when I was born on January 21, 1922, my first recollections of that iconic dream go back to when we lived on Simcoe Street. My folks later moved to McCall Street in downtown

It's rather worn out, but this is my grandmother on my mother's side. Naturally, the picture is an important family memento.

Toronto and again later to Chatham Avenue in the east end of Toronto.

While I don't recall being overly traumatized by racial issues at the time, they existed in abundance. Indeed, there was no doubt in me from

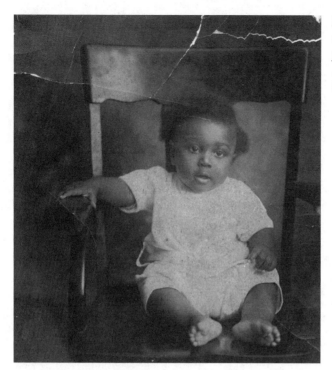

Here I am as a rather handsome young fellow in 1922 at age six months.

my earliest years of what it meant to be a visible minority, even though it would be decades later — in the 1960s and 1970s, in particular — before that term would become common. As a matter of fact, to the best of my memory I can recall only three other black families when I was growing up in the east end: the Abbotts, the Scotts, and the Berrys. When you consider the east end of Toronto of today, it is stunning to realize how much the city has changed in that regard.

Back then in Toronto there were certain places that, if you went there as a black, you had to be foolish. These places may not have been numerous, but you knew to avoid them. Nevertheless, as I would later discover, it was nothing like Harlem in New York, where I would spend almost three of my formative years. The scene in Toronto at that time wasn't violent, though you had to know your place and govern yourself accordingly.

So, not surprisingly, one of my favourite phrases — "black is beautiful" — just wasn't the case in those days. Getting work was difficult, if not impossible. Lots of black people were reduced to doing jobs such as plucking feathers from chickens, being maids, or taking on squalid and demeaning labour. In this respect, for many people, there was not a lot of promise in life. After all, this was the WASP Toronto of the 1920s, where people with my parents' and my colour of skin were barely sufficient in number to constitute a minority group. Blacks at that time made up a sliver-thin portion of the city's population, and racial prejudice abounded. That environment clearly defined for my parents the kind of employment opportunities they could expect. Theirs was not a world filled with workplace options, so they settled on careers that were largely the default jobs for blacks at that time. For my mother, it would mean toiling as a maid or doing similar domestic work. She chose to work as a maid. My father, Lincoln MacCauley Alexander Sr., was a carpenter by trade, but he had little hope of pursuing that career here in Canada. He took work as a railway porter and, from what I gather, thrived at it. In any case, both lines of work were better than not working, and they were not among the squalid options.

As if the odds at the time were not adequately stacked against them, more pressure soon arrived in the shape of the Great Depression, though it turned out that monumental economic catastrophe did not affect them greatly. Fortunately, they were both committed and industrious, and throughout that difficult time both my parents continued to work and provide a home for me and for my brother, Hughie, two years my junior. Despite the economic and racial pressures my parents encountered in those early years, or that I had to face as I grew up, I will say emphatically to the day I die that I am overwhelmingly happy that they chose to leave the West Indies for Canada. My mom was born in Jamaica and my father in St. Vincent and the Grenadines; their paths brought them to Canada, where they met and started to build a life. My mother, whom I remember as strong-willed and determined, came to Canada at the height of the First World War and risked being attacked by German U-boats to get to the North American continent. That experience alone should present a pretty potent illustration of her firm character.

As much as I idolized my mother, as a youngster I also had immense respect for my father, though later events would cause that respect to erode to a significant extent. He had arrived in Canada about the same time as my mother. To a little kid, my six-foot-four father was a source of awe. They called him Big Alex. He cemented that awe in me one time when Hughie and I were playing in the yard in front of our apartment building. Even though we had a balcony on our second-floor apartment, we often came down to the yard to play outside. A disheveled drunk had come wandering up the street, staggering and mumbling and talking to no one in particular. My father told him to move along and leave us alone. To the drunk's later dismay, I'm sure, he chose not to leave us alone, so my father decked him with one punch, and the guy went down like a ton of bricks, out cold. I remember thinking, *Wow, that was my dad. That was my dad coming to the rescue of his two little sons.* It made one heck of an impression on me.

After coming to Canada from St. Vincent, my father had tried his hand on the East Coast, where he had a brother, but he eventually moved to Toronto. As I understand it, he left the East Coast because he didn't approve of some of the things going on there: the folks there were involved in something illicit, such as rum-running or smuggling. So my dad gravitated to one of the few decent industries open to blacks in post-

war Canada — the railway. Working the rails took him away from his wife and family for days on end, but it provided us all with the necessities of life and a modicum of dignity.

In time, I was ready for school, and in Toronto I went first to Earl Grey Public School. I remember when it was time to go to kindergarten that first day another child came by, a nice black boy named Desmond Davis. (Desmond Davis later fathered Carl Davis, who is now an inspector in the equestrian division of the Toronto Police Service.) He was in Grade 2 and, being older, he came to take me to school and guide me across University Avenue. There were not a lot of cars back then, not like today, but there were

Me with my hot tricycle in the late 1920s.

Here I am in my Grade 1 class photo in 1928. I'm front row left.

still enough vehicles rolling along the streets to create some danger. I remember that event as clearly as if it were yesterday — my first day of school.

At the same time, I enjoyed another first: my first puppy love. I can still picture it. We were all in class sitting in a circle and — remember, I was the only black kid in the class — this little girl sort of took a liking to me, and she grabbed me by the hand and we walked around the circle. I forget what game we were playing, but it was typical of those games you play when you are in kindergarten. It's funny the memories you can never shake, no matter how young you were when they happened. And that is one I've never forgotten, because it really struck me, even though I was a young child, that this was such a warm, friendly gesture that this girl offered. Oh, my, I was in love.

Despite such gestures of friendship, dealing with being the different one among my classmates was a constant for me, and it was never easy. Far from it. Throughout my education in Canada, from public school to my secondary and post-secondary studies, I was usually the only black face in my class. Despite that, I can tell you that I never raced home from school and cried. That was unacceptable. What mattered was gaining respect, and with the right kind of support from family, certain teachers,

This was, I believe, my Grade 2 class at Earl Grey Public School. I'm third in the row on the right.

and other children, I was able to get that respect in a variety of ways. I can't fight anymore, of course, but as a kid I would often have to fight, and I'm not ashamed to say that I had my fair share of entanglements. I wish it could have been otherwise, but at the time I had to stick up for myself. That taught me to always walk tall, and with a certain bearing, so people knew I meant business.

In the 1920s and '30s, there were several hundred (although some estimates put it as high as seven thousand) blacks in Toronto, and racism was simply a grim fact of everyday life. You could be confronted with it anywhere from your job, to school, to out on the street. I felt I had to make it clear that I would not accept being called any of those insulting names — nigger, coon, whatever. If those issuing the insults couldn't accept that, I had to resort to duking it out, and I can recall throwing the first punch, commonly known as a sucker punch.

When I started high school in Toronto, I went to Riverdale Collegiate, and, not surprisingly, yet again I was one of only a handful of black students. I was often singled out for name-calling and other insults, and that meant I again had to fight for respect. The results of these altercations were always the same: I'd win because no one else could fight like me. Of course, what's wrong with that picture is the fact

I had to fight at all. From that time to the present, I've been required to take whatever measures were necessary to assert my dignity and my right to respect — from scrapping in the schoolyard to calling out the dean of my law school for a public racial slur. Like it or not, confronting racism is a lifelong enterprise in which I have been engaged both personally and at the organizational level.

When I was young, I started piano lessons, essentially because my dad wanted me to be the next Duke Ellington. I wonder what he would have thought about me meeting Count Basie and the Duke in Harlem and then later on in Toronto. My father loved music and he loved the jazz of those years. I can't recall whether he was disappointed to learn I just didn't have any interest in the piano. I imagine he must have been somewhat let down. It wasn't so much that I wasn't musical. In fact, I can say without boasting that I do have a musical bent, not with an instrument but with my voice. That has been evident from time to time, such as during my 1960 trip to Africa when my fellow travellers and the native Africans couldn't seem to get enough of my singing. But as a youngster, propped at the piano plunking away at boring scales, I'd look out the window and see the other boys playing softball and all kinds of other sports. Sitting in front of the piano was the last place I wanted to be when there was a ball or puck in sight. Some people have the right combination of talent and drive to play the piano, but I didn't. I was fortunate enough to realize that and to give it up. I'd like to be able to play the piano now, but I'd have to practise a lot, and I am not interested in taking the time for that. You have to want it more than I did.

Instead, as youngster, I was very involved in extracurricular activities. I loved sports, to the detriment of piano. I used to run the hundred-yard dash in track, and I also played soccer, hockey, and softball — I even boxed. I loved it all, though I recognized I wasn't all that gifted an athlete. I was tall and skinny with big feet, and as a result my co-ordination may not have been my strongest athletic asset. I was pretty good at sports, but, as a gangly youth, I didn't excel. Nevertheless, even today I have a real love of sport because I think there's great value in challenging yourself. Sport does that. It makes demands of you, and that can't be a bad thing.

I can remember as a child being out on an outdoor rink in Toronto all by myself. I loved to skate, loved to hear the sound of the blades cutting and slashing through the ice. I liked crossing over my feet making turns and hearing the crunch of the ice. I eventually got a very good pair of CCM skates, which greatly enhanced my regular visits to the outdoor ice palaces. I liked to stickhandle the puck, too. Moving in and out with that rubber disc, zigging and zagging at top speed — well, my top speed — was such a thrill, with that brilliant winter air filling my lungs. It's quite likely that the attraction was that being on the ice, with fresh air, speed, and exhilaration, delivered a fantastic sense of freedom.

I also tried lacrosse, but in recent years my greatest sports interest has become basketball, which is natural given my involvement with the Toronto Raptors Foundation, of which I am the chairman.

As kids, we used to walk from Chatham Avenue over to Riverdale Park to bobsled in the winter. We'd carve tracks out of hills and go careering like crazy, defying mortality. During the hot summer days, we would take that daredevil attitude and apply it to the track, where we raced our homemade go-karts. We'd make them out of old crates with roller skates for wheels, and we'd race them on the streets. I also did a lot of cycling when I was a kid. The point is that I was a pretty active youngster, as I think most children were at the time, and I worry that today children are not encouraged to get out and be active.

Me with a bunch of pals in Riverdale Park in 1931. I was nine.

One thing I can't do athletically is swim. I went for lessons once, and the instructors got the brilliant idea of moving the taller people toward the deeper end, which ended up being not such good planning from my standpoint. I went farther, then a bit farther, and then, as I went a bit farther and tried to stand up, I dropped like a stone. I'd reached the separation point between shallow and deep, and I was gone, hopeless, a deadweight. I remember the teacher jumping in to pull me out. As soon as I realized that swimming was life-threatening, it was assured that I would have a real short swimming career. I never did learn how to swim.

Generally, my childhood memories are pretty positive with regards to my family, particularly early on. We always had presents at Christmas, and as a youngster I remember lots of love in our home.

In those formative years, my parents delivered different life lessons and sets of beliefs. My mother was utterly convinced that education was the certain path to a good future and insisted that I work hard at my schooling. I was told, "Go to school, you're a little black boy" so often that I knew when it was coming even before she said it. And I have to say, all her lecturing paid off, because I became a pretty solid student in elementary and secondary school. I was at the top of the class a few times and I was consistently in the top ten with my marks. My strengths during my school years were arithmetic, English, and history, and it was no coincidence they were also my favourite subjects. In time, I also came to be fond of manual training, which was related to machine shop training, woodworking, etc.

Although I wouldn't shy away from a fight to earn respect, one of the central messages my father left me with was the value of getting along with people. It was his nature to behave that way, and the trait was valuable to him in his work as a railway porter. In fact, there were regular visible, financial illustrations of his ability to get along with people. When my dad returned from one of his lengthy railway journeys, he would deposit a huge pile of cash on the table, the product of tips gained from being charming and effective in his work. My father was a porter on the Canadian Pacific Railway in the years when the CPR passenger service meant something. It had history and authority and class.

One story he told me was how he and his fellow porters would often serve members of Parliament or other big shots of the day. When such people took the time to say hello or chat with the porters, to treat them with respect, they received the best services available (and there were a lot of them). One payoff was that the porters would introduce them to the women in the sleeping cars. But if they ignored the porters, their shoes would not be shined, or perhaps they would not be served whisky. Those porters knew how things worked. Thanks to my father's story, I always remember to be friendly when I meet people and to treat them with respect. If I see someone looking my way, I always say, "Hello! How are you?" That breaks the ice; the atmosphere gets warmer and the communication gap shrinks.

In our family, my father was the disciplinarian from a physical standpoint, and there was no doubt about it. He expected us to be on the doorstep at 9:00 p.m., for example; if we were even one second late, he'd dress us down. Hughie and I were afraid of him. He didn't hit us much, though he did now and again. He'd just beat us on the bum with his belt. Not to hurt us, but to let us know that when he said something, he meant it. As a CPR porter, he had a steady run from Toronto to Vancouver — and occasionally Toronto to Montreal — so he would often be gone five or six days at a time. My mom used to say that if we weren't good, she would tell him when he got home. Talk about protracted anxiety! He could still be several days away from getting home, and we were left to imagine our punishment the entire time. He would be coming in from either the Montreal or the Vancouver run and, along with covering the table with his tips, he would bring us a lot of things, ranging from eggs, chickens, and turkeys to Sweet Marie chocolate bars. These were things people would give him or that he would buy along the way if he found good deals. So while it was always exciting to see what he had for us, in the back of our minds we would be concerned about being punished for our youthful indiscretions. We'd be shaking in our boots. Fortunately, my mother many times would not tell my father of our misdeeds.

In the end, my father's strict nature was good because it taught me responsibility and discipline, even though he was a rascal himself. In fact, it was that rascal element in my dad's character that eventually tore our family apart. My parents were religious. They went regularly to the Baptist church on University Avenue in Toronto, and, as is the case with many religious organizations, it became the centre of their social life as well. As a

Hughie and me, ready for the annual Port Dalhousie picnic, the annual gathering of the black community in Ontario and parts of the U.S. My hand is in that position because I was covering a spot on my white slacks so my dad wouldn't see it. I ended up not having socks on and my dad sent me home, which brought on a torrent of tears.

result, I went to Sunday school every Sunday for years. But religious faith alone could not forestall what lay ahead.

My mother was like a lot of women in those days: she often just turned a blind eye to my dad's indiscretions, at least up to a point, and I imagine that her faith helped her manage such emotions. So it wasn't racism or poverty that marred my reasonably happy childhood. It was infidelity — my father's. I had always thought

My brother Hughie all decked out, ready for the annual picnic.

there was a lot of love in the house, and in many senses there was, but in truth things were far from idyllic, at least as far as my parents were concerned.

In some respects, if they were so inclined, railway porters were not unlike salesmen or sailors, with love interests in each of the "ports" they visited. That was my father's weakness. Over the years, he had a series of trysts in the many places the trains stopped. Eventually he was caught after he passed a sexually transmitted disease to my mother. That was unacceptable to my mother, and she was humiliated, so she resolved to leave him immediately. That shows you the kind of inner strength she had, and maybe that's where I got my strength. Imagine, in the mid-1930s, with the effects of the Depression still lingering, having the courage as a woman to strike out on her own.

On the morning my mother left, it was as if all hell were breaking loose in the house. There was a fracas, and I can remember going downstairs to the kitchen where I witnessed a physical battle. My mother was trying to get out the back door, and my dad was blocking her way. I recall screaming, "Daddy, Daddy, don't hit her." During the fight, I was hanging onto his bathrobe belt and I was very frightened. He slapped her and broke her eardrum, a physical exclamation mark that signified the end of their relationship.

One of my dad's weaknesses didn't rub off on me. He was a womanizer. That was a lesson I learned. Never put your wife in the position that my dad put my mom in. He had done a lot of running around and, as I said, she cast a blind eye up to a point — though I have to believe it hurt her deeply. But when he gave her that disease, it was the last straw. She headed to New York, to Harlem, where she had a sister, Iris Knight.

Along with the devastation of her departure, we had to figure out how to carry on. My dad mostly handled the Toronto–Vancouver run, which was a prize among the CPR porters. It produced plenty of extra tip money, so he was reluctant to give it up. But that meant he would be gone from home for several days at a time. As a result, Hughie and I became a problem, me at fifteen and him at thirteen, without a mother. To solve this, first my dad arranged for a niece of his, Isobel Gibson, to come up from Halifax to look after us. Eventually she moved to California, and even today I hear from her from time to time. After she left, fortunately for us a wonderful couple, Sadie and Rupert Downs, cared for us while my dad was away. They were like surrogate parents at a particularly rough time in our lives. They had a son, Ray Downs, who went on to become an internationally renowned jazz pianist. I taught him to play "I Love Coffee, I Love Tea," his first exposure to the key-board, so I guess you could say I helped launch his career.

Sadie and Rupert Downs cared for us until I was able to join my mother in New York in 1936. Hughie stayed behind and, from that point on, we never had a relationship to speak of, which is quite sad to me. My mom was in a difficult financial position at the time and could only afford for one of us to join her. That turned out to be me. Hughie was, quite naturally, jealous over the years and resented my mother's decision, and I made matters worse by ignoring him. In due course, as he grew older, he moved to Boston and we drifted even further apart. He was a hard worker, and when he did get to Boston, where he became a plasterer, the city was in the midst of a building boom. One trait he inherited from my dad was a taste for women, and he ended up going through three wives.

Even though my dad was a porter, the trip to New York was my first train ride. It was fun, but then everybody likes choo-choos. My mom came

My brother Hughie boxing with Ray Downs, the son of Sadie and Rupert Downs, who helped with our care after my mother moved to New York. I had followed her to New York by the time this picture was taken.

up to Toronto and took me back on the train. I remember as we were preparing to depart she bought me a Coke and a *National Geographic* magazine. That was my first Coke, and the *National Geographic* was my first magazine, and I find it interesting that she chose it. There had to have been lots of other choices for a fifteen-year-old, but she opted for *National Geographic*, which I think reflected her determination to make me adhere to my studies and learn.

We lived in the Sugar Hill section of Harlem, and I welcomed the move with open arms, since it put me back together with the person who had such a profound influence in my life, my mother.

Once I arrived in the Big Apple, one of the first things I did was pawn off for $12 those beautiful CCM skates my mother had sent me from New York because, as it turned out, not too many kids in New York were into skating, particularly black kids. My mother must have had a hell of a time finding them in the first place, because even at that time I wore a size 14.

Girlie, my mother's sister. She was a nurse in Jamaica, then later nursed in New York.

The note on this photo postcard says, "to dear Mae Rose from Con," one of my mother's three sisters.

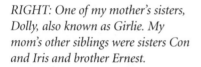

ABOVE: My Uncle Ernest, my mom's brother, in Kingston, Jamaica, in, I believe, the 1920s.

RIGHT: One of my mother's sisters, Dolly, also known as Girlie. My mom's other siblings were sisters Con and Iris and brother Ernest.

I enrolled at DeWitt Clinton high school in the Bronx, and I have to say the school has turned out a roster of impressive grads: playwrights Paddy Chayefsky and Neil Simon, actors Don Adams, Judd Hirsch, Burt Lancaster, and Tracy Morgan, composer Richard Rodgers, jazz musician Fats Waller, comic Robert Klein, and designer Ralph Lauren. In my time, I was about the only member of my gang to go to high school and, given the message about education that had been pounded into my head since I was a young child, the fact those kids didn't go to school was an eye-opener for me. In my mind, going to school was what you did; it was the right thing.

Beyond my studies, being in Harlem at that time turned out to be an incredible learning experience for me, although not all my experiences were positive. I had moved from a city where, as a black, I was the exception rather than the rule to a place where the exact opposite was the case. Black was everywhere, and it was important for me to see that. In all professions, in all walks of life, blacks were fully represented, and that was a stark difference from the limited career opportunities I'd come to expect in Canada. Mind you, much of that advancement was still primarily within the black community, largely insulated or isolated from the wider New York and American mainstream. Regardless, the sight of what all these blacks were accomplishing stiffened my resolve to be more than a porter.

At that time, my mom got me my first part-time job, moving around the clothing carts in the laundry where she worked. Then I got another life lesson. I was doing well and working hard when after two weeks, out of the blue, I was fired. It made no sense. I was devastated because I considered it a significant job and it enabled me to help my mother out financially. It was my first job, and I was a proud son of a gun, and then this guy up and fired me. I asked my mother how that could happen, and she said, "Well, the boss wanted to go to bed with me and I said no." I've never forgotten that. It affected me. It taught me that life wasn't fair. You can work as hard as you can, and then all of a sudden almost on a whim something can come upon you and you're gone, through no fault of your own.

I'll never forget that slimy excuse for a boss. I was getting used to seeing hustlers, con men, pimps, prostitutes, and rounders of all sorts taking advantage of people ... but when it affected me personally, and my mother, I was shocked and hurt. My mother took me aside and explained the facts of life to me with respect to the boss's request. I felt awful for her that she had to put up with things like that. She was a decent, moral woman.

I got my next job setting up pins in a bowling alley in the Bronx. As a relatively new arrival from Canada, I was really discouraged and disillusioned by the blatant racism in the United States. I remember saying to another black pin boy from Georgia how awful it was that in his home state, for instance, blacks couldn't go into restaurants or get work, and at that time blacks were even still being hung from trees in that part of the South. Incredibly, that young guy protested that I was insulting his home state, one of the worst states for racism in the United States of America. The reaction shocked me. It was hard to understand, and it taught me a couple of lessons. One, it's important to be proud of your birthplace, and two, get all the facts before you open your mouth.

Nevertheless, I got the New York experience, which is a very broad one when you are young. Those streets require you to mature very quickly and come to terms with what life is all about. You see how people are forced to live, often in the direst of circumstances. Back then in Harlem, you would regularly see a pimp beat one of his women for not turning over all her money. There were drunks lying on the sidewalks, knife fights, and many other illegal activities going on all over the place. When I hear people describe such settings as jungles, I have to agree. I feel safe in saying Harlem boys and girls of ten and twelve have seen and know more about the hard facts of life and suffering than young boys and girls in Canada in their late teens or even early twenties. That was true in the 1930s, and I am convinced it is the case today. There was no city in Canada to compare with Harlem before the Second World War. It was gruelling and grinding, it eroded your humanity, and it consumed your dignity. From that sense of personal emptiness, you begin to develop admiration for people who fight their way through that and have learned to hold their heads high.

Harlem, notwithstanding certain good points, faced a lot of poverty, crime, and despair, and there was little opportunity for the majority of black people to crawl out of that.

On top of it all, nobody — and by that I mean civic, social, and government people, those who could do something about it — gave a damn. It was debilitating. Life for black youth was bleak, and of course they didn't hang around on the streets out of choice. They were there because there was nothing else to do. And I will tell you that there were a lot of brilliant people on those streets. Given the opportunity, they would have been leaders in business, in politics, in government. That's proven by the fact that some, somehow, escaped the horrors of Harlem by becoming lawyers, judges, community leaders, politicians, professors, doctors, business leaders, and sports superstars.

They got out because of their own strong character, their determination, and their will, which made them able to sacrifice and not fall prey to the easy ways of life — crime or welfare. Seeing that was a very important lesson for me, and it reinforced much of the direction and encouragement I was getting from my mother.

My mother, Mae Rose, photographed around the time she left for New York. As I have pointed out, and as is obvious, she was a beautiful woman. The note says, "With much love to Linny, Mom."

My mother was a decent woman who always insisted on living a decent life. We lived in the relatively better part of Harlem, and I ended up being a regular, good student at DeWitt Clinton. Mae Rose had a lot of influence on me, and it was always clear her expectations of me were high. In turn, I had a great deal of love and respect for her and I realized how deeply it would hurt her if I let her down. Because of her I have always set my sights high. The fact that I was one of the few people from my gang attending school alone helped minimize my time on the streets. For as long as I can remember, I always wanted to be something, somebody.

After I went to New York, I really didn't go to church much, although I visited the church of Father Devine, the black American religious leader. Born George Baker in 1875 near Savannah, Georgia, he began preaching in the South in around 1900, and in around 1915 he moved to New York. There he founded his Peace Mission Movement and adopted the name Father Devine. This cult figure was a saint to the people of Harlem, and it was there I realized how religious many black people are. In retrospect, at the same time I discovered how vulnerable some people can be to persuasive talkers and how people can be consumed by cults.

The grim experiences I encountered in Harlem, fortunately, are not all that I remember. There are good memories. My first sexual encounter took place in Harlem, in the rumble seat of a car. It was a passing moment of youthful exuberance. These things happen. No matter how you cut it, the Harlem years are a part of my roots and have helped define who I am. I've gone back many times, including on my honeymoon. When I went back I would often see some of the gang I knew as a boy, still hanging around the same corners or sitting on their front stoops. When they recognized me, they greeted me with the same foul language and love they expressed back then.

In New York, I started a habit that would eat away at me for half a century and threatened my life at one point. I started smoking cigarettes. Back then, we used to "dinch," which means you choke off the lit end to save the rest for later. I kept my smoking from my mom, but I used to put the cigarette butt in my pocket, where she would find it when she was doing laundry. In some respects, I guess I wasn't too bright as a young fellow.

I played around a bit with reefers, or marijuana. The stuff was all over the place down there, and it was hard to avoid, so I tried it a couple times, but it just didn't work for me. Unlike Bill Clinton, I did inhale. I also started to drink while in Harlem. I didn't drink beer down there. Instead, the beverage of choice was Sneaky Pete wine, which is American slang for fortified cheap wine. There's a song about it, "Sneaky Pete" by Sonny Fisher. It's a classic:

> Well the old hound dog come a-snoopin' around my door
> Took a drink of Sneaky Pete, ain't seen that hound no more
> Like the little white rat he drunk on Sneaky Pete
> Told the big tom cat don't you even bat your eyes at me
> Well down in the hen house I thought I heard the chicken sneeze
> It was a big red rooster he was drunk on Sneaky Pete
> I wants a big fat woman, bottle of Sneaky Pete
> Now I'm a tellin' you boys that stuff just can't be beat

When I came back to Canada I had to learn how to drink beer because it was far more common. I soon discovered that I liked beer. It was easy to get and cheap. I can remember it being ten cents a glass.

Meanwhile, through the dirty thirties the world had slowly begun to turn its attention to Europe, where tensions were growing astronomically in the wake of the rise to power of the Nazis in Germany. Their racist policies and expansionist belligerence perhaps didn't resonate immediately with this seventeen-year-old, Harlem-living Canadian kid, but in time the dangers hit home. My mother grasped the threat, and as the Second World War was breaking out, she sent me home to Canada. I'm not sure how I would have turned out if I had stayed in Harlem. There were many negative influences and not a lot of hope for young blacks. In that regard, you could argue that the war saved me. We were in New York, but Canadians were being asked to register for the draft, so she told me I'd better get back to Canada and sign up.

Soon after I came back I began living with my father. None of the women my father knew were aware he had a son my age. He had never talked about me, and he told me not to mention I was his son (though

This picture was taken in Toronto, shortly after I returned from New York. I am nineteen years old.

we were known as Big Alex and Little Alex). One night I was going home with my girlfriend at the time, my first serious one, Eulie Abbott. Eulie was beautiful but possessive. Girls would surround me, because I was a pretty handsome dude, and she would yell, "Leave him alone, he's mine." That didn't sit too well with me because I don't like possessive women, so that relationship was doomed.

Anyway, as Eulie and I were going along Queen Street and looking up Spadina, I could see and hear a big fracas outside the beer parlour on Spadina where all the porters used to hang out. The ladies of the night used to hang around as well, so they could get to the porters (who had a pot full of money after returning from their runs) before they got home. I was told the next day that my father had been beaten up by a young guy named Wilfred Hayes in that fracas. Now, I remembered Wilfred as one big, tough dude and a boxer of some repute. I was fuming the next morning when I got up, so I grabbed my switch-blade, a souvenir from my recent term in Harlem, and went looking for Wilfred. There was nothing out of the ordinary about carrying a switchblade on the streets of Harlem. Most men and many women carried them there. But that wasn't the case in Toronto. I made my way over to Wilfred's apartment, near University Avenue, north of Queen Street. When he came down stairs and opened the

The dapper Alexander brothers, Linc and Hughie, shortly after my return to Toronto from New York.

door, he was surprised to see me. He hadn't seen me in the three years I'd been away. The moment he opened the door I flipped open the knife. "Wilfred," I said as calmly as I could, because I was angry, "I hear you had a fight with my father, and I'm telling you I'm here to cut your goddamn throat from ear to ear."

I was a mean son of a bitch and, having just gotten back from Harlem, I was very schooled in the facts of life on the streets, even though I wasn't a street regular. His eyes were wild with fear at the sight of the knife, and as he backed slowly and cautiously up those old wooden stairs, he was mumbling and stuttering. He started to cop a plea, apologizing and try-ing to justify how and why he would beat up an old man.

I said, "I'm sorry, Wilfred, I'm still going to cut your goddamn throat."

Eventually, he persuaded me to let him tell his side of the story, but that blade stayed a couple of inches from his neck. He was a boxer and a good one; that's why I had a knife in my hand. I let him tell his story and try to justify why he beat up my dad.

He said my father had started playing around with the girl he was going with, who was beautiful and shapely, and he was very jealous of my dad and worried about the embarrassment he would face if he lost her to an older man. When Wilfred was done I said I guessed he had some justification to beat my father up. In a way I was relieved, too, because using that knife was nothing I fancied. But I added, "Let me tell you here and now, if I ever see or hear of you molesting my father again, I'm going to cut your throat, I'm going to kill you, you son of a bitch." Then I backed carefully and slowly down the stairs and made my way along University Avenue. As I was walking away, I kept my knife at the ready and kept looking back over my shoulder to see if he was following. He didn't, and he never bothered my father again.

Later, I stepped into the bar where the fracas had happened and gave everyone there the same message: "Don't you ever touch my father, any of you sons of bitches, or I'll come after you with my switchblade too, you bastards." It hurt me deeply, a young man beating up an old man.

Another time — a non-confrontational one — my dad was coming off work and I went down to the station to meet him. This was in around 1940, not long after I'd returned from Harlem. Quite proudly, I think, my dad introduced me to his boss, A.B. Smith. Smith, trying to be positive and encouraging, said that I was a big and strong and would make a good porter one day. Now, I wasn't trying to be disrespectful, only truthful, but I replied that I would never carry anyone else's bags but my own. "You have the wrong man," I said. "I intend to go to school and see what happens."

Between returning from Harlem and preparing for war, I met Yvonne Harrison. I remember seeing her for the first time at a social event in 1940 in Toronto and saying, "Who the hell is that?" She was considered one of the "untouchables" — not necessarily aloof, but very shy and elegant. I

Here I am, the future Duke Ellington, tapping out a tune.

was just back from New York, bold and sharp looking. I said to myself, "That one is for me."

I was bowled over by her beauty, and I decided right then I would marry her. How brash is that? It would take time and effort, but I was prepared to make the necessary sacrifices to win her over. On returning from New York, I had taken some machine-shop training in Toronto and subsequently received assistance from Frank Barber of F.F. Barber and Sons Ltd. of Toronto. Barber had connections, and through his colleagues he was able to get me job offers in Hamilton or Ottawa. I chose a job in Hamilton, and I went to work as a machine operator with Otis Fenson, making the 40-mm Bofor anti-aircraft guns. I wanted a job in Hamilton, Yvonne's hometown, so I could be in a better position to woo her.

CHAPTER 2

The War Years

By 1942, I was ready to challenge the system. I stepped up. None of the three services at the time — army, navy, and air force — were interested in having blacks. The navy was the worst of the three. I wasn't keen to join the army; I didn't like their uniforms. So I opted for the air force. Besides, I thought I looked best in their uniform. Because of my poor eyesight, there was never a chance that I would go overseas, but nevertheless, in the air force I ultimately rose to the rank of corporal. At the start of my service I was a wireless operator ground, and my assignments involved training stints in Guelph, Ontario, and Lachine, Quebec.

From Lachine, after training as a wireless operator, I was shipped out to Number Seven Air Observer School in Portage la Prairie, Manitoba, where I flew on training missions. I worked in communications, flying in Anson aircraft with young men from the Commonwealth who would eventually become navigators. In total I spent about three years in the air force, with the majority of the time in Portage la Prairie. My pals and I had some good times out west, and we used to meet up with some very nice country girls in Winnipeg. I was a slick old boy.

One of the most interesting race-related experiences I've encountered took place during the war, and I wouldn't characterize it as negative. When I was in Portage la Prairie, there was this guy who just kept staring at me day after day. For the first while I didn't bother with it. But after a time, it became irritating, so I asked him what the hell he was

My wireless certificate, 1943.

looking at. And that poor country bumpkin replied that I was the first black person he'd ever seen. I was upset that I'd been angry with him — he was obviously naive and inexperienced — and I simply told him I was the same as anybody else. But do you see how much things have changed? Actually, it's amazing that even today there are people in Canada who have never seen a black person, except on TV.

One of the great rewards of my wartime service was in making new friends. After I joined the air force, my first stage of training in wireless was in Hamilton, and it was there that I forged another set of lifelong friendships. There were four of us — Charlie Chartrand, Gordon Bull, Walter Holtz, and I — and we spent the better part of our service time together. Our friendship started in the fall of 1942 at Westdale high school, where the air force was holding its initial wireless training course. After we graduated from the course in Hamilton, they shipped us out to Number One Wireless School in Lachine, where our talents were supposedly refined and we were groomed for service. It was after

Here I am with my fellow wireless operators ground (WOGs) based in Portage la Prairie during the Second World War.

completing that course that we were shipped out to Portage la Prairie, which was run by the British Commonwealth Air Training Program. Some pilots were trained there, but it was mostly for navigators and bombardiers. We left Portage la Prairie for Vancouver in the spring of 1945, when it was clear victory was imminent in Europe, but the battle was still raging in the Pacific.

Whether in Hamilton, Portage la Prairie, or Vancouver, we had some fun times. The people in Portage la Prairie were great with the air force personnel. We would regularly be invited out to their homes for Sunday dinner, which was a real treat after being so long away from home. In Hamilton, the four of us would go out on the town together and we were lucky in that regard. Holtz was a sewing machine salesman — Singer, I think — and he still had access to a car and gasoline. One of the places we used to like to go was The Brant Inn in Burlington, where they used to bring in some of the top big bands of the time. Ironically, it was a place that later on refused admittance to blacks. When we were in Portage la Prairie, one of the greatest events of my wartime experiences — if not the greatest — occurred when the jazz great Lionel Hampton came for a concert.

The four of us just kind of clicked and, though we didn't get together often after the war, the friendships forged during that time would last a lifetime. I'm still in touch with Charlie, who these days keeps a file on

Here I am with two air force colleagues, Walter Holtz (centre) and Jerry Comartin of Windsor.

my various exploits. One time he called to tell me he'd seen a picture of me on Wolfe Island, off Kingston in Lake Ontario. His wife was from the island — in fact, she is buried there — so they would go back often. He had come across this photo of me, as lieutenant-governor of Ontario, planting a tree. Every time he went to Wolfe Island after that, he took a picture of that tree and sent it to me.

Charlie often visited Ottawa when I was an MP, but I always had something going on. One time, we were set to meet for dinner and the House ended up in a debate over Prime Minister Pierre Trudeau's plans for an indoor swimming pool at his official residence, 24 Sussex Drive. I couldn't miss that session, so I couldn't see Charlie.

I also had some negative experiences in the air force. Toward the end of the war I was posted to the West Coast at Western Air Command. One time in Vancouver about six of us headed out for a night on the town. We went into one bar and ordered a round of beer, and the bartender scanned the bunch of us and then locked eyes with me. He paused, then said he would serve the entire group except me, even though all of us, including me, were in uniform. I exploded. I said to the bigot that if I wasn't going to

I can't remember the name of my mate here, but the note says, "Here is one of the aircraft we fly in. Ain't I a long rascal (ha-ha)." This was among the pictures I sent to Yvonne.

be able to have a beer, no one else would be able to either, and with that I swept all the beer off the bar onto the floor with my forearm. I leaned my six-foot-three-inch frame over the bar, grabbed the beer taps, and dared the bartender to try serving someone else. The incident had me fuming, so my pals and I left. It turned out several other servicemen, including some Americans, joined us and we did a pretty thorough tour of several more bars downtown, all without incident.

The next day, I reported the bartender's refusal to my commanding officer. I told my flight lieutenant it was his duty to stick up for his men. If I was fighting for my country, then the least the air force could do was set things right. There I was, defending the rights of the likes of that bartender, and he didn't have the decency to serve me. What kind of thinking is that? I also told him that if the air force couldn't represent my interests, it could very well release me from duty. From a military standpoint, perhaps my demands seemed impertinent, but I knew it was also the morally right course of action. I was obliged to speak out; he was obliged to act. But in the end, the air force did nothing. Within a couple of months, I had received my honourable discharge, though it turns out the paperwork had been completed some weeks earlier and was languishing on someone's desk somewhere.

I have a special bond with the people who serve in the Canadian Forces and for those I served with during the war. It troubles me deeply to hear the debates that arise annually over whether Remembrance Day is still relevant, or to hear people disparage what our soldiers have done for us. It's incredibly naive, and I think the irony is astounding — using the right of free speech that these people fought and died for to criticize the same people who defend us and strive to bring peace to the world. We live in a country rich in freedom and democracy, and it is important that we pause annually to recognize those people who have sacrificed so that we can enjoy such privileges.

Many times throughout my career I have had the opportunity to salute our armed forces. One of those came in 2001 while marking Remembrance Day as chancellor of the University of Guelph at the school's beautiful War Memorial Hall. It was just two months after the devastating terrorist attacks in the United States on September 11, 2001. "Together, we will battle against narrow perspectives, ignorance, and racism," I said in my address. "Despite history's searing lessons, our world is still torn by strife and anguish. September's tragic and horrific attacks in New York City have again brought the shadow of war to our doorsteps. Out of the horror of war can come peace, and it is for peace that we must strive. We shall not forget."

I noted the "terrible toll of suffering and sacrifice" that two world wars had exacted, and said that veterans must not be forgotten. "Their blood and tears were the awful price for the peace, comfort, and democracy we enjoy. The bullets that scarred the Earth, that churned fields into muddy graves and hammered cities into rubble tombs, also forever scarred our collective soul." I called the campus hall and its chapel "a lasting memorial to the generations of Guelph students, faculty, and staff who perished in the First and Second World Wars. They are also memorials to all Canadians caught up in these wars and the many conflicts since."

During my tenure as lieutenant-governor, I attended Toronto's old city hall for Remembrance Day services, and at those times I reflected on my days as a corporal in the Royal Canadian Air Force during the Second World War, remembering my comrades and those who had paid the ultimate price. I knew many who didn't make it back. "Whether it's one, or 101, that's not the point," I told the *Toronto Star*. "The fact is they

This was taken at a reunion of my air force colleagues in Hamilton. Good friend Charlie Chartrand is on my right.

went to serve, they went to do their best in order to try to preserve democracy and freedom, so that I, and so that you, could be free to worship, free to think, free to move. We should never forget. The torch of the past should be held high."

On VE-Day, I was in Vancouver. I had served 2 years and 302 days in the air force, and that time was certainly well spent. The air force experience taught me the value of self-respect, discipline, and confidence, and those are elements that have served me well throughout my life. They apply to all areas, whether the air force, the law, or politics.

After the war, those who were discharged were given grants to be used for housing or education. For me, that was a fairly easy decision, given the message my mother had been pounding into my head since I was a young child. As soon as I received my honourable discharge from the air force, I headed straight back to Hamilton and Yvonne. Aside from pursuing Yvonne, my main priority was to complete the courses I needed to go to university. I was going to go back to school, this little black boy.

CHAPTER 3

~

The Call of Higher Learning

After I settled into my university studies, I arranged for my mother to return to Canada from New York. She was quite a classy person, and one of the best examples of that is the fact that I can't recall her ever putting down or insulting my father, despite the fact he had cheated on her in the worst way and was the cause of the disintegration of their marriage. I had experienced the impact of his indiscretion, too. I watched the pain and suffering and indignities my mother faced. I ended up having almost no connection to my kid brother. I swore that I would never let such a thing happen in my marriage. I could see how it could destroy a family.

There was a good deal of pain still ahead. My mom started suffering pre-senile dementia shortly after coming to Hamilton, and she slowly began losing track of everything, including the people around her. Once another patient in the hospital came to me and said, "Do you really want to know what your mother looks like?" She lifted the covers to reveal my mother was now barely skin and bones. It was shocking to see her wasting away and covered in bruises and bedsores. It was with so much optimism that my mom and I were originally reunited in Hamilton, but unfortunately there was little joy to share after her return.

On one occasion, I went to see her and she screamed at me, "Get away from me. You are not getting into my bed tonight. Get away from me. Get away." I was shocked and for a moment couldn't figure out what was going on. She had never talked to me like that. Then I realized she had confused me with my dad. The incident made me realize the depth her illness and her suffering and the hurt that she had endured and held inside all those years.

In time, the hospital contacted me to tell me she had died, and I was deeply hurt, but not surprised, at the news. I was relieved that her suffering had been eased. My mother died in the Hamilton Psychiatric Hospital on my twenty-sixth birthday, January 21, 1948. She was not yet forty-nine years old.

When I look back now and see what she had to go through, cour-

My brother Hughie, along with my mother and Hughie's first wife, Lil Allen. Hughie was married three times.

ageously leaving her marriage and setting out on her own, it amazes me. She's been my source of strength, of confidence. In a 1988 research paper by Edsel Shreve and Darren Jack at the University of Western Ontario, when I was lieutenant-governor, I described my mother this way: "She was the one that encouraged me to go to school. She was the one that indicated to me that being black you had to excel and reach for excellence at all times; you had to be two or three times as good. I've never forgotten that trait, especially with respect to school. I accepted what she said and as a result of that I graduated from McMaster, I became a lawyer and all of that has helped me to reach this position. To try my best to play a role in the community in several ways … but basically it has been my mother who put the seed in my mind about education."

I paid a visit to my mother's gravesite shortly after she passed away. We were very close.

My dad's later years were equally grim. For the longest time, he remained bitter over the breakup of our family, actually blaming my mother for what he called "the Alexander family troubles." While I was prepared to fight for him — as in the time I went after Wilfred the boxer with a switch-blade — I can't say my father and I were very close. He and I got on as well as could be expect-ed, given the circum-stances, and I know he was proud of me when I was in the air force. That source of pride was twofold — first, that I was in such a highly respected uniform, and second, that I advanced through the ranks to become a corporal. In my service of Queen and country, as far as he was concerned, I had done the Alexander name proud.

His pride in the Alexander name was bolstered again when I head-ed off to McMaster, and when I graduated, he attended my convocation. He appreciated how rare it was for a young black man at that time to achieve a university education. Regardless of our difficulties in the past, I felt we had begun to make strides in rebuilding our relationship. Then, as happened with my mother, he didn't stick around.

He had finally cut through his walls of denial and admitted he was to blame for his marriage ending. I think the realization of this, the coming to grips with that truth, was just too much for him to bear. He had kept a lot of his own suffering inside over the years after my mom's departure, and it had left him mentally unstable. When he went to her funeral and realized she was dead — that was when, finally, like a slap in the face, he came to terms with his guilt. After that, he could never overcome it. In despair, he took his own life. He hanged himself with his belt in the old asylum at 999 Queen Street West in Toronto a week before Christmas 1951. He was fifty-nine years old.

Truth be told, I always realized in the back of my mind that suicide was a possibility for him. Once, I came home when he wasn't expecting me and as I came up the stairs I saw him standing in front of the bathroom mirror with a razor blade in one hand and his penis in the other. I screamed, "Dad, Dad, stop!" He was holding the blade to his penis, I assumed, because that was the thing that got him into trouble in the first place. I was afraid of him after that because I was never sure he wouldn't use the blade on me.

Another time, as I was returning from classes at Osgoode Hall law school, there were a lot of people and police milling about outside our apartment. My father had tried to gas himself, but someone had discovered him before it was too late. One thing that really upset me that day was

A rare picture of me with my dad, Big Alex. As usual, we were dressed to the nines.

the doctor who was on the scene. He refused to treat my dad until I paid him five dollars, which was not easy for us to come up with at the time.

So my dad had tried several times to take his life before he was finally successful and hung himself with a belt. I recall going to identify his body, and there was a deep black cut and bruise across his throat. It was chilling.

The fact both my parents died so young was troubling for me for some time because I worried I would die young, too. But I spent about thirty years on this Earth with them and, fortunately, I have lots of good memories.

I eventually learned I had a half-brother, Ridley "Bunny" Wright, born to my mother before she married my dad. He was about two years older than me. In our early years, we had little contact. My mother told me the barest details about the situation. She never talked about the circumstances of Ridley's birth. Ridley stayed with an aunt in Toronto because my dad refused to accept him and would never let him live under our roof. My mother brought Ridley to New York, and he was working and living with her when I joined her there. He moved out shortly after I arrived. I used to get very angry and frustrated with him. What upset me most is that he would come home with his paycheque and brag about all the girls and money he had, and then he'd give me a measly ten cents.

He came back to Toronto in due course, married, and adopted a son, Larry. I went to his house for dinner a few times. I had better contact with my kid brother, Hughie — although it was a distant relationship with little warmth. I used to envy the families who could have everyone together for Christmas and Easter, while mine was scattered here, there, and everywhere. That used to really bother me. It was all a hell of a mess. But I came out of it.

Among some of my long-standing friends in this life would be Alfonso Allen and his wife, Ona. This friendship dates to my early days in Hamilton. Along with Alfonso and Ona I socialized with Alfonso's brother Cleve and Enid Allen and Ray and Vivienne Lewis. One of the first places I lived when I first moved to Hamilton after the war was with Alfonso's mother, Rachel, and her husband, John C. Holland, the dynamic preacher at Stewart Memorial Church.

This was a fortuitous connection for me because, along with providing for a lifelong friendship, it also helped establish a good social and spiritual network, and it put me back in touch with Yvonne, who was involved with the church.

Ona was originally from the community of North Buxton, near Chatham in southwestern Ontario. The village is an important location and symbol for the black community in much of Canada because it was for many blacks the last stop on the Underground Railroad and a haven for fugitives of pre-Civil War slavery in the U.S. In fact, as chairman of the Ontario Heritage Trust, I will be visiting the community in the summer of 2006 to commemorate the existence of Uncle Tom's cabin.

Through the 1950s and my early career in law, I was active in the church and it gave me the opportunity to sing in the choir and participate in other singing activities organized through the church. Eventually that singing and church activity started to ease as my political career began to take off, but the friendships endured, as did my support for the church.

In the meantime, I was able to move ahead with my own life, personally and professionally. When I returned to Hamilton, I enrolled at Central Collegiate to finish high school. Many of us had been away from school for a long time, thanks to the war. We were placed in the "rehab" school on the third floor to top up our education. It was there, quite fortuitously, I met John Millar (whom I affectionately called Jack, or Jackie), who would turn out to be the most incredible and supportive friend for life and, in time, a partner in law. Along with Jack, I became good friends with Gary Lautens, a fellow student at the time who went on to become a popular columnist for the *Toronto Star*.

Central Collegiate was a classic school in the city centre, which might explain why it attracted a lot of war veterans like me. While I intended to go to university, it was not automatic that I would get in. Fortunately, I was successful in my classes, and in 1946 I was off to post-secondary education. McMaster in the city's west end was my university of choice, as well as Jack's, and my veteran's allowance made it possible for me to attend.

McMaster University in 1946 was another scholastic institution then experiencing the effects of returning veterans. Most were extremely conscientious and, because of their recent war experience, they were more attuned than many regular students to political and world events,

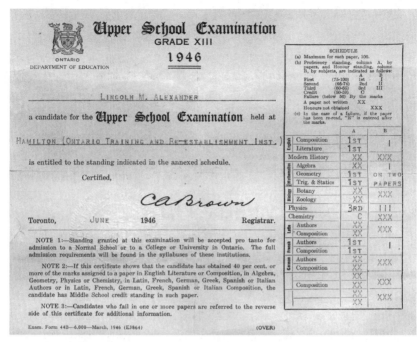

My high school upgrading marks report, June 1946.

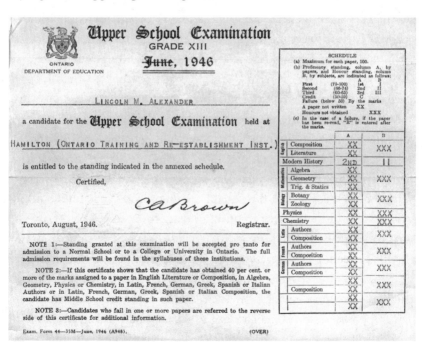

My high school upgrading marks report, August 1946.

which made for a vibrant intellectual atmosphere. Along with classroom sessions, there were organizations such as the politics club, which focused on issues that were important to the post-war world. It was a fascinating environment to immerse myself in.

Jack and I both studied history and political economics, which provided us with a perspective on post-war problems that was useful in our later careers. Frankly, I ended up taking political economics because I thought it would be easy. Both of us graduated in 1949, and the McMaster Marmor yearbook noted Jack had entered McMaster "with the intention of future study in the field of law," so it wasn't surprising when he enrolled at Osgoode Hall that same year.

At Mac, I ended up on the university football team. Now, a cynic might say I was recruited because, with my height and size, I could be a potent receiver, tight end, or even a lineman. Wrong on all counts. In football, I've always been enamoured with running backs, so at Mac I was a spinning fullback. It's a great position, and I imagined I could make great things happen lugging the ball for the burgundy crew. There was just one minor problem. Well, actually, major. You see, I hated taking a hit — which, in a great understatement, is a serious drawback for a fullback. Not only was I averse to getting drilled, it turned out my running style ensured I would be nailed harder and more often than other ball carriers.

The venerable Fred "Smut" Veale was our coach. He would harp at me over and over in practices and during games that when I was running I had to stay low to the ground and keep my head down. But I kept running upright, straight up and down, almost standing up, and by doing that, and being so tall, I used to get pounded. He'd say, "Get low, get low," but I never could make the adjustment. Not surprisingly, it was hard to miss this six-foot-three giant coming through the line standing straight up. And Smut was right. By staying low you are better able to keep your balance when you get hit because you have a lower centre of gravity. Instead, I was like a tackling dummy, emphasis on the dummy.

I think if I were playing today, with the game having changed as much as it has, I would be a wide receiver or tight end. Maybe tight end in particular, because I also weighed close to 250 pounds back then. Looking back, I imagine I would have preferred a receiver position, since you wouldn't have as much contact, but back then, the whole game was run,

run, run. Then I got married and decided I couldn't play anymore, so I told the coach my wife wanted me to study and that was part of the truth. But it was the fear of contact that actually prompted that decision. When you play competitive sports, you have to have a killer instinct, and I didn't have that. You can't be afraid of hitting hard, and I was afraid to get hurt.

The year I played was 1947, and our team went without a win, 0–1 in exhibition play and 0–6–0 in the regular season, finishing fourth. Under Smut, McMaster had won the Shaw Cup (Canadian Interuniversity Football Rugby Union), symbolic of the Intermediate Western Group championship, in both 1933 and 1934. Then he returned in 1946 and 1947. But his overall record was 7–18–1, and I'm sure my upright running style was no help in avoiding those numbers.

During my Mac days, dean of men Les Prince was remarkable to a bunch of us students. He took us under his wing and had a huge role in making our university days special and memorable. In my case, he did me a great favour during my less-than-distinguished experiment with football. Somehow, after scouring stores and other sources, he turned up a pair of extra-large football shoes for me. These were almost impossible to find, and he went the extra mile; I only wish I could have filled them in a way that would have better rewarded his kindness. Oh, well, at least he knew I tried. It wasn't the only time Les helped me out with my water-ski feet. Early on, even before the football shoe hunt, he had encouraged me to get active in general athletics at Mac. I tried to beg off and visited him in his office to confess that it was impossible to find sneakers, so I would have to pass. But he said, "Look, young man, when it's warm outside you can go barefoot, and then when it's cold and we are indoors you can wear socks. You can find socks, can't you? The physical activity is important for you, and it's good for making friends." It was sage advice that I took, and, as usual, he was right.

After I graduated from McMaster, I was intent on joining the white-collar workforce at Stelco in Hamilton. But that was 1949 and I again came face-to-face with racism. During summers while at university, I had worked in the open hearth at Stelco. Along with dozens of other Mac grads like me, I believed I had an advantage as a war veteran and a university graduate, and I had experience at the plant, so I applied for a job at Stelco. University graduates at that time were a relatively rare and valuable commodity. Stelco was falling all over itself to hire my fellow grads. The company was also willing to give me a job but, unlike the other grads, I was offered a position in the plant, back in the open hearth. I had applied for sales. I wanted what everybody else with a B.A. was getting. Everyone from my university assisted me, and even the city's mayor tried to help me to change the minds of Stelco's management, but to no avail.

The clear and unacceptable implication was that the company felt having a black in sales would harm its image. There was no room for a black among the white-collar types, university education or not. I suppose it would have been easy to take the factory job and keep my mouth shut, but my belief in education and what it could offer held firm. Largely as a result of this experience, I decided to become a lawyer and be with my friend Jack Millar.

Meanwhile, my life was changing in another important way, and so much for the better. Events were coming together that would have a profound, wonderful effect on me. These events came together through Yvonne. When I was young, I used to drink a lot. In the air force, for example, I figured I was immortal. I did everything a red-blooded young Canadian man would do — not all of it good, and a fair bit of it with the potential for causing trouble. I spent a lot of time on the dark side, smoking, drinking, and partying. It might not have seemed like the dark side at the time, but once you emerge into the light and look back, there were some things I'm not proud of. So, honestly, if I hadn't married Yvonne, I don't know what I would have become.

I have been fortunate to have two strong, intelligent, insightful women in my life: Yvonne and my mother. From the first moment we were together, Yvonne "Tody" Harrison became the most influential force in my life. Yvonne was the daughter of Robert Harrison and Edythe Harrison (née Lewis). Her mother and father were born in Canada, and her father was part Native Canadian. Yvonne's father, Robert, was a railway porter and, so the story goes, whenever he returned to town, Yvonne, his sweet little girl, would go down to the station to meet him. On one of these occasions, apparently, he coined for her the affectionate name "my little toad." Pretty soon he and Yvonne's sisters had spun that name into Tody, and it stuck for life. Yvonne was not fond of her nickname, but it was certainly used in fondness by others.

Yvonne and her three older sisters were fourth-generation Hamilton blacks, descended from American slaves who escaped to Canada through the Underground Railroad. The Harrisons were part of a small black community of about five hundred, most of whom worked as bellhops at the posh Royal Connaught Hotel or as janitors and domestics. Yvonne's father, as I've noted, was a railway porter, like my dad. Because he was half Native Canadian, he had straight black hair, and Yvonne had certain aboriginal features as well. She, too, faced discrimination throughout her life, particularly when she was younger. She graduated in secretarial training from high school but found it impossible to get work related to her education. She always handled such things with a quiet dignity that I admired and that, I think, in many ways defined her as a person.

The war had intervened after our initial meeting in 1940, and I left to join the air force. While I was away during the war, even though the other guys and I were fooling around with a lot of women, Yvonne had my heart. I always had Yvonne in the back of my mind. I wrote to her regularly, but she didn't write much, although she saved all my letters. When I came back, I made a beeline for Hamilton and we resumed our friendship. She was five years older than I, and she didn't want to go out with me because she thought people would laugh at her for robbing the cradle. But I knew she loved me.

I wouldn't be here, or anywhere else for that matter, without Yvonne. I had never met such a beautiful woman. She didn't like it, but I called her my first, my last, my everything. That's not my line, either. Some blues singer's. I was hopelessly attracted to her. I loved her very deeply. I treated her with respect. I had made up my mind that she was going to be my wife.

I proposed to Yvonne in a restaurant in east Hamilton in 1946. I gave her an ultimatum: she had to choose either me or her family. Her family considered me a con artist and looked down on me, but you don't have to get very high up to look down on someone. Yvonne was very shy, and her mother had taught her not to trust men. Her mom thought I was a womanizer, but I wasn't. I didn't like Mrs. Harrison. She wasn't too kind to my mother, and Yvonne had told her mother that her behaviour was not acceptable, but it took years before there was any sense of warmth from that woman. We were married on September 10, 1948, while I was still at McMaster. But even after we had been married for maybe five years, her family didn't like having me around the house.

They all treated her father terribly. Yvonne was the only one who treated him like a human being. Her mother had planted that seed of thought that men are no good, and the other sisters adopted that attitude toward him and me. Yvonne was the kind of woman who wouldn't buy into that stuff. She was a warm, loving person, while her mother and sisters — Juanita, Audrey, and Fern — treated Robert Harrison horribly. I used to hate it.

I didn't break through with that family until one day when I was coming home from law school. Yvonne was working, and I wanted to see our son, Keith. Her mother and sisters were looking after him, so I went to their house and told her mother enough was enough. But they never really accepted me until I became a lawyer. Then they bragged about me. How two-faced! In the long run, I became Yvonne's mother's lawyer, but we were never close.

We were married at Stewart Memorial Church in Hamilton and went on our honeymoon to New York, where we stayed with my aunt Iris. My wife was very pretty, and while we were there a man began flirting with her in an elevator. Yvonne was very naive. There were two handsome men on that elevator, and I realized they were pimps. One of them said, "I wonder what the penalty is if I touch her," and I said, "Death." They just clammed up. I wasn't going to put up with anything like that. I was a husband now.

We had a wonderful marriage. I'm very fortunate in that regard, because I have friends who do not have wonderful marriages. I did everything for her. I put her up on a pedestal. That's why I was so determined to succeed with my schooling. When I enrolled in law school, I knew I had to be somebody. As a lawyer, I knew I could be my own boss.

It was with much trepidation that I headed off to law school. I had a young family, and there were the ever-present worries about how I would be treated due to my colour. Some of that concern was eased immediately at registration when a friendly fellow first-year law student, John Mills, came over and introduced himself. His gesture certainly eased my inner tension, and who could have known that short incident would launch a friendship that was celebrated early in 2006 with the fifty-third reunion of our class. In the end, John, Ed Carter, and I spent a lot of our law school years together.

Studying law was a daunting challenge, not only socially but also economically. My veteran's benefits had been exhausted with the completion of my undergraduate degree, but I sought, and was granted, an exception to extend my benefits with the proviso that I remained in the top quarter of my class. I met this challenge and graduated from Osgoode Hall in 1953, at which time there were but a handful of blacks practising law in Ontario.

In law school, when I didn't stay with my father, I boarded in Toronto with a woman named Mrs. Roberts, and I came home to Hamilton on weekends. Yvonne and I had no money to speak of. I worked summers,

It was a very proud day when I graduated from Osgoode Hall in 1953. Pictured with Yvonne and me are fellow student Charlie Groves and his family.

mostly at the steel company. Yvonne worked in a laundry to help support our family. What always worried and motivated me was what my wife might think if I failed. She worked so hard to put me through school.

Yvonne worked until I became a lawyer and then for a while after I graduated. But when I graduated I told her I wanted her to stop working and stay at home, like other lawyers' wives. It wasn't all that easy to persuade her, though. At that time, most lawyers were white, and we couldn't be assured of a future. But she eventually stopped, and from 1953 to 1958 we lived with her mother. I didn't like being there, but it wasn't too stressful. My room was upstairs, and I spent a lot of time up there reading and working.

My law school friend John Mills helped me to partly manage these awkward and inconvenient early marriage years of living with Yvonne's parents. At one point, John and his wife, Helen, were moving into a newer apartment that included a fridge and stove. When I asked John what he was going to do with his fridge, he said he was selling it, so I told him I wanted to buy it. I think I gave him fifteen dollars. I got it back to Hamilton and tucked it in my mother-in-law's basement. That made no sense to John. Why go to all the trouble to buy a fridge and haul it back to Hamilton if it's just going to sit in a basement? I explained to him that Yvonne's mother was all over me about getting us a place of our own and the nagging was driving me crazy. The fridge was buying me time, because it convinced her we were preparing to move. Never did use it, but I appreciated the break it gave me. It was fifteen dollars well spent.

John understood the tension between me and Yvonne's mother and sisters. I told him of one incident that still makes him chuckle to this day. I've always tried to dress well and look sharp, even when I was in law school and had limited means. One Friday I was walking up the street to their house in Hamilton after being away the week in Toronto, and up pipes her mother, "Well, here comes Mr. Hotshot right now." Now that was uncalled for. John reminds me of that lovely moniker every now and then.

I chose law as a career after deciding that self-employment made the most sense for a young black man with ambition. Denial of white-collar opportunities at the steel company and the dismissive offer of a job on the shop floor — there is nothing wrong with that work, if one so chooses, but it wasn't what I had been trained or educated for — presented new decisions. The rejection actually strengthened my resolve to make education work for me. It turns out, coincidentally, that a similar rejection with racial undertones would lead another future partner of mine, Paul Tokiwa, to study law as well.

Early in my first year at Osgoode Hall one of those momentous occasions in life occurred. One day my dad called me and said, "You're now the proud father of a baby boy." It was 1949, and Keith had been born. It was a magnificent day because I suddenly realized I was now a father and family man and had to work very hard. I took the bus back to Hamilton and went into the nursery to see my new son. Then I started to cry. Keith was a pretty good-looking baby, and let's face it, most babies are pretty ugly. I suggested the name Lincoln MacCauley Alexander III, but my wife said no. She liked the name Keith. There was a player for the Calgary Stampeders at the time named Keith Spaith, and she liked the name.

A very special picture of Yvonne with Keith as a little boy.

While I eventually graduated from Osgoode Hall, an incident in my last year left me convinced for a time that I would never get my diploma. Addressing 250 would-be lawyers, Dean Smalley Baker used the expression, "It was like looking for a nigger in a woodpile." When I heard him say it, my head jerked to attention, as if someone had just slapped me across the face. Actually, my friend John Mills was sitting right beside me when Baker made that comment. You have to picture this. All of us soon-to-be lawyers were squeezed into this cramped room and, to make matters worse, we had those tiny old university desks that are connected together. John and I were literally shoulder to shoulder. It was an exercise in contortion for me just to get into the desk, let alone get comfortable enough to follow the instructors. But I had no trouble hearing Baker's slur, and John said afterward that he could feel my shoulders tighten up when the dean made that comment.

Dean Baker asked the class if there were any questions, and, without thinking, I stood up and said, "The one thing I don't understand is what does it mean to say 'looking for a nigger in a woodpile'?"

The atmosphere grew tense immediately. In this huge class there was only one other black student, Ken Rouffe. I'd say half my classmates were with me and half were shocked at my audacity. Dean Baker replied that everyone said it. I said, "But you can't say that because you have to show leadership. You're in a position of authority, a leader in the community. A leader has to lead and not be using such disrespectful comments without even thinking about them."

Then I called Yvonne and told her I had just blown it. She said she was behind me, but I was panicked for the rest of the year because I was sure he was going to fail me.

Back then, you discovered if you had passed by waiting to read the published results in the *Globe and Mail*. When the day came, I cautiously opened to the appropriate page, and there it was — my name near the top of the class.

When I met Dean Baker at a party at the end of the school year, he was offended when I told him I was surprised I had passed. In effect, I was questioning his academic integrity by suggesting that a student could be failed if he crossed his instructor. "How can you say that?" he shot back at me, clearly perturbed. "There was never any doubt in my mind that you would pass. You are in the top quarter of the class, for goodness' sake."

It was a good lesson in the difference between being black in a white world and being a member of that majority. As a black, I was so suspicious of the fragility of my rights that it seemed perfectly logical I could be failed for my impertinence. To him, his academic integrity and independence were unassailable, yet he could make a comment in class like that without grasping its impact. The episode reinforced for me — and I hope served to illustrate for at least some of the other students in that class — that racism was so deeply ingrained that even people who should know better would issue such phrases with the same ease with which they would order a cup of coffee. Imagine, the dean of the country's leading law school talking like that. And, in truth, I don't believe there was any malicious intent. It was simply so ingrained that people didn't even realize how wrong and hurtful it could be.

To me, an episode such as this one cuts far deeper than the comment itself. Imagine how often at that time black people bore the hurts of such comments and endured that pain in silence for fear of reprisals or punishment. Already greatly marginalized, they could be left in dire straits for fighting back. So they suffered in silence. It just so happened — whether because of my size or my courage or, some may say, my stubbornness — that I couldn't let such comments go without responding. I was always ready to defend myself, whether physically or, as I came to deal with more thoughtfully mature people, intellectually.

Every now and then I still dream that I didn't pass law school, a recurring nightmare not unlike the three hooded figures I talked about at the start of the book. These dreams keep me in line. But in any case, thanks to that confrontation, I'm convinced I influenced some attitudes in that law class. Whether it was the years in Harlem or the years in the air force or something else, I had a grounded understanding of what it meant to live in a white man's world. But I was not then, nor have I ever been, a token. Nobody can intimidate me.

CHAPTER 4

Called to the Bar

At the time I was called to the bar, there were few other black lawyers practising in all of Ontario, among them George Carter, Lloyd Perry and Oliver Holland (in Hamilton). Not only were we rarities, it was also difficult to make inroads in the profession because established practices were just not interested in hiring blacks. Despite the great cachet of the degree I held, there was a definite feeling of uncertainty upon graduation,

The first hurdle I faced was in securing an articling position, and the experience provided me with yet another example of the steep challenges minorities face. Articling jobs for blacks, women, and minorities in general were severely limited. I was fortunate enough to secure an articling position with Sam Gotfrid, Q.C., establishing a friendship that lasted through our lives. This course of action, it turned out, was common. The limited articling posts for minorities in Toronto were almost always with firms operated by Jewish lawyers. Almost inevitably, these lawyers had been confronted by the same obstacles I was facing. In one very obvious sense, through our limited articling options, we were already being removed from the profession's mainstream.

I wasn't in any position to make changes, at least not yet, and for now I needed work. I had a wife and a little son and a valuable degree to put into play. You have to remember that this was in 1953. As my articling experience quickly taught me, law firms not only didn't want black lawyers, they also didn't want female lawyers, and they certainly didn't want Jews. It was not easy if you didn't fit into that privileged class of the white male.

Obstacles aside, my experience with Samuel Gotfrid proved invaluable, and it enabled me to inch my way toward a genuine career in law. Getting started was no easy task. One of my first eye-opening experiences came after articling when I applied for a post as a junior lawyer with a leading Anglo-Celtic Hamilton firm. I presented myself quite correctly as an excellent law student. I had finished in the top quarter of the graduating class at the country's leading law school. Furthermore, I was a war veteran. These were exceptional credentials.

I had talked by phone with a representative of the firm and it had gone exceedingly well. As we were wrapping up our discussion, I asked somewhat casually, "Would it matter to you, sir, if I told you I was black?" The simple question was greeted with dead silence. To his credit, that lawyer did agree to meet with me, but in the end he said the firm's clients were English, Irish, and Scottish and would not accept me. That angered me, and it occurred to me that his was the easy answer of a coward, unwilling to make an honourable, bold statement for social justice, all for the sake of commerce.

That firm actually offered me financial assistance — to what end I'm not certain, though I suspect it was to get lost and start on my own practice — but was not willing to offer me a desk in its office. Though this experience rattled my faith in humanity, in a few years I would join a firm led by an individual who could restore that faith tenfold. But at the time, I applied for a post with a two-person Hamilton firm operated by a sister and brother, Helen and Edward Okuloski. Finally, after numerous rejections, I was working in my profession.

Okuloski and Okuloski was a new breed of law practice; the two partners had forged out on their own because they had been shut out of the mainstream law firms. Apart from being of Polish descent, Helen was also something of a maverick because there weren't many women practising law in Hamilton. But she was one of the best lawyers in the city at the time. The firm was in the east end of Hamilton, near the steel factory that had denied me a white-collar job. It was a valuable training ground for a young lawyer. Many Polish, European, and other post-war immigrants were settling in this part of the city and buying houses at that time, so I got an early introduction to commercial and real estate law. My experience with the Okuloskis was incredible, and I came to love the Polish and German people for whom we did so much work; many of them later voted for me when I started my political career.

What I appreciated about the Okuloskis was that I know they didn't hire me out of tokenism or sympathy because of my colour. Helen made it clear that her sole concern was whether I had the aggressiveness and mental tenacity to succeed in the profession, and as a professional, that's all you can ask for. In some ways, they took a chance because they hired me at least partly on the recommendation of Sam Gotfrid, with whom I had articled. Sam's reference said that I was quite competent, but also shy and inward-looking and lacking in confidence.

Actually, Gotfrid's was a fair observation, though it was not so much that I was scared to speak out in public. Those who know me might find it hard to believe, but there was good reason for reticence. I was still only the fifth black lawyer ever in Ontario and the only one in the city at the time (though not the first; Oliver Holland, the first black lawyer to practise in Hamilton, had retired). Given my minority status, it was wise, I concluded, to exercise discretion as much as I could. But Gotfrid's observation made me realize I had to stand up and be counted.

After getting my feet wet with Okuloski and Okuloski for a couple of years, I moved on to join Dave Duncan, described by many as one of Hamilton's most flamboyant and successful lawyers at the time. Because he was so prominent and visible, he really could have hired any lawyer he wanted, but he chose me, which was both rewarding and flattering. Dave operated a general law practice and had a reputation for being unyielding and outspoken. In the courtroom, he could put on a show. He was a great criminal lawyer and was highly regarded by the police.

His business practices did need some honing, however. My first encounter with Dave's business methodology was after we had received a $1,000 retainer, and he said, "There's $500 for you and $500 for me." But the money never ended up on the books. Eventually, he was audited and was fined. In his own defence, Dave went through the books with the auditors and showed them how much work he had done pro bono and how much he could have actually billed. In Dave's mind, that more than justified the omission of a few payments, but it didn't hold water with the auditors. In the end, I was able to draw on my experience with the Okuloskis to guide Dave toward proper accounting procedures.

Because Dave was so visible in the community, working with him couldn't help but get attention, so it was reasonable to expect that joining him would help advance my career. When we joined forces, I had the distinguished honour of being a member of the first interracial law partnership in Canada, Duncan and Alexander. We remained partners for nearly eight years.

Besides giving purpose, strength, and direction to my law career, Dave Duncan would eventually introduce me to another career — politics. Dave's political activities included serving as an alderman in Hamilton from 1954 to 1958. More importantly, he was active in the Progressive Conservative party, which led me to become more involved with the party locally. Dave, who backed Hamilton MPP Ada Pritchard during the 1960s, had also earlier worked on the campaign that led to Ellen Fairclough becoming Hamilton's first female member of Parliament in a 1950 federal by-election.

Politics was a way for a lawyer to raise his or her profile, but as a black, increasing involvement with the Conservatives had greater significance for me than it did for many others. The late 1950s was a time when blacks were beginning to find greater acceptance in politics as parties sought their support in a growing, multicultural Canada. I even received some national attention.

On the professional side, my partnership with Dave Duncan ended in 1962, when he became senior solicitor for Ontario's transportation department. I found it financially difficult to maintain a practice on my own. It was generally understood the best route to financial success was commercial law, and, not surprisingly, that area was not welcoming black lawyers with open arms.

Even the black community was reluctant to take a chance on a black lawyer — though since there were only 470 blacks in Hamilton in 1961, they would not have formed even the foundation of a strong practice. It turns out that that was a common experience for first-generation or visible minority lawyers in those days. Indeed, there are documented cases of lawyers from other minorities, such as Chinese and Native Canadians, who encountered difficulties building credibility and trust within their own communities. As in my case, many individuals shared stories of having to scrap and battle just so members of their own ethnic communities would put confidence in them.

In his paper "A Small United Nations: The Hamilton Firm of Millar, Alexander, Tokiwa and Isaacs, 1962 to 1993," Phillip Sworden, at the time an assistant professor in the Department of Law and Justice at Laurentian University, illustrated this reticence clearly. Kew Dock Yip, the first Chinese lawyer in Canada, said even his own people discriminated against him when he began practising law in Toronto after the Second World War. Yip said he had to "fight [his] way up" to earn the confidence of his fellow Chinese. He explained that the Chinese had been suppressed for so long in Canada that it was mainly after he began to win cases that their business came to him. David Nahwegahbow, an Ojibawa lawyer, concurs with this idea, noting that it took time to convince his own people that he was capable of doing the job.

At the same time as I honed my professional skills, my personal talents, such as they were, were being called upon in the murky field of parenting. I was the father of a busy young boy. Having been in Toronto studying at Osgoode Hall for the better part of Keith's first three years, when I returned to Hamilton it was time to build our relationship. Because she anchored the home life, Yvonne was the disciplinarian, and unfortunately, she got the short end of the good cop–bad

Keith in 1951, around age two, on my mother-in-law's backyard porch. Cute little fellow, isn't he?

cop stick. I really do think Keith looked up to me, literally and figuratively. Back then I was carrying something in the range of 250 pounds on my six-foot-three frame, so it was pretty easy to get his attention, if you know what I mean. Keith has said that if I told him to do something, it got done.

Over the next fifteen years or so, our relationship grew closer, though I don't imagine the things we did together were particularly different from other fathers and sons. Being back in town all the time

Keith at around age five, out for a walk on King Street in Hamilton.

meant we could do things like wander down to the corner store — it was called Baxter's — where they made first-class malted milkshakes. From my youth in Toronto, I could draw on my boxing experiences to teach him that noble art. I also drew from my stellar one-season football career at McMaster to teach him how to toss a football, and we dabbled in numerous other sports as well. And then we'd do things like go to movie matinees, especially for the cartoons, which he loved. What kid wouldn't?

After six years of my practising law, in 1958 Yvonne, Keith, and I moved into our own home at 30 Proctor Boulevard in east Hamilton. At the time of this writing, it is where I still live. Ironically, our Hamilton home has a covenant — which is illegal now — that prevents the sale of the house to blacks, Jews, Italians, Poles, Chinese, or foreign-born persons. Amazing.

Yvonne (right), Keith, and I along with Iris Knight (centre) and a friend of Iris's in New York in 1958.

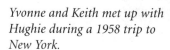

Yvonne and Keith board a train to New York in 1958.

Yvonne and Keith met up with Hughie during a 1958 trip to New York.

Me with Yvonne's father, Robert Harrison, in the late 1950s.

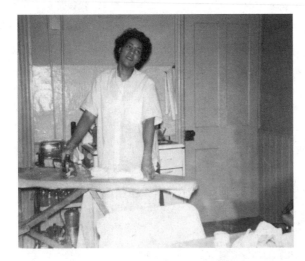

Yvonne up to her elbows in domestic chores in our new home on Proctor Boulevard in Hamilton in 1959.

This is me and Yvonne, circa 1959. Going to church was always a big part of our Mother's Day celebration, and was also an occasion to get a new suit and dress.

This is me (standing) circa 1960, with Keith (centre), Ewan Bell, my brother-in-law who was married to Yvonne's sister Audrey (left), and Robert Harrison, my father-in-law.

CHAPTER 5

~

Africa — A Journey of Self-Awareness

I had been practising law with Dave Duncan for several years when a unique opportunity came my way that would have a profound effect on my life. In 1959, the United Church invited the Reverend James Robinson of Harlem, the founder of Operation Crossroads Africa, to Canada to speak to a group that included a number of doctors. Robinson urged them to go to Africa to share their skills and expertise. The group took up the challenge, and nineteen visitors, including Yvonne and me, travelled to Africa in 1960.

The local inspiration for our trip came about largely from Dr. Alan Lane of Hamilton and Carl Zurbrigg, a United Church minister. They had attended a retreat at Elgin House, a United Church meeting centre in Muskoka, where the Crossroads founder was one of the guests.

I was included in the trip because organizers decided it would be a good idea to have a person of colour with them, and they were correct. But I didn't have any money — I was a poor lawyer at the time — so the trip organizers set out to raise the money for me. A member of the group, Dr. Jack Sibley, approached a Jewish car dealer in Hamilton, Hy Richter, for help, and he came up with $5,000 for our trip. Jack had done exceptional medical work for Hy's dad over the years, which was much appreciated. Hy provided us with that money anonymously, though I identified him publicly at the reception when I left Parliament years later.

I got a positive feeling about the trip, even before we left. We went to New York a couple of times in advance of our journey to meet with Rev. Robinson. On the first trip, after our meetings one day we decided to walk back to our hotel with Dr. Bill Lockington and his wife, Mike (it's a nickname derived from the first letters of her maiden name, Mae Isobel Kelly). Bill was the general practitioner among the group of doctors on our trip. We were in downtown New York and we walked along Fifth Avenue, some six or seven blocks, as I recall. When we got back to the hotel, I turned to Bill and Mike and said, "We're going to be okay."

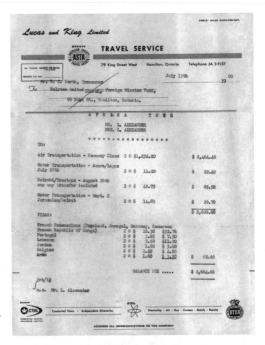

The bill for our trip to Africa in 1960.

They were confused. "What in heaven do you mean, Linc?" Bill asked.

"Well, we've just walked down Fifth Avenue, and you didn't walk in front of me, you didn't walk behind me, you walked right beside me. You told me an awful lot about yourselves in a few short blocks."

My remarks were sincere and heartfelt, and proof of that is the fact I remain friends with Bill and Mike to this day. In fact, Bill and I still share a nickname we gave ourselves on the trip. We address one another as Dudu, in honour of our first African driver on the journey in Dakar, who was blessed with that name.

On our journey, which would cover some twenty-three countries, one of our first stops involved a visit to a mission in Angola, and there we got an understanding of what those missionaries did. I used to think all missionaries did was go around with their Bibles trying to convert people. But these were doctors, agriculturalists, and community planners who worked alongside the local people. Sure, they had Bibles with them, but that was a small part of it. What they did, mainly, was share their specialized skills in hopes of aiding the people they met physically and spiritually.

The experience was an eye-opener for me, not only as a lawyer, but also as a human being, because I began to realize what black people could do. I saw that, unlike the Hollywood version, these Africans were men and women of significant talents. I became conscious of my blackness. I had come from a white world. Now we were in Africa, and I realized we are people of skill and creativity. I was a black man and I was a somebody. I started standing tall.

There have been a few incidents in my life that made me stand tall. That was one of them, as was not getting a job at the steel mill after McMaster, standing up to the dean at Osgoode Hall, and not being accepted at certain law firms after graduation. One individual who reinforced that sentiment of standing tall was Ralph Bunche, a black who represented the United States at the United Nations and played a major role in the civil rights movement of the 1960s. His accomplishments impressed me because I could relate to how much he had had to overcome to get there. In 1950 Bunche became the first African American to win the Nobel Peace Prize. (Fourteen years later, his fellow civil rights campaigner, Martin Luther King Jr., would become the second.) As principal secretary of the UN Palestine Commission, Bunche had obtained armistice agreements between Israel and the Arab states after almost a year of negotiations. The impact on the black community of the accomplishments of individuals such as Bunche cannot be underestimated.

When I got home to Hamilton, I was interviewed almost immediately — the next day, I think — and said I believed the countries of Africa were ready for independence. At the time, much of the talk was about "preparing" a country for independence, but I discovered that notion was really a way of sustaining colonialism, at least in my political assessment. How does one know when a country has been fully prepared? That kind of paternalism was not sitting well with Africans anymore. They were beginning to realize that independence wasn't pie in the sky but a legitimate wish and possibility.

The African people I had met were prepared to learn and to make their own mistakes. This was not racial chauvinism on the part of the Africans, but merely the legitimate aspirations of the people. I found ample evidence of that from people who expected and hoped for the involvement of whites in Africa. They recognized that the white community's expertise was essential, but the dynamics of the times meant change had to come, with Africans taking charge of their lives, governments, and futures. "White man must learn that, given the same training, the black man can do a job as efficiently as the white man," I told the *Hamilton Spectator* at the time.

Unfortunately, the notion of racial superiority was still predominant throughout Africa and would prove to be an almost insurmountable obstacle for decades to come.

The abolition of apartheid in South Africa is still a relatively recent event. My visit and observations happened three decades earlier. At that time, there were equally rigid colour barriers in countries such as Rhodesia, though some progress toward equality was taking place, for example in the Congo. We visited areas that had been under Belgian colonial rule, and our entourage discovered boundless instances of ways in which the Belgians had mistreated the Africans. "In many cases the Africans were treated little better than animals and they have been harbouring these feelings of bitterness and hate for years," I told the *Spectator*.

While these disturbing revelations did not rest well with me, the trip was personally rewarding beyond measure. In the January 1961 edition of the publication *Missionary Monthly*, one of the participants wrote an account of our journey: "The African people have been thrilled to the core. Personal contact is the superior way of breaking down race prejudices and differences. In the group was a negro lawyer and his wife from Hamilton [Yvonne and me].... What impressed many Africans ... was the fact that this negro was a Canadian and had travelled with other Canadians who were white. Everywhere Link [sic] went he would fall over backwards to meet the people and to get to know them and their names and their work."

There were plenty of examples of the advantages of having me on the trip. In one case, our party was crossing into the Congo and there was a huge bottleneck at the crossing. As it turned out, I towered over most of the people there, including all the Africans, and that seemed to gain me some sort of mystical respect. There was a large crowd milling around, including a large group of Americans, so I just sidled up, put my

Our entourage upon arrival for our visit to Africa in 1960. I am at the far right, while Yvonne, shy one that she was, is tucked in behind, seventh from the left.

Here I am with part of our entourage in Africa in 1960. From left are Dr. Bill Love, Corky Lane, me, Carl Zurbrigg, the United Church minister who was one of the organizers for the trip, and Morley Weaver.

arm around one of the border guards, and said, "Me and my buddies need to get through. Can you help us out?" I didn't speak the language, so I doubt he understood me, but we were whisked right through. Alan Lane still shakes his head and chuckles at that memory.

We ventured far off the beaten track to get to outlying communities, and those journeys could sometimes be quite harrowing. Navigating predator-infested rivers does not rank among my ideas of fun. Nor does managing heights. One time we had to cross a deep ravine somewhere in the depths of Angola. There was a precipitous drop to the river below, in which a significant collection of the aforementioned predators lurked. However, this was not an ordinary bridge. Instead it was like a loosely secured, railing-less catwalk, with a mere single cable with which to balance yourself. I was pretty certain my life was near its end, given my chronic fear of heights. Then this young lad, perhaps twelve years old, took my hand and skilfully guided me across. He had crossed hundreds of times and, it was abundantly clear, could do it blindfolded.

That wasn't the only hair-raising incident on the trip. Our arrival in Congo was not at the best of times, as civil strife and rebellion against the oppressive Belgian colonialists was reaching fever pitch. In time, the Belgians withdrew, and on June 30, 1960, the Democratic Republic of the Congo was formed under the quickly elected first prime minister, Patrice Lumumba, and first head of state and president, Joseph Kasavubu. Lumumba was reasonably popular, but he was extreme in his anti-white, anti-west, anti-capitalist views. The atmosphere caused Belgian administrators and technicians to flee, crippling the government and economy. Public order had disintegrated. The province of Katanga in the south had stayed relatively calm, however, and that was our destination as we flew across the country from Leopoldville to Elizabethville. Belgian troops had re-established themselves in the south, where the country's mineral riches were concentrated. Eventually Belgian commercial interests, backed by the Belgian army and intelligence, set out to force a partitioning of the country, separating the naturally rich parts of the Congo — Katanga and diamond-rich Kasai — from the rest of the nation. In fact, in Katanga, Belgian troops disarmed Congo government troops under guise of "peacekeeping." That was the backdrop as we waited to board our flight in Leopoldville. At the airport, I was extremely popular, as people identified me as a successful individual with outside contacts. They scribbled their names and contact information down in hopes that I could help in some way later on. Eventually, our commercial jet took off, and we were about halfway to Elizabethville when the pilot told us we had been ordered to land by UN troops. There was no airport between the two cities that could accommodate our jet, but that didn't matter. I gulped, then made a dash to the washroom to flush all those pieces of paper with names on them down the toilet. I worried that if they were found on me those individuals' lives would be in jeopardy and I, too, would run the risk of running afoul of authorities. In the end, UN troops boarded the plane and removed a person who later turned out to be one of Lumumba's people. And somehow, the pilot had managed to get the plane down and back up again.

It was a frenzied, panicked few hours, so we were all naturally relieved when we reached Elizabethville safely. Arrangements had been made for us to stay near the border between Congo and Northern Rhodesia, which became Zambia in 1964. The Federation of Rhodesia and Nyasaland (1953–63), consisted of Northern Rhodesia, Southern Rhodesia (now Zimbabwe), and Nyasaland (now Malawi). The next day, we drove into Rhodesia with great anticipation and relief. We had experienced the vile colonialism of the Belgians, and now we were excited to be in a country under British rule. In a little town across the border, Bill Lockington headed to the bank (he was our money man) and the rest of us made a beeline for a restaurant that boasted a huge sign advertising milkshakes. In the few minutes it took Bill to do his business, he met us already heading back up the street. The restaurant wouldn't serve blacks. My fellow travellers left with me and Yvonne in disgust. The British were blind too. They were no better than the despicable Belgians.

Thankfully, we were part of a committed and supportive group, and we continued to work hard in our outreach with the locals. Because we were part of an entourage supported by the United Church, we would from time to time sing hymns in the course of our travels. It turned out mine was the deepest, strongest voice, so I used to attract a lot of attention. Early in our trip, one of the missionaries we encountered translated one hymn into Unbundu, and when I sang in that African language it deeply affected the locals. Once, when we were visiting a hospital, I was invited to sing, and before long the villagers were standing three and

Yvonne and I (third and fourth from left) out for dinner in Cairo during our 1960 trip to Africa.

four deep outside the windows listening in what appeared to be awe. It was a remarkable moment. "He is a beautiful singer," the *Missionary Monthly* enthusiastically reported. "The children and adults literally flocked about him day and night. But when he sang 'How Great Thou Art,' translated into Unbundu … the people were so affected emotionally that they took minutes to return to normal again. And of course everywhere he went, his fame went ahead of him, and the requests for other singing were almost too great for him to carry out."

It was a flattering account of my vocal exploits, and the experience left me convinced that the emotional and intellectual awakening I witnessed and enjoyed in Africa powered my ability to communicate in song. As the *Missionary Monthly* pointed out, the most popular hymn, the one that was translated, was "How Great Thou Art":

> O Lord my God, When I in awesome wonder,
> Consider all the worlds Thy Hands have made;
> I see the stars, I hear the rolling thunder,
> Thy power throughout the universe displayed.
> Then sings my soul, My Saviour God, to Thee,
> How great Thou art, How great Thou art.

Then sings my soul, My Saviour God, to Thee,
How great Thou art, How great Thou art!
When through the woods, and forest glades I wander,
And hear the birds sing sweetly in the trees.
When I look down, from lofty mountain grandeur
And see the brook, and feel the gentle breeze.
Then sings my soul, My Saviour God, to Thee,
How great Thou art, How great Thou art.
Then sings my soul, My Saviour God, to Thee,
How great Thou art, How great Thou art!
And when I think, that God, His Son not sparing;
Sent Him to die, I scarce can take it in;
That on the Cross, my burden gladly bearing,
He bled and died to take away my sin.
Then sings my soul, My Saviour God, to Thee,
How great Thou art, How great Thou art.
Then sings my soul, My Saviour God, to Thee,
How great Thou art, How great Thou art!
When Christ shall come, with shout of acclamation,
And take me home, what joy shall fill my heart.
Then I shall bow, in humble adoration,
And then proclaim: "My God, how great Thou art!"
Then sings my soul, My Saviour God, to Thee,
How great Thou art, How great Thou art.
Then sings my soul, My Saviour God, to Thee,
How great Thou art, How great Thou art!

When I got back from that trip, the members of our group handled a large number of speaking engagements, since there was widespread interest in what we had experienced in Africa. In total there were about fifty such events, and Alan and I handled a significant portion of them. It provided a great opportunity for me to hone my speaking skills, as it was a topic for which I'd developed an immense passion.

To me, the most appealing thing about Rev. James Robinson — aside from the fact that he was a black minister from my old stamping grounds, Harlem — was his idea, adopted and acted upon by Alan Lane and other members of our group, that we can learn so much more about one another if we roll up our sleeves and work side by side with people in other countries. Ours was a highly professional entourage, packed with medical expertise, and members of our group worked closely with staff in the hospitals and clinics we visited.

Africa was a journey of self-awareness for me, a black man living in a white world where there was no inclusion of people of colour. Most often when it did include me and other people of colour, it was in a menial way. Going to Africa buoyed me up to not accept being treated like a second-class person. A lot of people feel that it's okay because other people permit it to happen every day, man's inhumanity to man. That's life, I guess, but it takes a terrible toll.

CHAPTER 6

The Millar Years

By 1962, my dynamic and conservative-leaning law partner, Dave Duncan, had secured an Ontario government appointment, and this left me at loose ends. My part of our partnership was not as substantial as Dave's, which made it close to impossible to carry on the firm. It had been difficult to build my practice, for reasons ranging from racism to mistrust to reluctance within my own ethnic community to take on a black lawyer.

Then one evening I was visiting my son in a city hospital, where he was being treated for a hip problem. I had noticed he was limping and mentioned it to Yvonne. It turned out to be a condition known as a slipped epiphysis, which causes the bone to keep slipping out of the joint. By chance, I bumped into Jack Millar, my old McMaster classmate and friend, who was visiting his father in the same hospital. Out of the blue, he asked me to join him as a partner in law. It was a huge break. I knew even then Jack was a very successful lawyer, and I was unsure of what I could offer him.

Jack was an incredible person. He thought black was beautiful at a time when black wasn't supposed to be beautiful. As we were working out the details of our partnership, Jack was approached by an individual from the Jewish faith who pointed out my colour and suggested it would be foolish to bring me into the partnership. Of course, he was wasting his time talking about such a subject to Jackie, but I still find the episode amazing. After all, this was 1962. Maybe this was expected in the southern U.S., but in Canada? It demonstrates how far we've come in a short period, though there are still miles to go. It is ironic that the same person went on to speak highly of me, though he is now deceased. I smile now when I see members of his family, and decency prevents me from naming him publicly.

Jack empathized with my situation, but he wanted me because he knew I was a good lawyer, not because I was black. He offered me diversity in practice, from real estate to criminal and family law. Paul Tokiwa had joined the office before I joined in 1962. So Jack's firm became the first law office in Hamilton — I would bet in Canada, too — with both a black and a Japanese partner.

Jack and I had really solidified our friendship at Mac, and we travelled in a pretty fun-loving group. Most of us were veterans, and the venerable Les Prince, the dean of men, was fond of us and watched out for us. He'd have us playing hockey, basketball, and a full range of activities. It was a great social component of my undergraduate days, and it wasn't just about sports. At the time there were but a few buildings on campus, and one of them was the old recreation hall. Jack could plunk a little piano, I had vocal inclinations, so with him tickling the ivories I would belt out the songs of the day, Dixieland style, all fueled by a tidy supply of booze. We'd all get involved. Jack and I were also at Osgoode Hall at the same time, and in summers we worked at the steel plant in Hamilton until we finished law school. So we already had a lengthy friendship when he invited me to join him.

John Sydney Millar was born in Hamilton on August 14, 1928, the son of a city policeman. He attended primary school in the city and focused on becoming well educated. He started his law career as a junior working for James Gage, where he soon developed his own expertise in real estate law. He worked there for nine years and became a partner. By 1962, Jack was handling the bulk of the practice's real estate work and he decided that he could set out successfully on his own. He departed that year to start his own practice.

People are naturally apprehensive about establishing their own businesses, including law firms, but Jack had developed some strong contacts among builders, lenders, purchasers, vendors, and others in the real estate business, and when he left, many of these people followed him. In that sense, he had built a strong foundation right from the start. This client loyalty reflected his competence.

In 1962, the city was enjoying a boom in real estate development, primarily from new housing in the Hamilton Mountain district; demographic changes and housing trends were transforming Hamilton. Jack acquired a substantial part of this market and quickly became deluged with real estate work. By the thousands, people were moving from the lower city onto the mountain, while the city's traditional British base was being augmented by immigrants from Europe and Asia.

Jack eventually cobbled together a firm perfectly suited for that new and growing market. On his own, and with a certain sense of the maverick in him, he was determined to put together a firm that suited his vision. That meant he veered sharply from the typical hiring practices of Hamilton law firms, which tended to choose white males. In building the law office that eventually came to be known as Hamilton's "United Nations" firm, Jack had hired Paul Yoshiharu Tokiwa, a Japanese Canadian who had recently arrived in Hamilton. Jack knew it would be prudent to hire another lawyer to handle family, criminal, and motor vehicle law, as well as other files neither he nor Tokiwa were inclined to do. I filled that position. We had a most unusual law firm. After we took on Peter Isaacs, a Native Canadian, as a partner in 1968, all four partners in the firm were of different colours. A Caucasian, a black, Japanese, and a Native Canadian. We were white, black, yellow, and red, we used to laugh.

So we were a law firm with connections. We were recognized as highly competent in real estate law, and we were all practising in a multiracial firm reflecting the new demographic changes of the time in Hamilton. Jack didn't consciously begin his practice as a multiracial firm, but as it became successful he saw no reason to change it. This was the culmination of many factors: his willingness to be among the first white lawyers to hire visible minority partners; his remarkable ability to anticipate changing times in post-war Canada; and his decision to remain within the structure of a classic small law firm of four partners in a smaller city. As the firm succeeded, he had many chances to enlarge it or merge it with other law firms, but he resisted, mainly to keep personal control over its business and multicultural direction.

In his paper "A Small United Nations," Phillip Sworden paid tribute to Jack's vision. "The legal profession may be headed by the recent emergence of the mega-firm, but the history of the former Hamilton firm of Millar, Alexander, Tokiwa and Isaacs shows that small law firms can still offer significant leadership to other lawyers. Specifically, this small firm was a leader in addressing the issue of race and the practice of law," he wrote. "It earned itself the title of Hamilton's 'United Nations' law firm, and was one of the first law firms to challenge the traditional law firm practice of hiring mostly well-connected white males. As such, it was an inspiration to other visible minority lawyers who have experienced many difficulties gaining access to Ontario's legal profession."

After beginning in our days at McMaster, Jack's and my already strong friendship grew tremendously closer. Aside from the support of Jack and our circle of friends, one of the things that solidified our relationship was the recognition by him and his wife, Marge, of the kinds of obstacles Yvonne and I faced. This bond between us strengthened further as we developed the practice.

As I've recounted, despite taking commercial courses in high school, Yvonne had not been able to break away from the old basic jobs available to blacks early in our marriage. She worked endless hours in a laundry to support us while I was in school. She was an elevator operator and helped her mother clean homes in east Hamilton. It was all menial work. Regardless, she had a strength of character that flew in the face of the racial obstacles thrown in front of her. Her dignity remained firm and untarnished, and Jack and Marge recognized this.

Marge reminded me about Yvonne's shyness, and sometimes, unfortunately, people mistook this trait for aloofness or arrogance. It was far from that. She was a very private person, most comfortable at home and within a very tight circle of friends. We holidayed on numerous occasions with the Millars, and they accompanied us to England when I went to meet the Queen after being appointed lieutenant-governor of Ontario. But Marge says it was like pulling teeth to get Yvonne out to do a little shopping. She was happiest at home and would almost always defer social decisions to me. If it was important to me, from a professional or personal standpoint, I would set the engagement. If it was nothing essential, she was content where she was.

An impromptu Alexander family photo taken in the early 1960s as my law career was on the upswing — thanks to Jack Millar — and my political career was looming.

In 1965, three years after we started building our law firm, I had the honour of being appointed Queen's Counsel. But, thanks to the lingering effects of Dave Duncan exposing me to politics, I was moving in another direction — politics. It was a direction that would consume much of my life over the next fifteen years. Politics was becoming my calling, and after campaigning and losing in 1965, followed by winning in the 1968 federal election, it was clear the political visibility was a tremendous help in pushing our firm to prominence. My fight to overcome prejudice and being an accepted part of the unique law firm Jack Millar had assembled was not lost on Hamiltonians during the election campaigns.

When I first ran for Parliament in 1965, we hadn't finished building the "United Nations" firm yet. I eventually won against the tide of the

Trudeau landslide in 1968, and then there was an opening in the firm. True to his beliefs and commitments, Jack added that fourth UN component when he brought in Peter Isaacs, a Native Canadian, that year. "We were a visual example of tolerance," noted Isaacs, "where these people felt comfortable." As a small law firm, we also had the advantage of dealing with these clients on an individual basis.

Through the media, our firm attracted both national and international recognition thanks to my successful election. The American black magazine *Ebony* followed my 1968 campaign closely and reported that "Canada's black member of Parliament" was "in partnership with three other lawyers — one British, one Japanese and one Canadian Indian." It pointed out that, at $18,000 a year, I was taking a stiff cut in pay compared to my law practice earnings, but I explained that I had been motivated by the belief that I could have an impact on Canada's future. The positive publicity for our firm continued in succeeding campaigns.

While I served as an MP in opposition, I was able to maintain my partnership in the law firm. However, when the Conservatives won the election of 1979 and I became minister of labour, conflict of interest guidelines required that I resign. This wasn't easy to do, given our firm's accomplishments. Paul Tokiwa left in 1983 to practise on his own. He died in 1994. The partnership finally dissolved when Isaacs left in 1993. He is currently an Ontario Provincial Court judge. However, the firm's name continues with Millar's two sons, who practise under the proud name of Millar, Alexander.

Jack believed in diversity, but he was great to work with for many other reasons as well. If I made a mistake on a title, I got guidance, not a reprimand. However, as much as I liked practising law, it wasn't my first love. I became a lawyer because I couldn't get a job at Stelco, so when I stepped down because of politics, I missed my law partners but I didn't miss the job. I wasn't the best lawyer in the city, but I certainly wasn't the worst. I mainly did real estate and criminal law, though I preferred real estate because there was money to be made and there were always interesting things happening in untangling deals.

At one time I fancied myself a Perry Mason, though that changed. I was defending a guy known as the Bongo Murderer, and I never took any murder cases after that one. I never thought I was good enough. I

*Our United Nations law firm a year after my election to Parliament. (From left)
Peter Isaacs, Paul Tokiwa, me, and Jack Millar, the visionary founder of the UN
firm. My note to him says, "To Jackie — My partner and friend who has made so
much possible and for which I am deeply thankful. Lincoln Alexander Oct 6/69."*

had this guy's life in my hands, and I decided I never wanted to be in
that position again. We ended up settling on manslaughter. Criminal
law, particularly involving murder, was taxing work. But in that case,
Harvey McCullough, Q.C., was the Crown attorney, and an experienced
one at that. He taught me a lesson in murder cases. At the last minute,
he brought in a witness who had seen everything, and it nailed my
client. I was shocked, at a loss for words. And Harvey just smiled. I was
cocksure I had won that case, because McCullough hadn't produced any
evidence. Then, wham! I've never forgotten the lessons of that day.

When I started practising law, I just wanted to do well, try as hard
as possible, commit to whatever I was working on completely, and not
be a phony. Now a new occupation was calling, and that was politics.

CHAPTER 7

Entering the Political Arena

As a black lawyer, the recognition afforded Oliver Holland, the first black lawyer to practise in Hamilton, had benefited me. His work inspired Hamilton's blacks and helped promote greater acceptance for them. Holland was also involved with the Conservative party in Hamilton.

That was part of my political influence. But my association with politics, specifically with the Conservatives, began long before I joined Jack Millar's law firm. Edward Okuloski, whose firm gave me my first job in the profession, was active for many years in the party. So, of course, was David Duncan, my first law partner. Therefore, my leaning, if you will, was directed toward the Conservatives. Then one day, John Diefenbaker asked me to run for his party.

Just as Hamilton's demographics were changing in the 1950s, so was its political scene. The Conservatives were in the vanguard of that change, which would see women and minorities assume prominent roles. Under the Conservative banner, Ellen Fairclough became the city's first female member of Parliament and later Canada's first female cabinet minister and deputy prime minister. In 1957 in Hamilton East, Conservative Quinto Martini became the first Italo-Canadian elected to Parliament. At the provincial level, Hamilton's Ada Pritchard became the first female Conservative member of the Ontario legislature. Both Fairclough and Pritchard had paid their political dues at the municipal level, serving on Hamilton's city

council. There, they were among the first women in the city to artic-
ulate women's concerns, such as equal pay for equal work. In 1962,
Victor Copps, a dynamic and flamboyant individual (and a Liberal),
very much in touch with the "new generation," became Hamilton's
first Roman Catholic mayor. The city's political landscape was going
through a grand transition, and the possibility of a city black getting
elected was growing more conceivable.

Changes at the provincial level were finally helping blacks and
other visible minorities overcome prejudice. In 1944, the Ontario legislature passed the first Canadian human rights statute. This Racial
Discrimination Act prohibited the publication or display of signs,
symbols, or other representations expressing racial or religious discrimination. In 1962, the legislature consolidated this legislation into
the Ontario Human Rights Code to be administered by the Ontario
Human Rights Commission, headed by Daniel Hill, a black.

*Here I am with an African bishop whose name I can't recall (left), Carl Rowan,
and Ellen Fairclough. I tried to rescue Fairclough from a blunder she made in a
comment about immigrants by arranging this photo op to show that Conservatives
were racially sensitive.*

The Canadian government had signed the United Nations Universal Declaration of Human Rights in 1948, and then later, as prime minister, John Diefenbaker led the crusade against ethnic and racial discrimination, both in Canada and the Commonwealth. After his Bill of Rights was passed in 1960, the following year, at a Commonwealth prime ministers' meeting, he publicly denounced apartheid in South Africa. Also helping to sensitize people to the impact of racial prejudice was Martin Luther King's civil rights crusade in the United States.

While Dave Duncan might have planted the first seed of political interest in me, it wasn't until after the six-week trip to Africa in 1960 that my political ambition blossomed. When I returned from that trip and was making speeches to churches and service organizations to raise money for African development, the potential power of political involvement started to become clear. My political activities began gaining momentum in 1963, when, while still actively pursuing my law career, I worked for Ada Pritchard in the provincial election. That was an invaluable experience, for I was exposed to politics down in the trenches, where you see all that is required of the candidate and the incredible army of supporters that is needed to get elected.

So my exposure to Dave Duncan, Ellen Fairclough, and Ada Pritchard, all Progressive Conservatives, drew me deeper into the party's circle. Who knows? If they had been Liberals, I probably would have become a Liberal, since until that time I had no party affiliation. For that matter, I never knew my mother's or father's choice of party. They never talked to me about politics.

Still, I almost didn't enter active politics. Two years before my first campaign, I heard through Duncan that Prime Minister John Diefenbaker wanted to appoint me to a diplomatic post. Diefenbaker met with me and explained he wanted me to become high commissioner to Jamaica. But apparently I wasn't well enough known to satisfy the Jamaicans — an objection that I still resent — and before the situation was resolved, Diefenbaker's government lost power.

Soon after, Diefenbaker sought me out again, this time as a political candidate. He said, "You know, it's time blacks should sit in Ottawa."

I was shocked. "Seek a seat?" I asked. I told him I didn't think Canadians were ready for a black member of Parliament, but he wanted to take the

A campaign stop during the 1965 election. You can see a picture of me on the wall at the back, one of three Conservative candidates in Hamilton.

initiative rather than wait for change to evolve. This grabbed my heart. Just as he had crusaded to sanction South Africa over apartheid, he also wanted to send a message in his own country about political representation of blacks.

I think there's a parallel between Diefenbaker persuading me to run for Parliament and Brooklyn Dodgers president Branch Rickey signing Jackie Robinson to break baseball's colour barrier. Rickey knew he needed a person of strong character to withstand the inevitable pressure and threats. Robinson not only had the character, he was university educated, not to mention his incredible talent. I think that Diefenbaker, probably after conferring with people such as Dave Duncan, felt I could meet the challenge.

Diefenbaker was a hard man to describe in a few words, but I gained immense respect for him. Perhaps he was interested in appointing me to such a position because he also saw himself as an outsider. He had boasted, "I am the first prime minister of this country of neither altogether English nor French origin." Twenty years later, when I was Ontario's lieutenant-governor, the *Toronto Star* reported my musings on

94

my first experiences with the Chief. I talked about how he felt I seemed to be just the man to show Canadians the Conservative party was open to all races and people of all backgrounds. While I realized I was a symbolic candidate, I also felt I could do a great job for the party. So I decided that if the Conservatives wanted to "use" me, I would use them for my own development. It was well known I had always been willing to stand up for my rights. I don't think I let Diefenbaker down.

In 1994, Conchita Tan-Willman and Shiu Loon Kong recounted my memories of Diefenbaker in Volume One of *Canadian Achievers and Their Mentors*: "His warmth, his interest in the plight of minorities, his ability to communicate, and his ability to have a vision captivated me, and soon I found myself talking like him.... He encouraged me all the way through. My mentors, more than anything else, gave me confidence and a respect for myself."

Getting elected can be a long, arduous process. It was hard enough to gain a nomination, much less to win a seat in Parliament, even if you were white. In 1965, I really hadn't even expected to win the party's nomination. For one thing, there were only a few hundred blacks in Hamilton, most of whom were, at best, on the fringes of politics. They weren't welcome in political circles and consequently had little interest in the whole process. So I knew I couldn't count on a lot of support from them.

At first, Hamilton East seemed the likeliest riding for me. It was being offered on a silver platter — and then the platter was snatched away. Former member of Parliament Quinto Martini asserted there would never be a black MP in Hamilton East. Because of my colour I could never win enough votes. It was senseless to nominate a candidate who was bound to lose at the polls, he said.

I was disgusted and furious at the way the riding association was run. I even threatened to go public, but then the riding of Hamilton West beckoned. Suds Stephens, Q.C., and Donald Cooper, the leader of the Conservatives in Hamilton at that time, wanted me to run in Hamilton West. The riding association had followed the dispute in Hamilton East and was prepared to back me. Because of its diversity — with McMaster University, middle-class Westdale, Aberdeen Avenue, and the working-class north end — Hamilton West was a candidate's riding, not a party one, if you know what I mean. That characteristic of the riding worked well for me because I thrived on personal politics. The nomination was contested, but I won.

Then, after I got the nomination, nothing happened. So my partner, Jack Millar, went to Cooper and Jim Fraser, both now deceased, and asked what the hell was going on. The problem was that as long as they had nominated a candidate, they figured their job was done. The local Conservatives didn't think Hamilton West was winnable, so they were just going through the motions until Jack shook them up.

When I began campaigning, the harsh realities of prejudice and racial taunts raised their ugly heads from time to time. But having taken on prejudice from downtown Toronto to Harlem to Osgoode Hall, I was not going to back down or cower. I fought back. Loud-mouthed louts and cowardly bullies that some people are, I would always be able to face them down. Beneath the surface I have a raw mean streak that can be triggered by such incidents. Fortunately, for me, this disposition almost always saw me through.

In the 1965 election, I ran against three other candidates. I remember what worried me most was that I might finish last. In the end, the Conservatives lost the election, but I came in second to Joseph Macaluso, the Liberal incumbent and also a lawyer, by 2,359 votes. When Diefenbaker conceded the election on national television that night, he singled out wrestler Whipper Billy Watson, the Conservative candidate in York East, and me, saying he was very sad we had lost. I was deeply touched that he would think about me at a time like that. In the enormity of his party's defeat, he was offering words of comfort to me on national television. I cried all night, but it made me stronger.

Running on the Conservative ticket under Diefenbaker's successor, Robert Stanfield, in the June 25, 1968, election, we expected to lose. Everybody, it seemed, was voting for the Liberals and their wildly popular new leader, Pierre Trudeau, whose political magnetism ignited the phenomenon dubbed "Trudeaumania" by the press. During the campaign, Trudeau came to Hamilton and introduced Liberal candidate Tom Beckett, another lawyer, as the giant-killer of Hamilton West. Well, it turned out I was the giant-killer, though I did just edge him by 342 votes.

I remember campaigning among the union members at the steel mills. It was dangerous turf for a Conservative in what is generally considered

New Democrat territory. But I wasn't scared of anyone. One time a few belligerent people were harassing me; one, in particular, was an overweight redheaded guy who had been drinking. He bellowed, "Get out, you black right-wing bastard." I didn't, of course, and I was prepared to fight him outside if I had to. But I know that many steelworkers voted for me. They couldn't say that out loud — that a union member would vote Conservative rather than NDP — but it was a fact lots did.

In 1968, we ran an aggressive campaign, with lots of gimmicks, from riding in a convertible with beautiful young women to hiring a marching band that played "Alexander's Ragtime Band." Jack Millar would later recall the pandemonium as telephone calls poured into our law office the day after the election and TV cameras arrived — the frenetic activity caused all the fuses to blow.

Henry Jacek, a political science professor at McMaster, used a student study of the 1968 election in Hamilton West to demonstrate the effects of political polling. The survey determined that if a candidate was only a little behind, making the poll public might energize his or her workers, but if the candidate was trailing significantly, he or she might simply give up.

My law partner Jack Millar and I in Ottawa in 1968 after winning my first election.

The McMaster students surveyed three Hamilton West polling areas and released the results about a week before the election. At the time, I was running second, slightly behind Beckett, the Liberal candidate. After hearing how close the margin was, our team campaigned hard over the final weekend. After the votes were tallied, I had edged out Beckett to become the first black Canadian elected to the House of Commons.

How significant was that win? I was the only Conservative candidate elected in an Ontario urban centre — and one of only four urban Tories in the country — as Trudeau and the Liberals captured 154 of the 264 seats in Parliament. In our immediate area, only William Knowles of Norfolk-Haldimand and I won seats for the Conservatives. I joked that my victory was the result of "Alexandermania."

I was not the only trailblazer for minorities in the 1968 vote. Liberal Leonard Marchand became the first status Indian elected to the House of Commons by winning the Kamloops-Cariboo riding in British Columbia. I remember saying at the time that I hoped my victory would encourage others to believe that they could be elected as well, regardless of their race, creed, colour, or religion.

During my victory speech, I was chatting away when all of a sudden everybody began roaring with laughter at my seemingly innocuous comment that I would do my best to fill the shoes of the last Tory to hold the seat. Well, that turned out to be the diminutive Ellen Fairclough, and her tiny size-four feet were significantly smaller than my snug size fourteens.

Parliament was still a white man's club when I arrived in Ottawa — Vancouver New Democrat Grace MacInnis was the only female member in the House — and I soon grew weary of being referred to in the press as the "black MP." I told the reporters to call me the MP ready to speak for anyone in my region who suffers from prejudice or some other injustice.

When you first go to Ottawa, you take a course within your own caucus to orient you to life as a member of Parliament. It was a crash course in Ottawa politics, and if one hasn't experienced it, it's hard to imagine what it's like. I'd liken it to jumping into the cockpit of a jet when you've never flown before and trying to steer the thing. It was a strange world, frightening because it was so awesome. And I was understandably worried and scared.

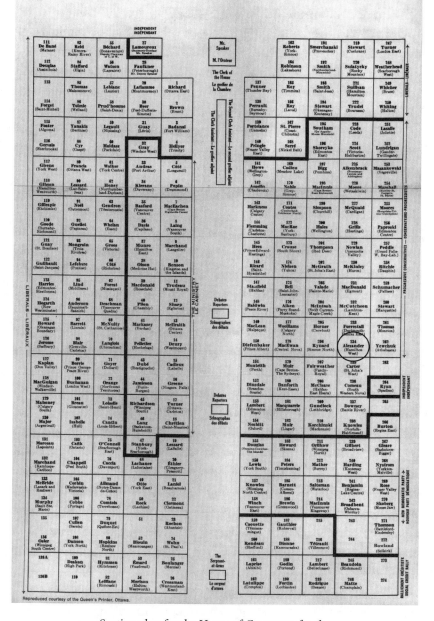

*Seating plan for the House of Commons for the
28th Parliament of Canada (my seat is circled).*

It was intimidating, that responsibility, and that's the central reason I waited so long to deliver my maiden speech — although from time to time you'll come across new MPs who can't wait to get up and shoot their mouths off. As a lawyer, you go to court in front of six to twelve people or a judge, but now you were in front of the whole country. I felt I could not fail. It is a humbling feeling and a powerful sense of responsibility. I had to remember that the whole point of fighting racism and asserting your rights is that you must not be intimidated. Otherwise, you let yourself be made to feel like a second-class citizen and become reluctant to demonstrate your talent and excellence. These days, much later in my life, my attitude is that I am as good as or better than most people, and to hell with you if you don't like me. But I had to work through all those internal, personal issues to prime myself for that first speech.

In the House of Commons, I eventually would have to speak, and remember, early in my law career one of the observations of Sam Gotfrid was that I was shy. As I said, it was less that I was shy and more that I was only the fifth black lawyer in Ontario. In any case, it took me six months to make my first speech in the Commons. I modelled my speaking style after people I admired, in particular John Diefenbaker and Martin Luther King Jr. The fact that I towered over most other members, backed by my deep, authoritative voice, helped too. Fellow MP Angus MacLean, whose advice and support was freely given and always welcome in our caucus, assured me I would do fine. (Angus, an air force war hero, MP from 1951 to 1976, Minister of Fisheries from 1957 to 1963, and later premier of Prince Edward Island, died in 2000.) After I made that first speech I told anyone who felt intimidated they shouldn't worry; they should recognize they were merely in the quagmire of hypocrisy and bullshit and they could deal with it.

As the first black MP to address the House, it was a very proud moment. Here is my inaugural speech to Parliament, September 20, 1968:

> Mr. Speaker, I wish to thank you for giving me this opportunity of speaking to this first session of the twenty-eighth parliament as the representative for Hamilton West. To me, this is a privilege and an honour which I

shall long remember because it is at this time that I feel a sense of involvement and belonging.

I begin by congratulating you, sir, on your election as Speaker and informing you that there can be no doubt in my mind, after listening to the many plaudits extended to you, that we shall continue to be directed by your excellent guidance and leadership. My congratulations are also extended to the Deputy Speaker, whose ability has been recognized. I, as well as many others, particularly those sitting in this House for the first time, have been very impressed with the way you have been discharging your responsibilities being knowledgeable, impartial and giving evidence of your wit.

My sincerest congratulations are extended to the Honourable Member for Madawaska-Victoria [Mr. Corbin] and the Honourable Member for Kamloops-Cariboo [Mr. Marchand], both of whom, because of their seriousness of thought and ability to communicate, have gained the respect and admiration of this entire House.

I would also like to bring your attention, sir, that at this moment I am very conscious of a meeting that I had in Toronto some time in 1964 with the Right Honourable Member for Prince Albert [Mr. Diefenbaker]. It was there that he, in his wisdom and experience, believed that I should be engaged in politics as a candidate because, as he stated, he had faith and confidence in my ability and believed that I could and would make a contribution toward the ultimate destiny of Canada. For this I am extremely grateful.

Some honourable members: Hear, hear.

I am also pleased to say that fortunately the electorate of Hamilton West were of the same opinion, and because of this faith and confidence, as expressed in many ways prior to the last general election, I now speak as the Honourable Member for Hamilton West. My gratitude is also extended to a former Honourable Member, Mr. Joseph Macaluso, who in his wisdom has helped me to be here this afternoon.

Some honourable members: Hear, hear.

Mr. Speaker, there are no words that can adequately express my thanks and those of my family for this great honour. Therefore, I can only say with deep sincerity and conviction that I am profoundly grateful for this unprecedented honour and I shall do my utmost to become a worthy member of Parliament under the leadership of the Leader of the Opposition [Mr. Stanfield], who has continually encouraged and counseled me, and the guidance of the many Honourable Members on both sides of this House who have expressed an interest in my political career, sanctioned, I fervently pray, by Him without whom all goals are unattainable.

I am privileged to say that I was born in Ontario, the province of opportunity, the province to which many people in Canada look for leadership because it has progressed so dynamically, welcoming all peoples, regardless of race, creed or colour, desirous of contributing to its phenomenal growth and sharing its wealth and the good life. Within that province is the city in which I live, the city that has adopted me and propelled me with jet-like propulsion to the House of Commons.

In the view of the time allotted to me, and because I would like to make some observations on other matters, I cannot recite a complete and adequate picture of the city of Hamilton, or in fact my riding of Hamilton West, [the only] one of four in the city that escaped Trudeaumania, much to the disbelief and bewilderment of the Grits. In any event, I find it necessary to speak about some of the important points of Hamilton because, as I understand it, a member is likely not to have another opportunity.

I would like to commence by pointing out to you, Mr. Speaker, and Honourable Members that Hamilton had another first in the person of Honourable Ellen Fairclough, Canada's first woman cabinet member, who no doubt is warmly remembered by many Honourable Members because of her outstanding contribution to this House.

Some honourable members: Hear, hear.

To her, I owe much, and I shall continue to rely on her wisdom and experience.

This city of almost 300,000 in population is the steel centre of Canada, producing more than one half of Canada's steel. It is interesting to note that iron and steel industry sales all across Canada make up approximately 2.7 per cent of the gross national product, therefore being even greater than wheat, which is 1.7 per cent.

Because of the importance of this industry to our economy, Canada's principal basic steel producers, among which Hamilton['s] steel industry plays an important role, are of course very interested in the new anti-dumping code agreed to by Canada in the recent General Agreement on Tariffs and Trade. Mr. Speaker, you will recall that something was said on this subject this morning. Industry regards dumping as a serious problem and is justifiably concerned about the potential loss of domestic markets to foreign competition at dump prices arising from Canada's acceptance of Article VI of the General Agreement on Tariffs and Trade.

Industry recognizes that competition on a fair trading basis is customary and, of course, challenging. However, competition at less than fair market value is disturbing and cannot be considered fair. In fact, it may result in irreparable damage to the domestic industry and to the economy. It is suggested that the onus of preventing undue disruption from dumping into the domestic market rests completely on the importing country. Therefore, I strongly urge that the government be very aware of the dangers of dumping, and in enacting any laws to bring the anti-dumping agreement into effect deep consideration and attention should be given to the scope of the legislation and the form of administration of the law because Hamilton, and indeed Canada, neither want nor can afford harmful effects on the economy.

Although steel plays a great role in the life of Hamilton, the manufacturing of machinery, electrical goods, rubber, chemicals and textiles also means a livelihood for many Hamiltonians. Hamilton can further boast of the port of Hamilton, which has a waterfront providing three miles of berthing space. It is a port of call for fifty shipping lines and it has agencies with services to and from one hundred world ports. Present trade trends suggest that the port will become an increasingly important seaport gateway through which an ever-growing volume of exports and imports will be shipped, thereby allowing it to continue to break records in terms of tonnage moved. In this connection, may I remind the Minister of Labour [Mr. Mackasey] that notwithstanding the fact that in a democracy one can expect strikes, Hamilton would take issue with him in the event there was a prolonged one in this area.

One cannot speak of Hamilton without reference to McMaster University, my alma mater, which has attracted and continues to attract students from all over the world who seek excellence in graduate and post-graduate studies. It is worthwhile mentioning that Hamilton's rock garden because of its floral display has received international acclaim. May I also point out, if anyone is in doubt, that Hamilton still has faith in the Hamilton Tiger-Cats football team.

The city of Hamilton is progressing with an urban renewal program, including a civic square, and Hamiltonians continue to expect, and in fact deserve, immediate, decisive and continued government leadership in that regard.

Of some concern to Hamilton at the present time are its plans for a cultural centre — the Hamilton Theatre Auditorium. Toward this end may I say that the people of Hamilton have made and met their financial commitments; the province of Ontario has made and is prepared to honour its commitment, and we now look to this government to become involved pursuant to the many requests made upon it so that a firm and early commitment may be expected. It is hoped that the government is as enthusiastic about receiving briefs and submissions on the project as are the Hamiltonians in presenting them.

Hamilton is no different from any other large city. Of course, it has its urban problems. Hamiltonians also are very concerned about housing, unemployment, inflation, air and water pollution, lack of mortgage moneys, high interest rates, and a lack of serviced land. These are the areas to which priority should be directed.

Hamiltonians, and indeed all Canadians, believed that the Speech from the Throne would indicate solutions to these problems with greater clarity as related to the just society, a phrase without definition and an election slogan that has frustrated and confused many. Canadians want solutions to the many social and economic problems which now burden this nation. They want them now, and will not be satisfied with the tokenism and expression of intentions for the future.

It is not unreasonable to conclude that because the Prime Minister spoke of the just society on the hustings and said, "follow me, give me a majority," Canadians have the right to expect and believe that this government would present to them a dynamic, inspiring and moving political manifesto in the Speech from the Throne. I can remember the arrival of the Prime Minister in Hamilton and I can remember reading about him and his smile when he said "follow me" and they walked. Then, he became famous for that which many of us younger ones would want to be famous and for which we feel some jealousy. The women said, "where do we go." He said, "follow me," and they walked.

No, it is implied that the government did not have to give this country leadership or direction in the Speech from the Throne. Apparently, in the mind of the government, this conclusion was unreasonable on the part of the people and reached without justification, much to the dismay and disappointment of many Canadians. I, too, am disappointed and in total disagreement with the utterances of many political experts who believe that it is inevitable that the Speech from the Throne should be dull, uninspiring and empty. Such speeches are not and never will be accepted. This is 1968, the jet-propelled age and not the days of the horse and buggy.

As a result of their disappointment, Canadians have changed. I say that sincerely. They are no longer uninformed, naïve and gullible. At this time an expression comes to mind which was continually referred to by the late Dr. Martin Luther King in speeches in which he quoted the ungrammatical truths of an old preacher, among which was the following: "We ain't what we oughta be, we ain't what we could be, we ain't what we should be, but thank God we ain't what we was." I say to the government: take heed and wake up before it is too late.

Mr. Speaker, since coming to this House I have become more and more aware of the tremendous responsibilities of a member of Parliament. He must grapple conscientiously and diligently with the many problems which face this nation. He must find with expediency the solutions to them. He must be concerned about the quality of life being experienced by all Canadians. He must create with enthusiasm and confidence a climate of proper direction to ensure the realization of our ultimate goal, that of a greater Canada in which we can all pray, live, work and play harmoniously while enjoying the fruits of full economic development. To these ends I dedicate my strength and my abilities and in this dedication my thoughts are directed toward many people in Canada about whom I and my constituents in Hamilton West are concerned.

We are concerned about the fact that four million people live in poverty. We are concerned about the fact that the dream of owning one's home has apparently become an impossible dream under this administration. We are concerned about the fact that unemployment is at the unwarranted high level of more than 400,000. We are concerned about the reliance on welfare by many. We are concerned about the fact that because of inflation the pensioners, the aged, the disabled and those on fixed incomes have very little purchasing power.

Does this government have the solutions to these basic problems that face this nation? If they have, let them kindly advise the country, because the country is waiting for the answers. I say to this government, this is the time to show greater evidence of its concern. This is unquestionably a time for reassessment, a time for awakening. This is a time for reflection on the past only to better enable us to determine the guidelines and direction that positive action for the immediate future must take, particularly in relation to economic development, research and technology. We would then be in a more favourable position to solve these problems.

It seems to me that in a just society it should be the continuing responsibility of this government to be constantly aware of and concerned about the degree of the quality of life that each and every Canadian is experiencing. If there is any disparity, no matter how little, then the government should immediately set itself to reducing it, thereby assuring that each and every individual can live a full productive life and become in fact an essential part of the mainstream of Canadian life for the betterment of all Canadians.

I should like to move now, Mr. Speaker, to another topic. I am the first black man elected to the House of Commons. This results from the fact that many Hamiltonians have accepted as a way of life a simple truism expressed by Adele Florence Corey long ago. She said that men should not be judged by the colour of their skin nor by the way they fight, love or sin, nor by the gods they serve or vintage they drink, but by the quality of the thoughts they think. How simple that statement is, but how unacceptable to many. Yet, if this way of life is not accepted, speak not to me of the Bill of Rights; speak not to me of democracy; speak not to me of the brotherhood of man or the fatherhood of God, because this then becomes hypocrisy. The black man also desires a place in the mainstream of life and because of this we read of his struggle, and struggle he must.

Listen to what Frederick Douglas, that great abolitionist, said back in 1857 about struggle. He said: "The whole history of the progress of human liberty shows that all concessions yet made to her august claims have been born of earnest struggle. If there is no struggle, there is no progress. Those who profess freedom, yet deprecate struggle, are men who want crops without ploughing up the ground; they want rain without thunder and lightning. Power concedes nothing without a demand. It never did and it never will. Men may not get all they pay for in this world, but they must certainly pay for all they get."

The negro has to struggle. Some say I have it made. Let me, standing here, be no indication that all negroes in Canada have it made. Let me say this: the negro has awakened with a new soul. He knows he is somebody. He is Thurgoode Marshall, supreme court justice, he is Dr. Ralph Bunche, diplomat extraordinaire. He is Carl Stokes, mayor of Cleveland. He is Dr. Martin Luther King, whose passive resistance has changed the nature of thinking of the whole free world. He is Leonard Braithwaite who, even though a Liberal, sits at Queen's Park in Toronto. He is the high commissioners and ambassadors we see here in Ottawa.

This is an impressive list, I know, but I wonder how many men of such calibre we have lost because of the deliberate rejection of people because of colour. I am not the spokesman for the negro; that honour has not been given to me. Do not let me ever give anyone that impression. However, I want the record to show that I accept the responsibility of speaking for him and all others in this great nation who feel that they are the subjects of discrimination because of race, creed or colour.

In conclusion, Mr. Speaker, I would say that our role in the building of the "just society," if it is to become reality, is that it must be involved with the hopes, the fears, the disappointments, legitimate aspirations and despair of each and every Canadian, ever mindful that involvement demands commitment in terms of actions and deeds, rather than words only.

As I look back at that speech, I find it amusing to see how many of the things I touched on still need attention today. Of course, the issue of race continues to dog us, whether it has to do with racial profiling by police or the plight of directionless young men in Toronto who have been killing one another at a horrifying rate. We still have far to go in that regard. Beyond the race issue, it is interesting that trade and protectionism concerns, especially because of the interests of Hamilton, were high on my agenda then. In this age of globalization and the debates and battles it has ignited, it leaves me convinced the matter of trade will forever pose challenges to us. And social concerns — equal rights for women, aboriginal issues, poverty, and affordable housing — continue to demand attention from all levels of government, along with greater promotion of education and research. My goodness, what foresight I had!

As a family, we considered moving lock, stock, and barrel to Ottawa, but those discussions ultimately didn't get very far. Being in Hamilton was important to Yvonne and Keith, even though my being away from home so much was not the easiest life for them. To me, it would have been self-ish to expect them to come to Ottawa, as though my life should be the only thing that defined their lives. They had schools, friends, social lives, and a home they were familiar with. Yvonne, as the youngest, was keen to stay close to her sisters, though I wouldn't have had any trouble mov-ing far away from them. In short, Yvonne and Keith had their own lives, and I'm convinced they would not have been happy with the move or, at the very least, it would have taken a long time before they ever came around to being happy with living in Ottawa. Besides, I could get my tail kicked out in any election and then we would surely find ourselves mov-ing back to Hamilton.

Yvonne did some constituency work and campaigning, and she came out occasionally to Ottawa for the bigger events. She was very ele-gant. When my wife walked into a room, people were astonished by her beauty. She was shy, but she always had very good bearing in public. I consulted her on political issues, and she always gave me good, com-mon-sense, practical advice.

I was home in Hamilton every weekend, although that became diffi-cult when I was a cabinet minister. Some politicians fail to realize that even after you become a minister, you've got to come back and maintain your bond with your riding. The people in Hamilton West told Yvonne that. She'd tell them I was spending more time in Ottawa because I had a cabinet post. They would say, "It doesn't matter. He should be here." It was an important reminder. You have to come home and be involved, walk the streets, meet the people. That's one of the reasons I hated winter elections — it wasn't easy walking the streets. It was valuable getting those observations from Yvonne.

The focus for any good MP should be his or her constituency, and their issues should be brought to the House of Commons in Ottawa. The issues that affect people are not in the House of Commons but at home, the place where the people who elected you live, work, and play. By way of example, at the federal level you don't deal directly with issues such as roads or education because they are not under federal jurisdiction. But as an MP, when a constituent raises a concern that is outside your jurisdiction, you still feel you have to get answers. Answers may not be solutions, but getting them is one way you feel able to help your constituents.

After I became an MP I didn't go to my church much anymore, but instead started going to everyone else's churches. I used to go for christenings, weddings, and funerals all the time, and this was important because it showed people that politicians were just regular people. To me, it was a genuine gesture. I don't believe you play around with people's emotions, and it was part of my training as a Christian. Now, I don't go to formal church much anymore, but I do go to church in my own bedroom. Unfortunately, I feel the churches are failing to capture people's imaginations, and as a result, they can't maintain solid core congregations. There's no vision in the leadership of the churches, and that's why so many churches are empty. But I digress.

Two people handled the day-to-day affairs of the Hamilton constituency office. I would touch base every time I came back to find out what the constituents were saying, and we would stay in touch with the constituency secretaries daily by phone. As for my election successes, I think it was more pro-Lincoln than pro-Conservative. Over the years many people have told me that the only time they voted Conservative was because of me. I never had any enemies. Even now, people say, "Come back, the country needs leadership."

The whole political experience illustrated for me how fortunate it was that I came to Hamilton rather than staying in Toronto. Because of the city's size, I always felt it was much easier to get closer to the people I represented, and my constituency office workers could readily look into problems in the city and communicate them to me so we could try to work toward a solution. I had a great constituency secretary, and we were always in touch.

The Hamilton West organization was one of the best in the country, as evidenced by the fact I defeated Liberal candidate Tom Beckett in the midst of Trudeaumania. We had a lot of good young people — it's estimated there were seven hundred to eight hundred young people involved in our campaign — mixed with a strong group of experienced leaders. They revolutionized campaigning and created a model for many subsequent campaigns. As the candidate, I would be out on the street and they'd be going door to door, inviting people to come out for a look or a chat. I loved campaigning. Still do.

In 1976–77, I served proudly as observer to the United Nations for Canada.

Life in the public eye is not without its rewards and, sometimes, its pleasant surprises. Such was the case in 1977 when, out of the blue as far as both Yvonne and I were concerned, I was given a testimonial dinner in Hamilton. The flattering invitation read as follows: "Linc Alexander has touched us all over the years in many ways, as a teammate, classmate, fellow serviceman, lodge brother, lawyer, politician, or

SOLID ROOTS

This sketch of me was on the cover of the program for a dinner in my honour in 1977, at which the organizers announced they had arranged for the discharge of the mortgage on our home on Proctor Boulevard.

just good friend. Some of Lincoln's many acquaintances have joined together to organize a reunion and testimonial dinner. A feature of the evening will be a presentation to Lincoln ..."

To have, at age fifty-five, a testimonial dinner was incredibly humbling in its own right, but what these people did for us was nothing short of shocking. It reduced Yvonne to tears and me, for many seconds, to speechlessness. I had to struggle to maintain my composure. These great friends and colleagues had arranged for the discharge of the mortgage on our home on Proctor Boulevard, which was still in the range of $8,000.

In a column on the event in the *Hamilton Spectator*, Stan McNeill wrote that friends totalling "500 crowded into the Royal Connaught ballroom to pay tribute to a man and his family who have endeared themselves to Hamilton in a way that few have ever matched." It's easy to see after an event like that why I have had such a bond to that community, for it has supported me in ways I could never have imagined. I hope I have been able in some ways to repay Hamilton's generosity.

113

Note from Flora McDonald at the time of the dinner for me in Hamilton in 1977.

That evening we had the good fortune to be entertained by Oscar Peterson, and I even got into the act with a little vocal performance with my church choir. It cost $6,000 to get Oscar, and his agent wouldn't waive it. Jack Millar paid the sum and charged it to my drawings from the firm. Although I was the sitting Conservative MP for Hamilton West, people from all political stripes, from every point in my past and from every walk of life, were there. Without engaging in excessive grandstanding, I truly believe an event like that tribute is a reward for my honesty and striving to be a people-oriented person. French existentialist philosopher Jean-Paul Sartre once wrote, "Hell is other people." I couldn't disagree more. The opposite, heaven, is the true subject of that statement.

At the dinner, I expressed much thanks to John Diefenbaker, who had dragged me into politics and was at that point sharing an Opposition bench with me in the Commons. I told our friends, "I would like to thank him for planting the seed that any goal an individual wants to attain is within his grasp."

CANADA

PRIME MINISTER · PREMIER MINISTRE

     I am sorry that prior commitments
prevent my being with you tonight to add in
person my sincere congratulations to all those
Lincoln Alexander receives.

     Being on opposite sides of the House
of Commons does not preclude the possibility
of mutual respect and Lincoln Alexander is one
of the members of the Opposition who has my
heartfelt esteem. I have always found him to
be a man of integrity, of wit and of wisdom.
It is parliamentarians such as Linc who bring
dignity and honour to the position. I am
delighted to have this opportunity to express
my deep admiration on this occasion.

     Please accept my warmest best wishes
and kind personal regards.

Pierre Elliott Trudeau

Ottawa,
1977.

Letter of congratulations from Prime Minister Pierre Trudeau at the time of the dinner for me in Hamilton in 1977.

The leaders I served under — John Diefenbaker, Robert Stanfield, and Joe Clark — were each as interesting as they were different. Stanfield was a very sincere, responsible, good person. That's why he is referred to as the best prime minister we never had. He was just not charismatic. And it was ridiculous the way that failing to catch a football in that famous newspaper photo cost him an election. Even if you have a great brain, if you don't have charisma in that business, it is a tough sell. You see people with charisma who aren't very bright, but people follow them. Stanfield would have been a great prime minister. He was a great administrator. The Diefenbaker people tried to take him down, and I didn't like that at all.

As much as I owed my political success to Dief, I was glad when he stepped down. It was time for him to go, both for him and for the party. There were too many MPs following Diefenbaker, and that made Stanfield's life very difficult. Diefenbaker's backers were going behind the curtains in the House of Commons, cooking up deals and spreading gossip, and it undermined Stanfield's authority. That is the stark difference, I think, between the Conservatives and the Liberals. The Liberals, no matter how deep the divisions and differences between individuals, would find a way to pull together and not implode the party. Too many Conservatives were unable to set aside their personal differences for the good of the party. They were self-centred prima donnas. People would ask me back then what I thought about all the intrigue surrounding and orchestrated by Diefenbaker and his gang — and remember, I had a fierce loyalty to him — and I would say, "I only have one leader, our party's leader, Stanfield." It reminds me of the thoughts of Tom Bell, one of the greatest whips the House has ever seen, who often said, "It's a whore's game, Alexander."

The selection of Joe Clark to succeed Stanfield was largely the result of the ministrations of Sinclair Stevens at the 1976 leadership convention. He was a kingmaker who swung his support to Clark, one of Stanfield's writers and a party man himself. But when I was told Clark was going to run, I thought, *Really*. As a leader, he came to demonstrate his thoughtfulness, depth of policy knowledge, and general political awareness, but at the time he was a political neophyte. Clark was very good on his feet, but when he talked he used to jab his finger — comment, point, comment, point, point — and people didn't like that. Clark used to fight like hell in caucus trying to bring Conservatives more to the centre, but the other MPs from the West, unlike him, were very conservative. And the thinking in some circles was that people didn't want to vote for us because Clark's wife, Maureen McTeer, hadn't taken his name. That amazed me; it was pathetic that people thought that way, and yet today a wife keeping her own name is so common. The Progressive Conservatives were a difficult party to govern because there were so many different views from within. The Liberals have similar wide-reaching viewpoints within their caucus, but they always pulled together. As prime minister, Clark had difficulty controlling the whole caucus, which didn't have the respect for him that he deserved.

It was during my first term in Ottawa that the FLQ crisis erupted in Quebec. I was in my bed, and somebody from the press called and said Trudeau had just introduced the War Measures Act. I didn't know what it was, but the reporter wanted me to comment, and fortunately for me I said that we might have to give up a few rights to save our overall rights. Trudeau got on the side of the rest of Canada against certain Quebec interests. Introducing the War Measures Act is a draconian choice, because you become *persona non grata*. But I believed at the time that in order to keep all our freedoms, we might have to give up some rights from time to time. We in the Conservative party voted for the measure, and the NDP didn't. On reflection, if I had to vote again I would vote against it, because the issue of limiting rights has far more serious implications than I thought at the time. You become vulnerable, grasped by the tentacles of government power.

I didn't hesitate to vote with the governing Liberals if an issue warranted my support. The controversial issue of capital punishment was a case in point when it came before the House of Commons on a free vote in 1976. It was called the "hanging issue." I supported the Liberals' plan to abolish the death penalty from the Criminal Code and replace it with a mandatory life sentence without possibility of parole for twenty-five years for all first-degree murders. I had received twenty or thirty letters urging me to change my position, but that wasn't much out of a constituency of ninety-five thousand. I was determined to be in the House to vote against the death penalty. In fact, there was extraordinary pressure being exerted on my constituents to try to get me to change my mind. There was intense arm-twisting going on, and it only strengthened my resolve that abolition was the proper course.

As it turned out, however, I was going through a bout of back problems severe enough that I had to be hospitalized. Flora McDonald, the former Kingston and the Islands MP and Conservative cabinet minister, was also an abolitionist. She contacted me in hospital at the time urging me to get up and come to Ottawa for the vote, and I was planning to do so, such was my belief in the abolition of the death penalty. But, boy, was my wife mad. Yvonne said, "If you go to Ottawa, stay there. We are finished." She couldn't understand why I wanted to go to Ottawa because I was in so much pain with my back and she had been subjected to all my complaining. In the end, I couldn't master the back pain enough to get to Ottawa and vote. I couldn't even get out of bed, so I was naturally relieved to discover that the bill did pass. I never felt that capital punishment was in any way a deterrent. And it's morally wrong.

Another case involved the so-called hate bill to introduce anti-hate legislation. The Conservative party opposed the proposed act, arguing it infringed on freedom of speech. I said, "Screw you on free speech" and planned to break ranks to vote with the Liberals. During debate on the bill, I asked, "Are you saying that you can call my son or daughter a nigger and that is free speech?" Prince Edward Island MP (and later senator) Heath MacQuarrie said, "I'm not going to let Linc stand alone on this," and together we led seventeen members of our caucus in support of the government.

I don't think freedom of speech has been eroded by measures such as anti-hate legislation. Speech is still free, but you've got to watch who you are hurting, and you've got to take some responsibility for your comments. I believe in free speech, but if it hurts someone, then to hell with free speech.

Breaking ranks with my party on occasions such as this was justified, in my opinion, not only because it reflected the wishes of my constituents but also because it involved voting on a matter of conscience. I think my willingness to take such a stance made it a lot easier for non-Conservatives in Hamilton to vote for me. Still, I didn't hesitate to take on the government like a belligerent terrier. On several occasions in 1976, when I was a member of the Opposition shadow cabinet, we were pressuring the Liberal government to take action on unemployment. When the manpower minister, Bud Cullen, announced spending the puny sum of $150 million, I denounced it as a stopgap measure. In May, in their budget speech, the Liberals had promised measures to create 250,000 new jobs. Our figures showed only half of that total, at best, had been attained, so I was after them constantly.

There was no shortage of challenging issues in Ottawa. While senior citizens didn't command the attention that they do today — as their ranks swell with baby boomers reaching the golden years — they were not forgotten when I was in Parliament. In 1976, I took a national tour with Alberta Conservative MP Arnold Malone to assess the needs of Canada's seniors.

In Parliament, every day was exciting. I always enjoyed the debates in the House and the cut and thrust of Question Period. Although anyone watching Question Period on television might find it hard to believe, MPs who tee off against each other on issues of the day often aren't as hostile as it may appear. At least, they weren't in my day. In fact, quite the opposite was often the case. I fraternized with members of the other parties, in particular the Liberals.

Personally, I think it is good to get somewhat close to the so-called enemy, but it is also harder to condemn them when you know them too well. You have a job to do, and you can't do it if you get too close. You have to find that tricky balance. For example, as a member of the shadow cabinet, I found that, because I liked him, I found it difficult to attack Trudeau's minister of state, Martin O'Connell. It's like those war movies where you see the enemy and look them in the eye and can't pull the trigger.

Alberta Conservatives Steve Paproski and Jack Horner and I would often hang around with Liberals. Some people in our party didn't like us socializing with the opposition because they suspected we were giving away secrets. Actually, we didn't talk much politics. It was mostly drinking and carousing. Our party wasn't big on fun. I used to say to my colleagues that I came from the big city, not from the bush. The problem was that at Liberal gatherings Paproski and I were getting more press than the Liberals themselves, and they didn't like that. A lot of the Liberals' wives were also upset with all the carousing going on, and they went to Trudeau and said they wanted it stopped. There was a lot of scandalous behaviour going on, to be sure.

Beyond that, Paproski and I attended the Christmas parties in Santa suits and put on a bit of a show. We were extremely popular. Then, in 1977, Horner crossed the floor to join the Liberals, and I didn't want to talk to him anymore. They gave him a cabinet post. To this day I don't accept the actions of recent floor-crossers such as Belinda Stronach, who defected to the Liberals, and David Emerson, who joined Stephen

Harper's Conservatives immediately after the 2006 election. You don't cross the floor for any reason, least of all personal gain. You stick with your party or get the hell out. If everybody crossed the floor, what kind of system would we have?

After Horner crossed the floor and became a cabinet minister, I questioned him in the Commons one day on some topic and he shot back at me with a racial slur. Though he later denied it, I know he said "nigger." Everybody within hearing distance knew he had said that word. We had had such a long-term friendship that I was shocked he would insult me like that. I remember that the NDP's venerable Stanley Knowles was stunned too, and was stirred from his slumbers to call out in his usual way, "Order, order, order."

In February 1971, Newfoundland MP John Lundrigan and I accused Trudeau of mouthing "fuck off" at us during a discussion in the House of Commons on training programs for the unemployed. It sparked a storm of controversy. Outside the House, Trudeau asked if the two of us were lip-readers. He told reporters he had mouthed some words and made a gesture of derision. Trudeau said, "If these guys want to read lips and they want to see anything in it, that's their problem. I think they're very sensitive. They come in the House and make all kinds of accusations and because I smile at them in derision, they go stomping out and go crying to mamma or to television that they've been insulted." Instead, he claimed, he had mouthed the words "fuddle duddle."

That's politics, I suppose. When Trudeau died in 2000, I wrote in all sincerity to his sons Justin and Sacha, "I was deeply saddened when I learned of the passing of your father. Pierre Trudeau was a man of remarkable strength, courage, intelligence, reserve and charm whose name will never be forgotten." Regardless of those warm sentiments, that doesn't change one small detail: He definitely told us to fuck off.

I still contend you can be friendly with your opponents. I don't want to hate an opponent because it serves no purpose. It's like an athletic competition. Good opposition makes you better, stronger. Every now and then we might have a fracas in the House, but when it was over we'd say, "Let's go downtown and have a couple of drinks and a steak." Now, I think, TV coverage has really changed the atmosphere for the worse. You get these showoffs on the floor of the Commons making every issue into a Shakespearean soliloquy, and because it's being done for effect, it does get personal and mean, and all for the cameras. It's just not productive.

Meanwhile, racism continued to be something I tackled as the need arose. In 1978, while a member of the Opposition, I told delegates to a black history conference in Toronto that it was essential they get involved in politics because there is a greater opportunity to fight successfully for change from the inside. All the marches and meetings and street-corner protests in the world will only take you so far. Whether at the local, provincial, or federal levels of government, I argued that you must go where the power is and become part of it.

Some agitators call that selling out. I wonder if those people really do want change or if they thrive on confrontation. I still firmly believe that there is no stronger way to bring about change than to become involved positively in the community, lead a decent life, and understand how the system works. You have got to be there where the influence is. You must understand the aims of political parties. It doesn't matter if you are a Liberal, Conservative, or socialist, so long as you're involved. I can appreciate that some people don't like the system, but in order to improve things one must understand what they are about. I never addressed politics or anything else from a feeling of inferiority, as one who has sold out.

Looking back at my years in Parliament, I like to think I made it easier for others to follow my lead. When I was first elected to Parliament in 1968, I believed that if I could become an MP, then it would mean that a lot of people who thought that perhaps they weren't wanted could make it too. No matter your colour or religion or sex or how your name sounds, you can say, "Well, hell, if Lincoln Alexander can do it, then I guess that I can too." As a matter of fact, when I talk to children in schools, I ask them to repeat after me: "Lincoln Alexander. He did it. I can. I will."

This is what I hoped would be the feeling taken from my success. It means that everybody has an equal chance, provided they work hard, believe in themselves, and have confidence.

CHAPTER 8

On the Government Benches

On May 22, 1979, one of the most exciting events in my political career occurred. The Conservatives won the federal election and would form the next government, although it would be a minority. A first it was such a feeling of euphoria. I was so thrilled that at long last we had it made. And it didn't take me long to remember that there was a reasonable possibility I could be made a cabinet minister. That led to the immediate revelation that I didn't have a clue what being a minister was all about, and I became very worried. I realized that I was now going to be attacked and challenged the same way I had attacked and challenged Liberal ministers when I was in Opposition. I thought, *God, if they do the same to me as I did to them, I will be finished.* I was scared.

When our party came to power under Joe Clark, he appointed me his minister of labour. My pride was overflowing. I quickly threw myself into the task. It was a huge commitment of time and energy. I would arrive at the office no later than 8:00 a.m. and would still be going full out at 10:00 or 11:00 p.m. At first, this went on seven days a week. That meant there were many weeks that I didn't get home to Hamilton. Fortunately, I soon started to feel more comfortable in the role and was able to manage my time better. That was good, since even after twelve years in Ottawa, I could not get over being away from my family. When Parliament was sitting, I would phone home three or four times a day.

Throughout the twelve years I served in Ottawa, Yvonne and Keith remained at home in Hamilton. Even though we saw one another most weekends, it was far from the ideal family life. Yet as a unit we hung together and remained fairly close. For Keith, it can't have been easy having a parent very much out in front of the public while he was busy trying to maintain a happy life as a young adult. That this was managed, as far as I am concerned, is yet another example of the strength, compassion, and willpower of Yvonne.

My diplomatic passport as Minister of Labour.

In my absence, Yvonne was a pillar, looking after Keith and taking the role of the disciplinarian. As a youngster, Keith was always a good boy and never got into real trouble or caused me anxiety. I remember disciplining him once when he found two-dollar bill in somebody's home. I told him that when you find money in someone's home, you take it to the owner. If I had been able to spend more time at home, he could have had the guidance of a father, but he was fortunate to have a wonderful mother, and they were very close. I taught him the same things my father taught me: to be friendly, to respect people, to be honest … and to love your mother.

Keith was fortunate compared to me in that I came from a broken family. Despite the responsibilities falling on Yvonne during my years in politics, she was supportive and never complained. Yvonne took little part in my political career, but besides looking after our lives, she constantly encouraged me. When I was labour minister I used to tell people she was smarter than I and should have had the portfolio herself.

Getting more secretaries and assistants comes with the territory in assuming a cabinet post, but you lose the intimacy with the people that you enjoy when you are a backbencher. Naturally, a cabinet minister's workload is much greater. In addition to the demands of caucus, in the case of my ministry there were meetings with the press, labour leaders, provincial labour ministers, and many others who sought to bend the minister's ear.

An October 1979 *Hamilton Magazine* feature article, under the headline "Lincoln Alexander — Hamilton's Tough Guy in Ottawa," reported that I was embarrassed at being addressed as Mr. Minister. Naturally, I accepted the title as part of the job, but I wasn't one to put on airs, and that took a lot of getting used to. One of my Italian constituents once asked me whether I was still a beer drinker. Of course, what he was really asking was whether I had joined "the scotch and champagne crowd," I said in the magazine article. "Would I still drink beer with my friends or had I become a big shot? Had I changed?" I certainly had not.

We assumed power from the Trudeau Liberals under difficult circumstances. In the aftermath of the election, voters faced a quandary: They had rejected Trudeau, yet they had not really accepted Clark. With the election over, they had time to consider the inexperience of the new prime minister and to ponder his campaign promises: to disband Petro-Canada, Canada's only control over its major energy source; to move Canada's embassy in Israel from Tel Aviv to Jerusalem, a promise that brought protests and threats from other world powers; and to discharge approximately sixty-four thousand government workers without any plans for their alternative employment. Clark had repeated these promises throughout the election campaign, but voters had not been listening. Now the voters had to be wondering if they had jumped from the frying pan into the fire. They could only wait and see.

As it turned out, with Clark's decision to govern as if we had a majority our time on the government benches would be short-lived. As our fragile grip on power was wavering, the Social Credit party indicated it was willing to support our federal budget if the proposed gasoline excise tax was increased by only nine cents a gallon rather than the planned eighteen cents. Stubbornly, we insisted on eighteen cents, and our minority government was defeated 139–133 in a confidence vote. Three of our 136 members were not in the House, and all five Social Credit members abstained from voting. The combination of those two factors was enough to defeat us, as 112 Liberals and all 27 New Democrats voted against us.

There were a lot of tears and anguish when, just a few months after the election, our government fell. How could this possibly happen? Critics laughed and said we didn't know how to count. As for our three members who were elsewhere, I can't recall where they were or who gave them permission to be absent. There was blame everywhere. Clark had insisted that we govern like a majority and refused to make deals with other parties, but we know now how wrong that could be. We fervently believed the Liberals would not try to defeat us. We never thought the Liberals and New Democrats would risk sending voters back to the polls so soon after the previous election. We thought that voters would be angry with those two parties and infuriated by the economic waste of forcing another election so soon and that they would then punish those parties. We were wrong.

After all those years in Opposition, it was a great disappointment that my term as labour minister would last just nine months before the winter election of 1980. I didn't get a chance to prove myself on the cabinet benches or to accomplish as much as I wanted to in my portfolio. And we were misjudged. Our party was wrongly accused of trying to remove the right to strike in amendments we had proposed to the Canada Labour Code. In fact, the legislation I had proposed was simply to empower the government to order a twenty-day cooling-off period before public service unions could begin a legal strike. The Liberals pounced on that, as did the NDP, but I still think it was a reasonable proposal. As a party, we just didn't have time to sell it. I still wonder if I would have been considered a good minister, an average minister, or a dud.

While the party's prospects were grim in Ottawa, there were plenty of positive things emanating from my hometown. As labour minister, I settled two labour disputes in succession, and *Hamilton Magazine*, which called me "one bright ray of hope" for the Conservatives, reported that my name was being whispered as a possible future party leader. Some political observers were predicting my popularity would rise on the national scene as quickly as it had in Hamilton. I remember being afraid to pursue the leadership when Clark won, because I was worried I wouldn't succeed. After all, I would have been following Stanfield. I regret that now, but I didn't want to put the party in the position of losing again. There were even Liberals who were prepared to back me, under the table, because they were disenchanted with their own party. I'll keep their names quiet.

I have always considered honesty to be my greatest virtue as a politician, and the lesson never to deviate from that path — even to bluff — was driven home early in my political career. Shortly after the 1968 election, I was speaking at the University of British Columbia, where a student asked me about collective security with respect to the Warsaw Pact and NATO. It caught me totally off guard and unprepared. Instead of admitting that, I tried to answer him. When I finished, the young man accused me of not understanding the question and said I had a lot to learn. That was rather humbling, but from then on I resolved never to try to deceive anybody. Though it may feel awkward, it's much better to admit you don't know and that you will try to learn more and get an answer. You'll get respect for admitting your shortcomings, but you will get — and deserve — disdain when you try to mislead people. That's arrogant and condescending.

It's funny how these notions are sustained throughout your life. Just recently, I was forwarded a letter to the editor from a weekly newspaper, the New Tecumseth (Ontario) *Free Press*. The letter writer, T.D. Allamby, was commending the local council for being forthright about an issue involving the community arena. In his letter, he said, "I fondly remember the philosophy of a Great Canadian who I had the honour of serving as his Executive Assistant [at the Workers' Compensation Board of Ontario (WCBO)] by the name of the Hon. Lincoln Alexander, Q.C. He always said, 'Allamby, the people have the right to know when we do good and even more so when we do bad.'" To me, it's sad so many voters think all politicians are dishonest. Consequently, if you try to fake it, you reinforce their suspicions. The public was cynical forty years ago, and given what has transpired in recent years, their cynicism has only deepened.

A case in point is the sponsorship scandal, inherited from Jean Chrétien's decade in office, which deeply undermined Paul Martin's Liberal government. I'm a Conservative no matter what. To me, the Liberals are devious and manipulative. I think the Conservatives are making progress, but a lot of people still won't accept Stephen Harper. I think he is attractive, he has programs and a vision, and I expect he will win a majority next election because the vision is becoming more appealing. He's a leader, and I am convinced honesty and frankness is what reinforces that.

The election of a Harper minority on January 23, 2006, brought the first Conservative government since Kim Campbell's brief stint as Canada's first female prime minister in 1993. Unfortunately, she had to carry Brian Mulroney's baggage. Mulroney was charismatic, and his comment to John Turner on patronage appointments during a campaign debate — "You could have said no" — resonated with voters. He was an accomplished politician, but he saddled Campbell and the party with plenty of voter antipathy when he stepped down, leading to the humiliating defeat to the arrogant Liberals, an arrogance that almost led to the loss of the referendum vote in 1995. Chrétien was asleep at the switch.

After losing my first federal campaign in 1965, I won the Hamilton West riding for the Conservatives through five successive elections — 1968, 1972, 1974, 1979, and 1980 — which I think is a rather impressive run. During my last election many political opponents conceded that

A colourized portrait of the gorgeous Yvonne Phyllis Harrison as a young woman.

A rare photo of me taken when I was seventeen years old and living in New York.

This was my Hamilton West campaign headquarters in 1968.

When we campaigned we cruised the streets of my riding looking to talk to whomever we could find. My campaign workers would go door to door and invite people out for a chat.

Here I am, with my size 14s, vowing to fill the shoes of the last Conservative MP, Ellen Fairclough (size 4) during our exciting election win in 1968. The voters of Hamilton West had elected the first black member of Parliament in Canada. I was going to Ottawa.

Here I am with my son, Keith, in 1974.

Ellen Fairclough, who was one of my political mentors, hams it up with me in 1982.

Me in my office in my early days as head of Ontario's Workmen's Compensation Board, with pictures of various friends, colleagues, and famous people from my political life on the wall behind me.

This family photograph was taken during the early part of my time as lieutenant-governor. Shown along with Yvonne and me are Keith, his wife, Joyce, and our first grandchild, Erika.

At a reception in 1985 in London, England, during our trip to visit with the Queen were (from left) Ontario Trade Commissioner Tom Wells, Yvonne, my former law partner Dave Duncan, me, and Marge and Jack Millar.

In 1986, Yvonne and I welcomed Princess Anne upon her arrival in Canada.

Yvonne and I arrive by landau at Queen's Park prior to the Throne Speech in 1986.

As lieutenant-governor, I greeted His Highness Prince Karim Aga Khan at a dinner and reception in his honour in 1987 at the King Edward Hotel in Toronto.

Here I am reading the Throne Speech in the Legislature at Queen's Park in 1987.

Prime Minister Brian Mulroney, who put my name forward to become lieutenant-governor of Ontario, and I attended the Harry Jerome Awards together in March 1988.

As lieutenant-governor, I welcomed the Duke and Duchess of York (Prince Andrew and Sarah Ferguson) in 1987. With Yvonne and me are (left) Michael Wilson, representing the federal government, and Premier David Peterson.

In 1988, I was part of the head table at a dinner in Toronto honouring British Prime Minister Margaret Thatcher, here addressing the guests.

With my McMaster co-conspirators during my tenure as lieutenant-governor: (from left) Vince Miller, Brigadier-General (Retired) Jack Gibbons, Jack Millar, me, Professor Les Prince, Victor Cassano, and Carle Kiel. My security person is behind Les.

With Marge Millar and Yvonne, I met Prime Minister Eugenie Charles in Dominica in 1989.

Yvonne and I shared some wonderful times with the Queen Mother during her visit in 1989.

Yvonne and I had the privilege of welcoming Princess Diana and Prince Charles in October 1991. Diana's untimely death was an immense tragedy and one I felt personally.

My granddaughters Marissa and Erika and I admire the official portrait of me as lieutenant-governor.

In 1995, I met former American president George H. Bush at an advisory board meeting for Barrick International, to which I was invited by former prime minister Brian Mulroney, who is behind Bush.

I was fortunate enough to be invited to participate in activities around the visit of Nelson Mandela to Canada in 1998. Here I am with Prime Minister Jean Chrétien, with Ontario Premier Mike Harris in the background.

One of my pleasant annual duties each spring is to start the Great Ride for Cancer, which runs along the Lincoln M. Alexander Parkway.

In uniform, in 2004 I participated in ceremonies recognizing the Allied landings in France sixty years earlier. With me is Bill Parker, former Ontario superior court judge.

Ed and Anne Mirvish have become dear and close friends, dating back to my lieutenant-governor days when I often attended Mirvish theatrical openings.

Steve Stavro and I became great pals, but, as happens all too regularly these days with my friends, he died suddenly in the spring of 2006 as I was putting the finishing touches on this book.

From sharing smokes to seeing his government's stunning loss to the NDP, David Peterson and I have shared some interesting experiences; happily, we continue to be great friends to this day.

Hamilton Police Service Inspector John Daniels, centre, and I shared a moment with Queen Elizabeth during the her stop in Hamilton in 2002. More than 16,000 people were at Copps Coliseum for a ceremony honouring the Argyll and Sutherland Highlanders.

Hamilton's is one of the police services for which I am an honorary chief, a posting in which I take great pride.

This is one of my very favourite times of the year, convocation at the University of Guelph. Behind me over my left shoulder is President Alastair Summerlee.

Here I am greeting Prince Edward and Sophie Rhys-Jones at a reception in 2004.

Even long after leaving the lieutenant-governor's post, I still enjoyed many opportunities to hobnob with royalty. Here I am with Prince Philip and Hilary Weston.

Look Who's a Grad !
B.A.S. 24 Feb 2005

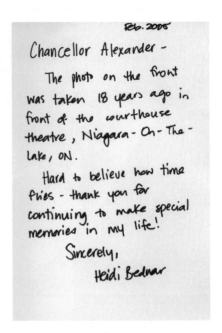

Feb. 2005

Chancellor Alexander –

The photo on the front was taken 18 years ago in front of the courthouse theatre, Niagara-On-The-Lake, ON.

Hard to believe how time flies – thank you for continuing to make special memories in my life!

Sincerely,

Heidi Bednar

This is a rather special card given to me at convocation at the University of Guelph in 2005. It was given to me by Heidi Bednar, a graduate that year; the picture of her with Yvonne and me had been taken eighteen years earlier. In her note, Heidi added, "Hard to believe how time flies — thank you for continuing to make special memories in my life." Wow.

This is the picture taken at our fifty-third Osgoode Hall class reunion in June 2006. To my left is John Mills, whom I encountered on our first day at law school; we remain close friends to this day.

my riding was the only safe seat in Hamilton. Former Liberal party whip Gus MacFarlane once said no one would ever take my seat. Norm Marshall, a well-known Hamilton newscaster and former Liberal candidate, acknowledged that I deserved to win and that I had the makings of a party leader. I had no enemies, I believe. When I left Ottawa I got three standing ovations in the House of Commons.

That is not to say my political opponents never criticized me. New Democrat MP John Rodriguez once said my approach to issues showed more flair than substance. During my tenure as labour minister, he said, I wanted to be a friend to both business and labour but satisfied neither. Sometimes, he said, they saw me as an actor in the House. "Linc would huff and puff during debate, stab his finger across the aisle, and shout in that booming voice of his, 'I want the minister to come clean — no bamboozling or flimflammery!'" But that was just livening up the debate, which doesn't mean that there isn't significance to your message. Further, I am not convinced that having cordial relations with both sides in a labour dispute is wrong. I'd rather be trying to find common ground than exacerbating differences.

Sometimes after your leave a job you gain perspective in looking back. After I left politics in 1980 to become chairman of the Workers' Compensation Board of Ontario, I took that opportunity in an interview with the editor of *Spear* magazine, Stanley Anson. When he asked me how I saw my role as a black member of Parliament, I told him I didn't think about representing only blacks, but instead, all the people who elected me. I said I would never dare call myself the spokesman for blacks. It doesn't mean I wasn't concerned about blacks, but you should lead by example. One is not elected to government to be a spokesman for any particular segment of the constituency.

During my last campaign, I was asked if colour was a political advantage. "What colour are you talking about?" I replied. Another racial issue I recall arose after Stanfield planned to appoint me immigration and manpower critic in his shadow cabinet. Someone from Vancouver sent a letter to the editor to newspapers across the country complaining that my appointment would open the door for a lot of blacks to enter the country. I talked to Stanfield about it, and he told me not to worry about it, such a notion was nonsense. He was a great Canadian.

Of course, blacks are not the only people to be considered in promoting equality. Once, as labour minister, I was scheduled to attend a media conference at a club in the Maritimes. As I approached the door with my staff, somebody asked how I could go in there. I said, "What do you mean?" They'd noticed that women were not permitted in the club at that time. I immediately had the venue changed to a local hotel. There is also age discrimination. I was interested in trying to end mandatory retirement at age sixty-five and would have pursued it if I'd been around long enough. As it turns out, that has now happened. It sickened me that after you turn sixty-five, you're declared useless.

While I was re-elected in Hamilton West in the 1980 election, the Conservative party lost and I was relegated to the Opposition benches again. Shortly afterward, then Ontario premier William Davis offered me the post of chairman of the WCBO, prompting me to resign my seat and end my political career. I left the House of Commons after an emotional farewell from fellow MPs of all parties, with a New Democratic Party member saying I had served with distinction. I didn't really want to leave politics, but Yvonne never took to life in Ottawa. She came up for formal occasions and some weekends, but reminded me I was getting older and working too hard. I had been promising her I wouldn't run again, so when Davis made me the offer, it was time to go.

In the years that followed, people would be kind in assessing my impact as a politician. Former Hamilton Mayor Bob Morrow told the *Toronto Star* I had "a tremendous depth of understanding of people. His own personal standards are very high and he has become an example to those around him and to those who observe him. We all love him very much."

While I loved politics, I have gained satisfaction in many aspects of my life. As I told the *Hamilton Spectator* in an interview in 2000: "Ottawa was interesting and exciting at all levels, but generally my life has been satisfying and rewarding. I am lucky to have been in the position to counsel. I've gotten satisfaction from that. I still do."

One of the perks of an MP's job is the people you meet, and Perrin Beatty ranks as one of the most interesting individuals I came to know during my time on the Hill. I always saw him as one of those rock-solid

Parliamentarians. His wife, Judy, is a charmer and a great cook. He came into the House of Commons after my first re-election, in the 1972 Liberal win that produced a minority government. He was twenty-two at the time, and I was close to thirty years older, but we established a rapport early on. Part of that was because, even though he had had a rather charmed upbringing — Upper Canada College and all — there was no condescension or arrogance to him, but instead a willingness to learn the job and a determination to be good at it. And that he did, becoming, while still in his late twenties, the youngest person ever appointed to cabinet when Joe Clark made him his minister of state for the Treasury Board in 1979. Later, in the Brian Mulroney government, he would serve in the portfolios of minister of national revenue and minister responsible for Canada Post, solicitor general, minister of defence, minister of national health and welfare, and the now defunct minister of communications.

Perrin represented Wellington-Grey-Dufferin-Waterloo, which was a substantial, largely rural riding, and he would joke that it was less a riding and more a bus route. I visited his riding on a few occasions. In one instance, he had brought me in to speak. A black man addressing a primarily rural riding wasn't something that happened every day. Perrin had cautioned me about this, not so much that there would be significant problems but rather that the reception would be cool. That, of course, was an invitation to Mr. Icebreaker. "Good evening, ladies and gentlemen. Thank you for having me here to speak," I began. "I've just returned from down south, where I've been working on my tan." There was a bit of a pause, maybe the odd titter, but in general people were caught off guard and didn't know how to react. "What," I continued, "you don't think I tan?" It was like giving people licence to laugh, and they did. Reveal your humanity — and is there a better way than with humour? — and you can start to cut through invisible obstacles.

Another time I was speaking in Perrin's riding, and he made the mistake — which he will readily admit to — of inviting a former politician to introduce me. It turned out this individual had a great list of things to say ... about himself and his political career. He went on and on before he finally got around to introducing me. I got up and said, "Refresh my memory. I'm not sure if I'm being introduced or if I'm to thank the guest speaker."

In a milieu such as Parliament, it's easy for people to let their egos run wild, especially today, it seems. But to be effective, whether in caucus, committee, or the House, I think you have to shelve those egos and avoid the mean and bitter attitudes we see today. I've been on the receiving end of too much meanness and bitterness to engage in it. I think that is what lay behind the warm sendoff I got when I left Parliament, and Perrin was one of those who made it clear that my departure would be felt acutely not just by the Conservative caucus, but by Parliament in general. "If you could clone him and make fifty more, Parliament would be a much better place," Perrin kindly said of me.

I didn't have to look far from my home riding for another good friend in the House of Commons. I speak of Gordon Sullivan, who was elected as a Liberal in the riding of Hamilton Mountain in the Trudeaumania sweep of 1968. I don't think politicians today have anywhere near the respect for one another that we did, and this was less than forty years ago. Then, we didn't grandstand for the television cameras and we were more preoccupied with being effective. And it was no sin to be on good terms with members of other parties. My relationship with Gordon serves as an illustration of that.

He, too, was a lawyer, and our paths frequently crossed for many years before he was elected. Our relationship began as we closed real estate deals or some other legal matters, but there were good grounds for a long-term friendship being laid. These days, Gord tells me I was one of the most trusted lawyers in Hamilton, though it didn't always feel that way, especially as I was trying to build my practice. Gordon is a person of great honesty and integrity, and, quite properly, one gravitates toward such people. It was natural and right that such a person serve on the bench as a judge, as Gordon did with distinction after he had served just one term in the House. I recall Gordon being very concerned because he thought by voting against the government (he voted against an amendment to the criminal code to change the rules on abortion) he would not be considered a candidate for the bench. I approached former prime minister John Turner, then minister of justice, about this issue and he told me not to worry, that Gordon would get the position, which I related to him.

While I was running for the Conservatives and he was a Liberal, I have to confess that there were parts of me pulling for Gordon to capture the Hamilton Mountain seat. Despite the cynicism of the electorate, it is a difficult and daunting decision to run for office. So, in some respects, I wanted to help him. One of the things my people had discovered in that 1968 campaign — I had an outstanding team — was that more than 60 percent of the time we knocked on a door, no one was home. Other politicians would more often than not just move on to the next house, but we determined that we could still make contact by leaving a card or note saying something like, "Sorry we missed you, but please consider supporting Lincoln Alexander." We blanketed neighbourhoods with about ten to twenty people using this technique, which turned out to be quite effective. We were making contact with virtually every voter in those neighbourhoods. As a result, one day I quietly picked up the phone and suggested that Gord and his team try it. While the Trudeau juggernaut was central to Gord's win, he'll tell you to this day that those cards helped him win. Glad to be of service.

During that campaign, I came to one home on Wellington Street where an elderly woman lived. We chatted, and she invited me in, and eventually it turned out she was Gord Sullivan's mother. That may well have been the longest visit I made on that campaign, but it clearly mattered to her and it was a good investment of time for a friend such as Gord. Even if the odds are that she voted Liberal. It's not all about the vote.

One night we were in the Commons during a quiet, empty session, and across the way was Gord, sitting at his seat on the Liberal bench. I knew him pretty well, and just by looking I could see something was on his mind. I am pretty certain this was in our first year as MPs. I wandered across and said, "Gord, you look like you've lost your best friend."

"Well, it's not quite that," he said glumly. "But it's my birthday, and I hate being away from home."

Like Yvonne, Gordon's wife wasn't enamoured with Ottawa and had stayed in Hamilton. "It's my birthday, too," I said, and it was. "Let's get out of here and head to the Château for a drink and some dinner." That invitation was a hit with him — and, as I said to him on the way home, we wouldn't have been missed in the nearly empty House anyway; if there had been a vote, we would have cancelled each other out.

Gord reminds me that I was fairly popular around Parliament, and I think that was partly me and partly the times. There was much greater respect and camaraderie among the various parties than you see today. An example of our ability to overcome party boundaries and work together was our committee work. Naturally, I served on a variety of committees during my time in Ottawa, and early in my career as an MP I served on the justice committee. John Turner was the minister of justice at the time, and Gord was also on the committee. Gord's recollections mirror mine: we would negotiate hard and debate forcefully, but it never became personal. Everyone in that room — Liberal, Conservative, NDP, or Social Credit — wanted to reach a productive result.

It is intriguing the effect television and the media in general have on affairs in Ottawa. Television's effect is particularly invasive today, with insufferable showboating in the House. But even before television, it was fascinating to watch the media coverage. I'm not naive. I know they had to sell newspapers. Gord and I lived near one another, and often on our way home we would joke about the fact that the big story of the day was something we couldn't even recall happening in the House; instead, it was something that would make a good headline. This happened with disturbing regularity.

After he left politics for the bench, Gord and I continued to keep in touch. We still do. And every time I changed jobs after serving as an MP, Judge Sullivan would call to remind he was still working as a judge and was enjoying it quite nicely. He told me he wanted to make me a judge, and I said no. His wife recently passed away, and Gord was in a state of shock; I shared his grief and told him how I'd handled Yvonne's death.

Another politician, this one at the municipal level, who became my friend was Hamilton city councillor Bernie Morelli. When I first met him, he was a student riding the bus to Cathedral High School. That is evidence that during my years practising law in Hamilton, I was pioneer in the fields of environmental awareness and public transit. Or perhaps it was my aversion to and fear of driving, rather than that loftier purpose. But I was a bus rider, and I loved the social interaction that came from sharing a ride with lots of other people. Bernie reminds me of my daily stride through to the back of the bus, where I would share greetings with my fellow travellers and offer a smile or two to brighten people's days. I, too, was relegated to the back of the bus, but unlike the heroic Rosa Parks, the back seat, right in the middle, was my choice. It was the only seat where I could find comfort for my wide body and stretch out my long legs.

It was refreshing for me to be able to talk with young people and high school students such as Bernie, not that I was an antique at the time. Such relationships were instructional, for they gave me insight into the issues and concerns that youth of the day were facing. Their enthusiasm was invigorating, and I think my discussions with them helped lay the groundwork for my interest in youth issues throughout my political and post-political careers, especially after I'd moved into positions where I had influence.

I won the 1968 federal election because I attracted some staunch support away from the Liberals. There had evidently been some disappointment in the performance of Joe Macaluso, the Liberal who had beaten me in 1965. We had turned in a strong showing then, and in the intervening years key individuals who had backed Macaluso migrated to my camp because they felt he had ignored them once he got to Ottawa. I welcomed the quiet help I received from many people in the Liberal camp, such as Charlie Cupido, Nicholas Zaffiro (who supported me with money under the table — out of sight of other Liberals), and Shirley Fiola, among hundreds of big Liberals who helped. Theirs were among the key efforts that helped put us over the top.

With the exception of my last two elections (in 1979 and 1980, when Stan Hudecki squared off against me both times), the Liberals threw a variety of candidates against me. I wouldn't go so far as to call Hamilton West a safe seat for the Conservatives while I was representing the party (I only won by about five hundred votes in 1980), but given the working-class nature of our community, it has to be considered an impressive run. What I draw from friends is a distinct pride in our city and its working-class roots. My parents and my long ties to Hamilton have taught me that you don't put on airs — you accept people as they are. I identify with such roots, and in them I can see my strengths and trace my successes in public life.

That sentiment makes me recall a newspaper article recently brought to my attention that discussed a uniquely Canadian trait, the "who-do-you-think-you-are?" trait. It says basically that if any of us get a little too big for our britches — no matter how big those britches might be — there'll always be someone there to ask that question and bring us back to earth. As it turns out, most of us Canadians have internalized the question and do a good job of self-monitoring. I think my success in winning five of six federal elections had something to do with my down-to-earth attitude and my ability to communicate, both as a speaker and in one-on-one conversations with people on the street. From my very first campaign in 1965, I had always felt most comfortable with the politics of personal contact. If we could meet face-to-face, I believed earnestly that I would win your vote. It was very much the politics of the street, if I can coin a phrase. I've travelled in some rather heady circles, and where I've come from has held me in good stead in these encounters.

When I was first elected in 1968, my riding consisted of eighty thousand constituents, and among that entire number there were only about two hundred blacks. Back then, an interesting fact was discovered regarding speaking engagements. I'm not sure who compiled these figures — and I can pretty much guarantee that they are no longer verifiable — but apparently there was only one Conservative who received more speaking invitations than me, and that was John Diefenbaker. Dief was an ardent supporter and advocate for equal rights and the father of Canada's Bill of Rights, and I suspect he relished the fact that a protégé of his was gaining visibility. In 1985, I was given the Canadian Award, part of an annual program of the John G. Diefenbaker Memorial Foundation. The prize is a large statuette of Dief. I quite liked that symbolism, and there was a nice sense of symmetry in the way he had helped shape my political career.

One of the steps I've taken that has been personally and professionally satisfying was developing a reasonable relationship with the media — not a sycophantic relationship either, but ones of mutual respect and honesty. Bill Kelly, a Hamilton city councillor and a semi-retired broadcaster (if you are a broadcaster, do you ever really retire?), is a three-and-a-half-decade example of one of those relationships. Bill was a broadcast student at Mohawk College when we first met in 1972. His family's Liberal roots went back beyond Sir Wilfrid Laurier, an unswerving commitment that we Progressive Conservatives couldn't hope to penetrate. Regardless, we struck up a friendship that has endured and that certainly transcends politics. He tells me I've never seemed like a Conservative, whatever that means.

Bill tells me that he's modelled elements of his political philosophy on things he felt I reflected: caring about your community, being concerned for people, and treating people with dignity all the time. He says he looks at me and realizes that the negative clichés about politicians are not always the case; I dispel them and personify what people should look for and rightly expect. He's one hell of a politician. You know, you can raise yourself up as high as you want in this country without thinking you're better than anyone else.

While my political career is now long behind me, the passage of time — and of Hamilton people who were fixtures on the national political scene for years — is reflected on the obituary pages. Two of Hamilton's better known MPs have died in the last few years. When former Hamilton East Liberal MP John Munro died in 2003, I told the *Hamilton Spectator* that politicians on either side of the House had helped define who I was, no matter the nature of our relationship. John Munro had an effect on my work as a politician. He was a "politician's politician," and I was careful in how I dealt with him because he was Liberal icon and a serious scrapper, in the best Hamilton tradition.

In November 2004, my long-time friend and supporter Ellen Fairclough died, two days after suffering an apparent stroke at St. Joseph's Villa in Hamilton. A trailblazer herself, as Canada's first female cabinet minister, Ellen was just two months shy of her hundredth birthday at the time of her death. "She was as tough as nails. She had no problem telling people where their place was, and that was behind her," I said in a story in the *Spectator*. "But she was very compassionate and understanding and willing to assist those who were less fortunate or needed help. She did so much for Hamilton, so much for Canada, in fact." And she helped me immensely in my political career.

After that career wound down, former prime minister Brian Mulroney said my departure from Parliament was a deep loss for the party, not just because Hamilton West had been a reliable seat for the Conservatives, but also because my impact, visibility, and campaigning skills were valuable for the party from coast to coast.

After weighing all my options, the time eventually did come for me to step away from Ottawa. My last day in the House of Commons was May 27, 1980. Prior to my final address to the Commons, Bill Yurko of Edmonton East rose with this comment, recorded in Hansard (the Speaker of the House at this time was Jeanne Sauve, who served in that role from April 1980 to January 1984): "Madam Speaker, I wish that I had two opportunities to put a motion today, as I would like to recognize the service to this House of the hon. Member for Hamilton West [Mr. Alexander] who is spending his last day in this august assembly." I received a standing ovation.

Finally it was time for me to make my final address to the House. As recorded in Hansard:

Resignation of Hon. Lincoln M. Alexander
Hon. Lincoln M. Alexander (Hamilton West): Madam Speaker, I hope you that you will forgive me if I take a few moments of time of the House. I know that there are matters of significant importance which must be debated, but I feel that it is necessary, after having spent 12 years in this House, to give some credibility to what is already a fact, that I will be leaving my "family", as I would like to have it known, this House of Commons, because I have accepted a position with the Workmen's Compensation Board of Ontario.

I wish you well, Madam Speaker. I saw that you were being tested today. I think that you have the fortitude and excellence of mind to handle yourself in your new position. I am sorry that I did not have an opportunity to become more involved and to challenge you as well, but I thank you for giving me this opportunity to speak to the House.

I have been touched by the excitement of this place. I have been moved by the challenges and touched by the joys and disappointments. But what is more important to me is that I have been touched by the friendships which I know I have made, because I have received so

138

many letters wishing me well. When my friend from Edmonton East [Mr. Yurko] triggered that standing ovation, it was a good thing that I did not have to speak at that time because there were tears in my eyes. I am not ashamed to say that I was not able to control myself. That was a great tribute and one I will never forget.

That is why I feel so sad at this particular time. This is a great family and a tremendous institution. When I think of the criticisms which come from all quarters, I say to my colleagues, "Forget it, because you are serving". Let those who criticize try to get into this place. There are many who try to get in, but who cannot make it.

However, I have been blessed. I am grateful to three or four people, who I would like to single out, with your patience, Madam Speaker. The late Right Hon. John George Diefenbaker is the one who asked me to run, who believed that I should be here in the House and who believed that I had a role to play. No matter where he may be, I hope that I have not disappointed him.

I remember Bob Stanfield. He plucked me from what is called the back benches and honoured me by making me a critic in the shadow cabinet.

Of course, there is the right hon. Leader of the Opposition [Mr. Clark] who made me a cabinet minister. Madam Speaker and my dear colleagues, I stand here naked because in my wildest dream I never believed I would represent my country as a member of Parliament or that it was possible I would represent my country as a cabinet minister.

Yes, I will have some very fond memories of this place, but I think it must be recognized that there are many around us who make our lives more successful. It is not only the "me's" and the "I's" who are fortunate to be sitting here temporarily, but I think of those who are involved in Hansard, the maintenance department, the office of the Clerk, the Sergeant-at-Arms, security, the

post office, public servants and even the media —
although there are a couple I would like to mention
specifically, but I will let them know that I have love and
forgiveness in my heart! Frankly, I could not care less
what they think of me anyway.

I care about what the hon. Members of this House
think of me, and I care about what the people of
Hamilton West think of me. I am pleased to have con-
crete evidence that they thought enough of me to send
me back to this House on five occasions. But to those
people to whom I made reference, I would like to say
thank you, because with their assistance to help the
Alexanders and anyone else you would like to mention,
Madam Speaker, would not be effective in this House of
Commons. They are the people who protect us and
who look after us. I would like publicly to thank them
now for looking after me for the past 12 years.

Some hon. Members: Hear, hear!

Mr. Alexander: These people have made my task very
easy and pleasant. I would like to extend a special
thanks to Labour Canada. Although I was not there
long, they did keep me out of trouble, and I thank them
from the bottom of my heart. I wish them well because
they are a fine group of people. When a new government takes charge and new ministers are appointed,
there are some who believe that perhaps the public servants are not on their side. I can stand here and say that
I had the confidence of my department, for which I am
very grateful and I thank them.

Last but not least, I want to thank the constituents
of Hamilton West who gave me their confidence, loyalty, and faith over the years. It is in this area that I feel a
little confused and a little sad because they were count-
ing on me. However, I will not disappoint them in the

future because I am going into another area of service. I can advise them, as I can advise my colleagues here, that you expect much of me, that you want me to do a good job and I will not disappoint you, as I have tried not to disappoint you in all the years I have been here.

In conclusion, Madam Speaker, I would like to tell you in all sincerity and from the bottom of my heart that I will miss this place. But I think having served in this place I am a much better person, and for that I am grateful. Thank you very much. [Editor's note: Mr. Alexander received a standing ovation.]

Madam Speaker, I would now indicate to you that I resign my seat in the House of Commons for the constituency of Hamilton West effective midnight, May 28, 1980.

Tributes to Hon. Lincoln M. Alexander

Right Hon. Joe Clark (Leader of the Opposition): Madam Speaker, I think this is one occasion on which I can truly claim to speak on behalf of all members of the House of Commons when I say to the member of Parliament for Hamilton West [Mr. Alexander] just how very much he will be missed in this assembly, in the work of Parliament and of government. I think it is true to say that no member of Parliament is better liked in this House and that no member of Parliament will be more sorely missed by his colleagues.

The hon. Member for Hamilton West served here with distinction for 12 productive years. He became a symbol of Canadian democracy and a spokesman for Canadians in need across this land. He served his constituency with care and sensitivity. He served cabinet as an outstanding minister of labour. But more importantly to him and to us, he won the respect and affection of all who were associated with the House of Commons.

We all wish him well in the new responsibilities which he has accepted, but this House of Commons will miss Lincoln Alexander and will long remember him as one of the outstanding individuals ever to have served in this Parliament.

Hon. Stanley Knowles (Winnipeg North Centre): Madam Speaker, the right hon. Leader of the Opposition [Mr. Clark] was perfectly correct when he said that on this occasion he was speaking for everyone in the House of Commons. I should just like to make that very clear and very certain by associating the New Democratic Party with the sentiments that have been expressed.

I rise to speak on behalf of my leader, the hon. Member for Oshawa [Mr. Broadbent], who, like the hon. Member for Hamilton West [Mr. Alexander], first came here in 1968. I also speak on behalf of all my colleagues.

We enjoyed the remarks the hon. Member made today in his final speech in this chamber. I think what appealed to us most — at least, it appealed to me — was his emphasis on the friendships he has developed in this assembly, friendships that he will carry with him through the rest of his life. We have not always agreed with the hon. Member. He and I have had some interesting discussions, but more often than not we have agreed we have common interests. He has served this place with distinction. He has put forth his best effort and he fully deserved the tributes we have been paying to him in these few moments today.

We say goodbye to Lincoln Alexander from the House of Commons and we wish him the very best through all the years that lie ahead.

Some hon. Members: Hear, hear!

Mr. W. Kenneth Robinson (Parliamentary Secretary to Minister of Justice and Minister of State for Social Development): Madam Speaker, it is indeed a pleasure for me to have the opportunity to say a few words in tribute to my colleague and friend, and my colleague from law school as well. We both went to Osgoode Hall law school and got to know each other very well over the years. Of course, he has been much more successful than I, and I guess he was more successful in law school as well. He has certainly been more successful politically. Although we were both elected in 1968, I sort of took a sabbatical from 1972 to 1974 while he continued to serve here. We have both been around since that time, Madam Speaker.

On behalf of this party I want to echo the sentiments of the right hon. Leader of the Opposition [Mr. Clark] and the hon. member for Winnipeg North Centre [Mr. Knowles] who spoke for the New Democratic Party.

I have enjoyed working with the hon. member these many years. He is going on to his reward with a new career — a career with the Workman's Compensation Board in the province of Ontario. As a member from Ontario, I know that I shall be working with him and seeing him from time to time. I can only say au revoir, good luck, and God be with you.

Some hon. Members: Hear, hear!

Hon. Bryce Mackasey (Lincoln): Thank you, Madam Speaker, for permitting me this opportunity of adding my voice to those of the leader of the Conservative party and others in paying tribute to one who is best described as a very personal friend.

When the hon. gentleman arrived in this House in 1968, I was then the minister of labour. In a comparatively short period of time I was very much aware of a rather brash, talented new member of the opposition party. In no time at all, as I recall, the hon. member became the Official Opposition critic of the labour portfolio. One day I called him over after a rather tough question or two and expressed the opinion that he had perhaps been a little unfair. He reminded me that he had patterned his particular style after mine, which made it very difficult for me. He is a very charming individual.

I repeat what has often been said, that this is a very unique institution. I recall the hon. member and his wife coming with us to the ILO convention in Geneva in the early seventies. I had an opportunity to break bread with him and get to know him well. I must admit that I have always had a particularly soft sport for the hon. gentleman, particularly since he is the member of Parliament for the riding in which my mother lives. I am not just sure how she voted in the last election, since very early in the campaign she received a personal visit from the hon. member.

In conclusion, I want to say as one who left this House in 1976 that it is not at best a very easy decision. If we are selfish we tend to remain here because we enjoy the company of members, the challenge and the unpredictability of the House of Commons if you are a House of Commons man.

I recall on a similar occasion the hon. member for Winnipeg North Centre [Mr. Knowles] expressed the wish that perhaps one day fortune would be such that I would be back in the House of Commons. I hope that what happened to me does not happen to the hon. gentleman.

I know, from the hon. member's record in this House of Commons and particularly from his compassion when he was minister of labour for those wonderful Canadians who do manual work for a living,

144

that he is more than adequate to fill the role of head of Ontario's Workmen's Compensation Board. I bridled and went to the defence of the hon. member when, shortly after his appointment, it was suggested by certain members of the press that he lacked the qualifications for the job. I think, Madam Speaker, that the qualities which the hon. gentleman has exemplified so many times here — compassion, concern, curiousity, willingness and devotion to work — are all the qualifications he needs to fill this very sensitive position, and I wish him well.

Some Hon. Members: Hear, hear!

Mr. Mark Rose (Mission–Port Moody): Madam Speaker, I will be very brief. I know that all of us in this House would like to pay special tribute to the departing member for Hamilton West [Mr. Alexander]. We are extremely fond of him. As a matter of fact, I do not think it would be too much to say that we love him.

He is one of the four surviving members of the Conservative part of the class of '68; I am one of the four survivors of the class of '68 in my own party [the NDP].

Mr. Nystrom: Retreaded.

Mr. Rose: Recycled and retreaded, I should like to tell him that I express no flim-flam at all when I suggest that the kind of friendship he has developed with all members of the House on both sides is unique. He is unique in a lot of ways. He is a person with drive, intelligence, forcefulness and a tremendously big heart.

We plan to have a meeting of the survivors of the class of '68 on June 25, which is a very important anniversary. Although he intends to resign from this

House today or tomorrow, I should like him to know that we intend to award him special status and hope that he will be able to come to Ottawa and join the survivors of '68. There are some 25 members left out of approximately 100 who were elected, which tells something about job security around this place.

We offer the hon. member congratulations on his new career and want to let him know that we will certainly miss him. I know that he will miss us, and I hope he comes back some day.

Some hon. Members: Hear, hear.

Hon. Yvon Pinard (President of the Privy Council): [The following was translated from French.] Madam Speaker, on behalf of my colleagues I also want to pay tribute to the hon. member for Hamilton West [Mr. Alexander)] His contribution to the Parliament of Canada has been exceptional. He dedicated 12 years of his life to representing his constituents and Canadians as a whole in the best way he could, and I believe the circumstances justify that, on behalf of the government, I should offer him our best wishes, good health and a successful career outside this House.

I do not want to add further to what was said by those who knew him more intimately, but I would like to say that I personally had the opportunity to come in contact with him on several occasions. He proved himself to be a seasoned parliamentarian but always polite and always aware of that spirit that must stir us of being adversaries, of course, but at the same time people working for a common cause — the improvement of the well-being of Canadians as a whole.

[The following was in English.] In conclusion, Madam Speaker, I have recognized a good sense of humour in the hon. member for Hamilton West. I am sure he will agree with me when I say that the House of Commons will have a "missing Linc".

Some hon. Members: Hear, hear!

And it was over. No matter how you cut it, I had a good life in politics, and I walked away knowing it is possible to make a difference. Here are the voting totals of the six federal elections I contested for the Conservatives in Hamilton West:

1965
MACALUSO, Joseph, Liberal, barrister —13,247
ALEXANDER, Lincoln M., Progressive Conservative, lawyer —10,888
DOYLE, Tom, NDP, sales manager — 6,297
JAMES, Reynolds H., Social Credit, clergyman — 199

1968
ALEXANDER, Lincoln M., Progressive Conservative, lawyer —13,580
BECKETT, Thomas A., Liberal, barrister —13,238
BRUCE, Patricia, NDP, teacher — 6,809

1972
ALEXANDER, Lincoln M., Progressive Conservative, lawyer —19,837
BURGHARDT, Jack, Liberal, broadcaster —12,204
LEPPERT, Peggy, NDP, housewife — 5,420
JAGGARD, Bob, no affiliation, bus operator — 218

1974
ALEXANDER, Lincoln M., Progressive Conservative, lawyer —15,421
LEWIS, Milt, Liberal, lawyer —13,162
HOLMES, Gordon, NDP, labourer — 4,890
DEME, Louis, Social Credit, cement mason — 363
JAGGARD, Bob, Communist, bus operator —138
MOORE, Nola H., Marxist-Leninist, teacher —117

1979

ALEXANDER, Lincoln M., Progressive Conservative, lawyer —19,661

HUDECKI, Stan, Liberal, surgeon —13,859

SIMPSON, Miriam, NDP, librarian — 8,512

MCDONALD, Edward, Communist, organizer — 161

DALJEET, A.P., Marxist-Leninist, labourer — 138

1980

ALEXANDER, Lincoln M., Progressive Conservative, lawyer —15,500

HUDECKI, Stanley M., Liberal, surgeon —14,929

SIMPSON, Miriam, NDP, librarian — 9,330

ABZALI, James E.S., Rhino, student — 304

DALJEET, A.P., Marxist-Leninist, unemployed — 139

CHAPTER 9

∾

Life after Parliament

Leaving politics in 1980 after twelve years and six elections — winning five of them — wasn't easy. It was a tough decision to accept Premier William Davis's offer to head up the Workers' Compensation Board of Ontario. I had a lot of great friends and colleagues in Ottawa, and I loved the job. I think Yvonne saw that I was hesitating, took it as an indication I might be ready for a change, and urged me to take the job. It would certainly be much closer to home in Hamilton.

As I said in an interview with *Spear* editor Stanley Anson: "After so many years, I thought it was about time, I started to look for new challenges. I thought, well, this is another opportunity to test myself — I've always had the attitude that I could do any job. I've never hung around the dark corners of the closet, thinking [that] because I was black I couldn't compete. As a matter of fact, I love competition, but I also know that you have to be prepared. You just can't be mediocre and expect to make it, no matter who you are. So I said yes to the job."

Not everyone was as convinced as Davis that I was the right person for the post. Organized labour and the provincial NDP said I had no experience in the field. When my five-year term ended, New Democrat MPP Bob Mackenzie was quoted as saying, "Linc was always very approachable, but he didn't make any of the changes the board needed — like indexing pensions to the cost of living." But the criticism didn't bother me. As a politician, I was used to it. Besides, he was wrong. We moved the organization forward significantly in that period, developing and introducing policy and improving our services.

One of the highlights of my tenure was a major overhaul of the board, a process that was conceived in a report by renowned Harvard labour law scholar Paul Weiler entitled "Reshaping Workers' Compensation for Ontario," commissioned by the labour minister in 1980. By June 1981, the report and the subsequent government White Paper, which included twenty-one major proposals mainly drawn from it, were released for public discussion, along with draft legislation. By December 1984, the legislature gave third and final reading to Bill 101. The act represented the greatest changes to Workers' Compensation in Ontario since the organization was introduced in 1915. So I think my record sufficiently rebuts Mackenzie's criticism.

Another of my initiatives at the WCBO was sanctioning the use of chiropractors, albeit over the objections of doctors. Chiropractors are becoming more popular every day, and today doctors refer their patients to them.

We also created the Workers' Compensation Appeals Tribunal, an independent external tripartite tribunal, to serve as the final level of appeal for board decisions, replacing the internal Appeal Branch.

The organization moved forward significantly, but fitting into the job did not come easy for me. After I left Ottawa, my old friend Bernie Morelli said it seemed a voice had been silenced around Hamilton, and it had. Accustomed to the excitement of Parliament, I found my new job lonely. I tended to be isolated in my office for great parts of the day. As a person who enjoys people, this was a difficult transition. But over time I adjusted, and I think we accomplished a lot during my tenure there.

As Stanley Anson would report, after an interview in my office at the WCBO, I had brought a lot of Ottawa with me to my new job. Anson wrote, "It illustrates the status of the individual in it. The walls are decorated with pictures of John Diefenbaker, Joe Clark, Prime Minister Pierre Trudeau and Governor General Edward Schreyer. In addition, there are pictures that tell of the man and persons he has come to know as a lawyer and a politician." I wonder if, besides serving as a visual record of some of the events in my life, they also fed those parts of my heart and soul that missed Ottawa.

During my term at the WCBO, my personal life was enhanced when Yvonne and I became grandparents, as Keith and Joyce had first Erika and then Marissa.

Looking back, I can see that I was pretty naive about pregnancy and its complexities and risks. When my daughter-in-law became pregnant, my eyes were opened. I was motivated to read more about childbirth and, in doing so, gained a whole new appreciation of the process. But the research also left me anxious and concerned that everything would work out.

The experience also gave me the chance to look back on Yvonne's experience and the birth of our son. I had been in Toronto studying law while she was managing her pregnancy alone, except when I came home on weekends. Her family was nearby, however. In 1949, mind you, the medical system's handling of pregnancies was vastly different from today. Then you would be in hospital for days; now they hustle you out as soon as you're able to move, and I'm not saying that's a bad thing. In 1949, the role of the father was positively medieval compared to today. No Lamaze classes, no handholding and coaching during labour, just nervous pacing in smoke-filled waiting rooms. Given all those circumstances, perhaps my being away at law school wasn't such a bad thing.

In any case, Joyce's pregnancy went well, and we were blessed with a beautiful granddaughter.

My term as chairman of the Workers' Compensation Board of Ontario ended in 1985, but a new and exciting opportunity awaited me.

CHAPTER 10

Trail-Blazing in the Lieutenant-Governor's Office

W hen I was sworn in as the twenty-fourth lieutenant-governor of Ontario on September 20, 1985, it marked the first time an African Canadian held a vice-regal position in Canada. My appointment came eleven years after Pauline McGibbon, whom I considered a mentor, had become Ontario's first female lieutenant-governor. To the province's black community, the significance of the rise of the son of a railway porter to lieutenant-governor was profound. Ontario ombudsman Daniel Hill said it represented a "new Ontario, the new Canada. It's a symbol of the fact that racial intolerance is becoming less acceptable."

The year before, Brian Mulroney had become prime minister, and it was on his recommendation that the Governor General appointed me as the Queen's representative in Ontario. Although my parliamentary career didn't overlap with Mulroney's, he was very involved in the Conservative party and the affairs of government while was I an MP and cabinet minister. Once Mulroney was elected prime minister, among the leadership initiatives the party undertook was to pressure for an end to apartheid in South Africa. That pleased me immensely, and subsequently he and I would discuss progress in this area from time to time. In that sense, I was on his radar as the time was approaching to appoint a new lieutenant-governor.

I had first met Brian Mulroney during the Progressive Conservative leadership convention at Maple Leaf Gardens in Toronto in September

1967, at which Robert Stanfield was chosen party leader. I was chief returning officer for the convention and Mulroney was a key aide for candidate Donald Fleming. Actually, I ended up quite upset with people in that camp, though I don't recall Mulroney being part of it. As chief returning officer, it was my job to enforce the party constitution's rules as they applied to leadership conventions, and they were flagrantly ignoring them. As I recall, it had to do with liquor and when or where it could be distributed. So I had to go into their headquarters and let them know in no uncertain terms that they had to start obeying the rules.

When Mulroney offered me the post, one of the first things I asked was whether he viewed it as a way to get blacks to vote for him in the future. I had asked Bill Davis the same thing in 1980 when I was offered the Workers' Compensation Board job. I wasn't being impertinent; instead, I was asking a question I felt I had to ask each time an opportunity came along. Mulroney replied, "No, it's because you're competent." He said he had put my name before cabinet, and across the board the ministers from Ontario fully supported his choice, as did Ontario's Liberal premier, David Peterson. In the end, he said, the decision was his and his alone.

"Linc, you're my first and only choice," he assured me.

"Mr. Prime Minister," I said after a brief pause, "you've just made the best appointment you'll ever make."

I remember that around the time of my appointment there was a lot of discussion about tokenism in government appointments, and the suggestion really rankled Mulroney. Patronage and government appointments were a potent issue in the previous election campaign. We all remember the telling moment in the national leaders' debate when Mulroney chided John Turner and told him he did have a choice to reject Pierre Trudeau's appointments. "You could have said no," he said. Mulroney's position at the time was that minorities must reach for power and influence, and on at least one occasion he pointed to me as an example. That was gratifying, though not surprising, support.

When he called to offer me the post, Mulroney outlined certain of my traits that he felt would make me a good lieutenant-governor. Among other things, he pointed to my communication skills, which had been put to good use in the Commons. Indeed, at the time of the appointment, he made it clear that my impact on Parliament, both within the party and as a cabinet minister, was substantial and that I had played a key role in the 1979 election campaign that saw the Conservatives win and Joe Clark become prime minister. Mulroney told me my overall skills and service to my community and country, coupled with the changing dynamics and demographics of Canada, meant I would be a superb choice.

Chatelaine magazine would write, "As Canada's first black MP and later, first black cabinet minister, Alexander is well accustomed to being a symbol, but the appointment was a personal triumph, the culmination of a life spent being a team player and working within the system to give himself and his family a better life than that of his parents and the generations of Canadian blacks who preceded him. Yet, he says, 'It's something I never thought could happen to me. My wife keeps asking if it's sunk in yet.'"

On installation day, onlookers greeted Yvonne and me with applause as we arrived at Queen's Park. The police had closed the northbound lanes of University Avenue for our motorcycle-escorted trip by landau from the Royal York Hotel to the Ontario legislature. There we were greeted by Premier David Peterson and his wife, Shelley, along with Cabinet Secretary Robert Carman. Then I received a salute from a hundred-member guard of honour made up of the Royal Hamilton Light Infantry and the Argyle and Sutherland Highlanders of Canada, also from Hamilton. (I had arranged for both to come because I wasn't about to choose one over the other.) I took the oath before the 125 MPPs, their spouses, and about 250 invited guests. After a fifteen-gun salute from the 11th Field Regiment of the Royal Canadian Artillery, my first official duty was an inspection of the troops. I remember telling the *Toronto Star* after the ceremony (and a pause to ask protocol staff if they would permit me to have a cigarette), "I'm still excited, still elated and still nervous. It's something I have seen on occasion, but it's a little different when you are one of the participants."

When I looked out over the audience at the ceremony, I was proud to see people from all backgrounds and races. That is what Ontario is all about. I told the guests my appointment was recognition that "Canadian society has changed immeasurably over the last thirty years" and added, "I hope I will be supported if, from time to time, I … address the aspirations of our youth, and the concerns of many, who, for whatever reasons, are not in the mainstream of life in Ontario. In these areas, I have strong convictions and I intend to speak about them, as befits my office, in a dignified, but forceful, whisper."

Premier Peterson said the duties of the lieutenant-governor "will rest comfortably on the shoulders of Lincoln Alexander. I am completely confident you will handle them with ease. You will do it your way and you will do it well." Peterson noted that we were members of opposing political parties but that he had known me for some time and was looking forward to working with me. "There's absolutely not a shred of partisanship in these things. It's not the way he is and it's not the way I am. I'm sure that Linc will be a first-class lieutenant-governor."

Former Minister of Indian Affairs David Crombie, who represented the federal government at the swearing-in ceremony, noted, "We have come a long way, but we have a long way to go." He described me as "a man with a mission. His honour will be a symbol to this province that in this province there is a place in the Ontario sun for everybody."

It was exciting and uplifting to witness the responses to my being named lieutenant-governor and to see how people interpreted the significance of it. My former law partner Peter Isaacs told the *Toronto Star*, "His appointment is like waving a flag to [black] people, that you can do it in Canada. His personal abilities have been honed to a fine edge in his dedication to the community."

The lieutenant-governor performs functions similar to those of the monarch and is beyond partisan politics. My official duties included summoning and dissolving Ontario's legislature, reading the Speech from the Throne at the opening of each legislative session, and giving assent to bills passed by the legislature. I made it my personal goal to bring the role of lieutenant-governor closer to all Ontarians, and I also made youth and education issues key parts of my mandate. I made good on the education component most certainly, as I spoke to students at more than 250 schools during my tenure. I drove home to them the importance of education, telling them to stay in school and to stay away from drugs and alcohol. It's a simple message and one I still share with young people.

Race was another issue I wanted to address during my term. About a year into my mandate, at a conference with about eight hundred Roman Catholic educators from the York Region, I recounted my encounter with my Osgoode dean over his use of the phrase "nigger in

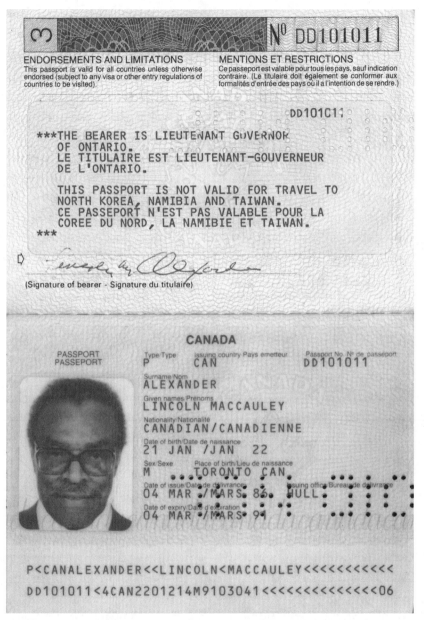

My diplomatic passport as lieutenant-governor.

a woodpile" to demonstrate how insidious racism can be. I challenged these educators not merely to go through the motions when it comes to racism but to accept their responsibility and lead. That was their role. Just like my dean at law school, whether they were teachers, trustees, or administrators, they had to accept the fact they were leaders and that people, especially young people, looked to them for guidance.

In my first two years of my term, I visited 314 places outside Toronto, hosted 381 receptions, and had about 31,000 guests in my suite. I attended more than 1,800 functions and had to decline another 1,744 invitations because of scheduling conflicts. I also met 104 ambassadors and royalty, and I visited 90 schools and 114 different communities.

Yvonne was exceptional at official functions. Even back when I was involved in election campaigns, she was very selective about the activities in which she participated. My appointment as lieutenant-governor changed that somewhat for her. She was involved in a great many more official functions, and, as our friend Ray Lewis once noted, with her proud, regal air she fell quite naturally into her new role. For a person who protected her privacy with stark determination, it was awe-inspiring to see what Yvonne was capable of in public. Such dignity. The prime minister once remarked that when he made me the vice-regal representative, he got two for the price of one.

My first official meeting with royalty was to welcome Princess Alexandra, the Queen's first cousin, to Ontario for a five-day visit. I was flabbergasted at her great charm as soon as I met her at the airport. She made me feel at ease, and it was eye-opening to experience such grace and dignity. The princess was visiting Toronto with her husband, Angus Ogilvy, to attend the 125th anniversary celebration of the Queen's Own Rifles of Canada, of which she is colonel-in-chief.

Coming from St. Vincent, where there was a substantial British influence, my father brought a fascination with the Commonwealth with him to Canada. Perhaps I inherited it. I admired and was always comfortable with the monarchy, so when my vice-regal appointment came along I'm sure that, if it were possible, it would have made my father sit up in his grave.

I had to greet any royalty who visited Ontario. The Queen, Prince Edward, Prince Charles, Diana, Princess of Wales — I met all members of the royal family when they arrived. Every so often I would host a dinner, and there was always an exchange of gifts. I would give things like pens and my picture, and I would get their pictures signed. I must say that the gifts they gave to me were much nicer than the gifts I gave them.

Theirs would be nice silver and gold items that might not be extremely valuable in their own right, but they bore the royal stamp. And they all signed my guest book.

I went to London when I was first appointed, so the Queen would have an opportunity to see who I was. We chit-chatted. The people around the Queen are exceptional. By the time you walk in to her presence, she has been thoroughly briefed about you. As a result, she can talk to you as if she has known you all your life. I also met her in Ottawa when she was here to meet with all her Privy Councillors, 150 to 200 people. She gave a great speech and thanked us for our role. She's been queen since 1953 and has had the ear and counsel of many prime ministers, so she is a walking encyclopedia. I love her. I think she is the most exciting woman in the world today, her kids notwithstanding.

In London, we were worried about protocol, since this was all so obviously new to us, but everything down to the last detail was lined up for us. It was my first time in London, and I was only there two or three days. My aide-de-camp was there with his wife, as were my wife, my law partner, Jack Millar, and his wife, Marge. We saw Big Ben, the House of Commons, and House of Lords. We stayed at a wonderful hotel, and we could see the Queen Mother's residence from our window.

"Your honour, you're next," said one of the Queen's officials as Yvonne and I sat waiting in an anteroom. We were both so excited, but I was the nervous one. We got all gussied up to go and meet her. Yvonne had bought a new dress, and I had bought a new morning suit. I was shaking, literally. Then I was coached by people who said to relax and that I would be surprised at how warm and intelligent she is — and they were right.

The palace was huge. We went in a door on the right side of the building, and as we walked through, it just seemed to be endless halls. We were told that when the door opened for my official visit, there would be an old mat there — and there was, a very old mat — and when we got to it, we should bow or curtsey, then walk fifteen feet and bow or curtsey again. We were to go in, sit, and wait for the Queen to say something to me, then to Yvonne, and then we could engage in conversation.

Here was living history. I knew the role and she knew the role, and I have to say the Queen exuded charm, elegance, and dignity. She disarmed me, and in the end I did not find her intimidating at all, but quite warm and able to relate. She made us feel at home. It was very personal. She knew where my mother was born, where my father was born, and what they did. I thought of my parents and how remarkable it was their son was in such a place and time. I mean, how many people meet the Queen? I was emotionally drained when I left because of the opportunity I had had, all because my mom had said, "Linney, go to school, you're a little black boy."

No one has ever told me what the Queen's assessment of me was, but I met her three times and she always greeted me warmly and always remembered me, including once when she visited Hamilton.

I listen to the debates people engage in about having a queen and having a monarchy. It's my feeling — and I'll acknowledge my bias — that the Queen is very important, no matter what others argue. The Queen is our representative, and in the scheme of things, I don't think it costs the taxpayers a lot of money. Believe me, the Americans would love to have a monarch. Those royals know how to operate; they know how to have a parade. We can always look to the Queen as someone who has shown leadership, through war and through crises at home. Her kids, well, something went wrong. They seem to have forgotten who they are, and they have put the Queen in many awkward positions.

I think it would be dangerous trying to put in place an alternative political structure, and I worry about people being appointed to some quasi-official post similar to that of the governor general. Then it becomes political. In England, the monarchial system is productive and those in power are far more accountable — unlike, say, the so-called experts and advisers that make up George W. Bush's entourage. The Brits don't make the kinds of blunders we've been witnessing from the U.S., from flawed presidential elections to questionable justifications for going to war.

I hear all the calls for Canada to end its relationship with the monarchy and choose its own head of state. Those who object to the monarchy suggest that maintaining it is a sign of our immaturity as a nation. I think that is a naive interpretation and would argue exactly the opposite — that it's a reflection of our maturity. The monarchy, because it is not elected, is beyond the reach of politics. As a result, the monarchy and its representatives serve as a safeguard against tyrannical governments. Scoundrels can be controlled.

As with the visit to London to meet the Queen, the Millars and Alexanders often vacationed together. After I became lieutenant-governor and made Jack an aide-de-camp, he and his wife would sometimes accompany us on official trips. We made a few trips to the Caribbean, both official and personal, and I loved going down there. I felt that I was reconnecting with my past, poking around in my roots. I've always been an early riser, so I'd often head to the beaches early in the morning as life was awakening. Usually the fishermen would be preparing to head out for the day, and it was always enjoyable and instructional to find out what was on their minds, what the issues of the day were for them. That too provided insights to my past.

We were fortunate that the Millars enjoyed travelling with us. Since our trips sometimes had an official component, they got their fill of meeting high commissioners, ambassadors, and the like. Our trip to meet the Queen was an example. The Mulroney government was in power in Ottawa, so I had a fresh and full slate of friends in significant positions. For instance, Roy McMurtry, the former attorney general of Ontario, who later returned to law and became chief justice of Ontario, was Canada's high commissioner in London during the first three years of my stint as lieutenant-governor. It was exciting for us to share these experiences with the Millars — even though I had to insist they pay their own freight, which they did willingly. The taxpayers of Ontario could not finance something like that.

Not long after we had met the Queen, we hosted Princess Anne during a four-day visit to Toronto. Then, in the summer of 1987, it was Prince Andrew and the Duchess of York, Sarah Ferguson. Given my personal traits and inclinations, I loved these events and, as the official representative of the monarchy, I was bursting with pride to display our wonderful people, province, and country to such visitors.

I also enjoyed the time I spent with Diana, Princess of Wales, whom Yvonne and I met on several occasions. We were tickled pink to have the honour of meeting her. Despite living in a fishbowl of constant media and public attention, Diana was, I think, a shy person at heart. She was, of course, attractive, but also intelligent, warm, and interesting. She didn't intimidate me when I met her. Instead I was impressed that, despite all the trappings of royalty, she was very much like an ordinary person.

As for her tragic death in that horrific accident in France in 1997, I remember feeling terribly sorry for her children. It came as a complete shock, and I just thought, *What a terrible tragedy*. She was so young and she had many clear and honourable goals, such as her work with children in hospital care. There is much she would have accomplished. People recognized that about her. She would have done good things, and with a visceral passion that people could sense. That's why her loss was so sad to people and why there was such an outpouring of anguish when she died. I remember thinking that perhaps it was about time those boorish photographers who hounded her to her death might learn something from the tragedy and give other famous people a bit more room, but I realize that was too much to hope for.

The end of my tenure as lieutenant-governor in 1991 would not be my last contact with Queen Elizabeth. In 2002, we met again when she came to Hamilton as part of a royal visit and I was one of the guests of honour. In fact, that wasn't the only time we met during that visit. I remembered she had a smooth reserve but was not without a warm sense of humour, which I decided to play to. As she was leaving the event, held in Copps Coliseum, she noticed me. "You again?" she asked, then asked what I was doing there and hadn't she seen me at a banquet in Toronto the night before?

"Indeed, you did, Your Majesty," I said. "Better yet, you'll have the good fortune of seeing me again tonight." We were due to attend an event at Roy Thomson Hall back in Toronto. She got quite a chuckle from my witty repartee.

CHAPTER 11

The Lieutenant-Governor's Role

My goals, as I told the Queen when I visited her at Buckingham Palace, were to advance the cause of youth, fight racism, and advocate on behalf of seniors. When I spoke to schoolchildren, I often related the difficulties I had faced with racism. Young people are the ones we have to work tirelessly with to send the anti-racism message. On one of my earliest visits to a school, Palmerston Avenue Junior Public School in Toronto in February 1986, I established a theme that I would repeat regularly through my tenure as lieutenant-governor. I told the children to stay in school as long as possible and to be wary of people who wanted them to do or try bad things. I told them to love one another and said that because each of them was made in the image of God, they all were equal. I urged each and every one of them to always stand tall, to never throw around insults or call people names, and to show everyone respect and recognize we all have the same rights.

Aside from such advocacy issues, the lieutenant-governor's role involves everything from gala dinners and community visits to meeting with the governor general once a year. I also spent a lot of time in my office at Queen's Park, as the lieutenant-governor signs provincial legislation. As well, there are duties ranging from reading, reviewing, and writing letters to signing other documents. I mention these somewhat more mundane tasks to illustrate that despite the great volume of pomp and ceremony, it was not all glamour.

While I aimed to demystify the role, there was still much awe and interest in the glamour of the position and the trappings that go with it. The grandeur of the lieutenant-governor's suite is not lost on those who visit it. Its deep red carpeting projected a regal feel for anyone who entered the two-storey vice-regal suite. The high ceilings and rich oak panelling infused the setting with a noble atmosphere where one would expect affairs of state to be carried on. The suite also boasted a library and formal reception rooms.

I had seven staff members to handle appointments, scheduling, and correspondence, along with two stewards, a housekeeper, a chauffeur, and fifty aides-de-camp. That substantial staff vetted all of the huge volume of requests that came in. As with the many invitations I still get today, I'd joke that they fit into one of three categories — come, give, or do. Keeping in mind the demands of protocol, timing, and necessity, my staff would review the various invitations and requests to ensure they suited the role of lieutenant-governor. In some cases, before I accepted an invitation, they would go on advance scouting missions, so to speak. The purpose in such surveillance was to make sure I didn't get involved in something that might embarrass the Queen, whom I represented.

Along with administrative support, I also had a series of aides-de-camp. In fact, it was the existence of that position that enabled me to repay, at least in part, one of the people who had been so supportive of me over the years, Jack Millar. It came as no surprise to me that my friend and former law partner served in that role with the same dignity, poise, and pride as he did all things.

The licence plate on my car was 1Crown1, and my drivers were always Ontario Provincial Police officers. They would come to Hamilton to pick me up and take me wherever I had to go, and I would have security and aides-de-camp with me wherever I went. I had a two-bedroom suite in the Royal York Hotel in Toronto. I liked that suite, but I always preferred home, where my wife was, which was just sixty kilometres away.

People have told me they've found inspiration in me, which is flattering. I too have benefited from inspiring individuals on a few occasions. One of the events I presided over was the awarding of a Junior Citizen of the Year award in 1988 to a teenage girl, Susan Mitchell, from Muskoka, who had an inoperable brain tumour. It was an emotionally powerful event, one where hope and optimism replaced what could easily have been despair. To me, this young girl's story represented so much about life, what a gift it is, and how we should behave. Despite the debilitating effects of her illness, she was active in her community and in her school. She was a leader. In my speech to her high school, I said, "Many people have said I act as a role model, but what you have done in your sixteen years has taken me sixty-five years.... To you, the students, the message is this: you have to emulate your friend. You must pursue excellence. You must be concerned about the happiness of others. You have to believe in yourselves. She's telling you that you must not rely on alcohol or drugs. She's telling you that you must stand tall."

Sadly, Susan died at age sixteen in March 1988. She was a study in courage for such a young person and really represented the message I and others constantly wanted to deliver to young people. In that way, she lives on.

As lieutenant-governor, I presented a brave teenage girl, Susan Mitchell, with a Junior Citizen of the Year Award. She had an inoperable brain tumour, but her determination and fighting spirit were inspirational.

165

I always liked to speak to school kids. I remember telling one group that I couldn't count how many times I have been refused things because of my colour. Fortunately in my case, the central message of how to deal with such setbacks was never far away — get an education. It will carry you beyond such obstacles. At Midland Secondary School in June 1987, I told the students they were the future, our agents of change. I used the slogan, "He did it, I can, I will." Soon, the whole gymnasium was chanting along. That was a moving moment.

During one visit to Sault Ste. Marie, I said how blessed we are to be Canadian, which is abundantly evident when one looks around the world. That was the case in 1987, and that is equally the case today. One technique I enjoyed using when I spoke about Canada was to recite the national anthem and then to insert between some lines various observations about our country's great grace in being a haven for the world's oppressed.

At a school in Cambridge, one of the students said he appreciated that I didn't talk down to the young people but rather talked to them as equals. I consider that an accomplishment and a compliment. It's natural to assume that you will get young people to engage if you demonstrate respect for them and their intelligence, rather than preaching to them.

With the above series of encounters, you'll note I've used examples from different parts of Ontario. Generally, these were my constant messages, whether in Toronto, Midland, or Sault Ste. Marie. Not surprisingly, it was the frequency of public appearances such as these — more than eighty of them in an average month — that contributed to my popularity. In my first two and a half years as lieutenant-governor, I estimate I had maybe two weeks off. Most days, between the time I left Hamilton in the morning and the time I returned at night, my workday lasted from 7:00 a.m. to 11:00 p.m. or midnight. I also had commitments most weekends.

While my energy did wane from time to time, it was as if I had hidden stashes of adrenalin that I could draw on as the need arose. It's important to have that in reserve. "He comes to life having people around him," Jack Millar once told the *Toronto Star*. "He could be dead tired, but when the door opens and he starts to greet somebody, he will be back in top form, taking charge." People who are excited to have you as a guest don't deserve to deal with a tired old sourpuss. That's not to say, however, that I wouldn't be nodding off moments after my backside hit the back seat of my car.

One of the perks of the job was the people I met and got to work with, including the two premiers who led the province while I was lieutenant-governor. Although David Peterson and I came from different political backgrounds — he a Liberal and I a Conservative — we struck up a friendship almost immediately after my appointment. David assured me that when Brian Mulroney called him to tell him I was being considered for the post, he told the Prime Minister, "Great choice." If he thought otherwise, he did a great job hiding it. We put together a strong professional relationship, along with a personal bond that continues to this day. And that relationship washed from one end of the spectrum to the other and everywhere in between. One evening we would be sharing a table at a command performance dinner with royalty from other nations and the next day he'd be popping down to my office to bum a smoke and chew the fat. He was perpetually quitting smoking, so my cigarettes provided a reliable supply.

One thing David and I had in common in our jobs was the incessant demands on our time, whether for presentations, speeches, or dinners. Over time, despite the work we put in to keep these events upbeat and enjoyable, they had the capacity to get quite tedious. Making conversation is hard work, and that's from someone who is good at it. As a result, I know David would conspire to be seated with me, and I with him, whenever possible. Then we could have fun, and we shared a lot of laughs together. Our table was always the one you wanted to be at.

One time, not long after I had become lieutenant-governor, the premier and I found ourselves at a plowing match in Stirling in eastern Ontario. Especially early in my term, my forays into rural parts of the province could generate a lot of curiosity among the locals. Even then, in the 1980s, seeing a black man in rural Ontario was not an everyday occurrence — especially one the size of me. So this was a tentative but polite crowd, enduring the chilly fall rain and mud baths that often accompany these events. I needed to connect with these people, and they needed to know the guy in all the regalia was "regular folks" like them. Finally, the ice still waiting to be broken, I said, "Well, now, you're my kind of folks." David reminds me of that event from time to time and how the once tentative crowd immediately burst with excitement. It was a few simple words and we had forged a bond. And David had gotten an early taste of me in action.

In my conversations in recent years with him, it has been interesting to explore our shared working time in retrospect. Although in our political lives we came from different parties, the issues of the day as we had to deal with them never broke along party lines, even indirectly. I know that he supported and endorsed my actions on those occasions when I had to step beyond my vice-regal role and speak out. Unlike some people, I am not perpetually on the lookout for a fight, and the premier indicated he respected that in me. At the same time, I will not hesitate to speak out when I feel the issue demands it.

During my term as lieutenant-governor, the issue of racial tension and racial profiling bubbled to the surface again, as it does all too frequently to this day, and I felt the need to speak on the subject. I made the case directly to the top, as it were, by telling a meeting of the powerful Toronto Board of Trade to get off their collective butt and get involved in resolving this matter. My point to these community and business leaders was that if they thought they were untouched by this issue, they were pathetically naive. I urged them to strike a committee and lead the way.

Peter Wren, a senior executive with the Bank of Montreal at the time, called my pitch "unusual and unexpected," as well as "rather courageous." He said that, if nothing else, it got the business people talking about the issue. Not everyone agreed. One man said that I, as the Queen's representative, should not be making such statements and should stay out of politics. But injustice doesn't recognize venues or titles, and that attitude, to me, smacked of the superficial thinking of those who believe merely closing a door makes a problem go away. It doesn't, and perhaps it even exacerbates the angst. This was a special opportunity for a black in a leadership role, with a prominent platform from which to continue to advocate on race issues. I would argue it was not a political issue, anyway, but one of human decency. As such, and as lieutenant-governor, I was eminently qualified to discuss the subject. It was part of my self-assigned mandate.

The board of trade wasn't my only forum to discuss the issue. In 1990, I agreed to meet with several officials and community leaders over racial unrest in Metropolitan Toronto. I had been invited to intervene to help ease tensions between Metro police and members of the black community. Police Commission chairperson June Rowlands had presented a letter to me signed by twenty-four people representing church, university, professional, and community groups, both black and white. The letter invited me to "lend the prestige of your high office to a consultation process to restore the feelings of trust and rapport."

In 1988, I was sixty-six but still felt the need to keep busy. I had been working since I was sixteen, back in that laundry and then in the bowling alley in Harlem. So I understood all along that hard work would deliver success, and over the years my inclination toward going all out just came naturally. I may never have been a fitness freak — how could I be if I've smoked for sixty years? — but I did try to watch my health in some respects, such as getting adequate sleep, and I watched how much I drank. I brought that attitude about hard work to the lieutenant-governor's role.

To many people, I've referred to myself as a "dignified populist." I love people, and that has always been central to the way I behave. My father taught me to always show respect toward other people, to say hello or say good morning or ask how people are, and I've never forgotten that. In that respect, it's easier to understand why a lot of people have taken me under their wing, the vast majority of them white. I have been lucky in that regard, and hard work has underpinned that.

Among the messages I gave young people was the one about hard work, but I also encouraged them not to get frustrated and to be optimistic, to see the glass as half full, not half empty. I told them to focus on their strengths and on the fact they could be as good as anyone, and to shoot for excellence and challenge themselves. I attributed my success to being committed to be the best I could. And that doesn't mean you have to finish first, either.

During my years as lieutenant-governor, I received many honours recognizing my lifetime achievements. It had been almost twenty-five years since I graduated from Osgoode Hall law school, and even longer since my McMaster convocation, when I was pleasantly surprised to learn that the University of Toronto was going to award me an honorary doctor of laws degree in 1986. The degree was given in recognition of my public service, and it was exciting to address that audience of bright young students and their parents. Shamelessly, I encouraged them to believe in themselves with that familiar slogan, "He made it. I can. I will." I challenged them, as potential leaders, to stand up and be counted when racism raises its ugly head. In subsequent years I have been graced with honorary degrees from McMaster, the University of Western Ontario, York University, the Royal Military College, and Queen's University.

The year 1986 also saw me honoured by the Hamilton Jewish National Fund. What made it special was that it marked the first time in its thirty-three-year history that the fund had so honoured a non-Jew. Once again, in my acceptance address, I mentioned that such recognition was important in promoting race relations. As I frequently explained at that time, my dad was a CPR porter because, in the 1920s, that was about all he could hope for as a career. Sixty years later, in the late 1980s, my granddaughters could say their grandfather was lieutenant-governor of Ontario. That timeline and the transition it defines tell an important story.

Then, at age seventy, I was honoured to be named a Companion of the Order of Canada. The citation at my induction said: "Motivated by his continuing concern for social justice, he has led an exemplary life as a lawyer, politician and Lieutenant Governor of Ontario. He has broken many barriers during his lifetime. Known for his good judgment, tolerance, compassion and humanity, he has served the citizens of Ontario well, striving to instill these values in young people and working tirelessly for improved race relations."

While I chose to stress work with youth and create awareness for better race relations, my predecessor, John Black Aird, placed his focus on the disabled. Those in the position of lieutenant-governor can make great use of our visibility toward advocacy for many good causes. Aird left his mark by becoming involved with Variety Village, a haven for children with disabilities, and he used his influence and his own financial resources to help raise funds for this great institution, which I later joined, as did Hilary Weston and Hal Jackman, subsequent lieutenant-governors.

Pauline McGibbon has been everyone's favourite lieutenant-governor because she always reached out to people, and her infectious smile made them feel comfortable. She was very committed to the arts, raising its visibility and helping arts organizations by approaching wealthy people for support.

Still — and this is important to stress — while I did push hard on the race relations issue, I was ever cognizant that I was a role model and symbol not only for blacks but for every single individual in Ontario. I aimed to remove the mystique of the office and to bring people together.

One of my greatest personal achievements occurred when I was lieutenant-governor, and it was long overdue: I quit smoking in 1989. I had chain-smoked for years, and I always acknowledged its addictiveness. I didn't smoke in public, obviously — it looked undignified, and I didn't want to set a bad example — but I would have a couple of puffs before events, and I would smoke in my office. I've been blessed in many ways during my lifetime, not the least of which has been my good health, even though I smoked two packs a day for years and didn't quit until two years before I left the lieutenant-governor's post.

CHAPTER 12

∽

Balancing Family and Vice-Regal Life

One of the most difficult adjustments to becoming lieutenant-governor was that I wasn't able to see my new granddaughter, Erika, anywhere near as often as I would have liked. We talked on the phone, but it was not the same as being there. And she always said, "I love you, Baba" (she called me that). That always left me on the brink of tears. But as for the rest of the lieutenant-governor's role, I would tell everyone that I should have had the job twenty years earlier; it was that enjoyable. That's the reason, when then Prime Minister Brian Mulroney asked me in 1990 to stay on for one more year, it was easy for me to say yes. I loved it. It was my dream job.

Sometimes, with the many public appearances, the days seemed endless, but there were perks. I told someone in 1988 that being lieutenant-governor paid $75,000 a year and all I could eat. There were a lot of dinners. Still, the job affected our private life in other ways. We had to have a security system added to our home in Hamilton. Dining out with friends involved being chauffeured by Ontario Provincial Police security; they were always very discreet, but their presence made Yvonne uncomfortable.

Throughout my years in Ottawa, and even while I was with the Workers' Compensation Board of Ontario, Yvonne carefully protected her private life. She would appear with me in public at very important events and, of course, from time to time during the election campaigns.

By the time I was named lieutenant-governor, she started to somewhat enjoy the public activities and became more involved. I think the reason was that in this capacity her involvement was meaningful and her role legitimate. Whether meeting dignitaries and royalty or visiting schools in Northern Ontario, she had a part to play. In earlier years, as the wife of an MP or cabinet minister, she wasn't interested in being an adornment, and I certainly can't fault her for that.

I knew I'd never sit still when I left the lieutenant-governor's suite, but I used to joke that I also knew I also wouldn't sit around in Yvonne's kitchen. It would have been rather presumptuous to invade her domain after I'd left her to it all those years. Not that I don't know my way around a kitchen. I mean, at eighty-four I cook for myself and do all things required to run my own home, though I do have a cleaning lady whom I describe as my domestic engineer.

As for my family loyalties, my son Keith once quipped: "His first priority is my mother, his second priority would be my kids. I'm around somewhere in the middle." But he also said once that if he was having a bad week, if he spent a half-hour with his mother and me, we would we have him laughing, and that was gratifying.

As it had been back in 1980, when the time had come to leave Parliament, it was sad for me when I left the lieutenant-governor's post because I enjoyed the role and its responsibilities so much. All things must pass, but that doesn't mean it has to feel good or be easy. In any case, in departing I could draw comfort in the belief that I had demystified the role and brought the job out in front of the people of Ontario.

Several years after I left the job, Hilary Weston paid me a great tribute. She had followed Hal Jackman into the lieutenant-governor's job; he in turn had followed me. Hilary said that I was her role model in the vice-regal position and that I had displayed great dignity. Then, during a visit to Hamilton in February 1998, she commented, "Not only has Linc done so much to forge the road for me, but he in fact has a whole parkway."

She was referring to the Lincoln Alexander Parkway, which was opened in 1997 and eases traffic across Hamilton Mountain. (A parkway is within city limits; a highway is outside the city.) It's a well-known parkway, since I've met people from all over Canada. It was, of course, an honour to have it named after me, but, like Hilary's quip, it has led to the occasional joke, including some by me. There's also the irony of the fact I've never driven, yet I have had a parkway named after me. In an interview with the *Hamilton Spectator* in 1999, I was asked if I thought the parkway bearing my name should be extended. I replied that of course it should be extended, "all the way to heaven."

As my term as lieutenant-governor wound down, Yvonne seemed destined to take over as my chauffeur, since I don't drive and never have. I'm afraid of cars. I always sit in the back, real low, so I can't see what's going on. Keith jokes, however, that while I never learned to drive, I never held back from telling Yvonne how to do it.

When I wasn't signing legislation for the provincial government or representing the Queen at the many public functions a lieutenant-governor attends, I was involved in other matters of government. One of the shockers came when David Peterson walked into my office and announced he wanted to dissolve the legislature just three years into his mandate. His party's approval rating in the latest polls was a staggering fifty-four percent, and that made Peterson and the Liberals confident they could cruise to a strong majority if he called a snap election.

I had good relationships with Peterson and NDP leader Bob Rae, but I can't say they had much use for each other, even though they had worked together to end about four decades of Conservative rule in Ontario. In the 1985 election, Frank Miller, who had succeeded Bill Davis, led the Conservatives to one of the narrowest of victories, capturing fifty-two seats in the legislature. The Liberals under Peterson won forty-eight seats, and the New Democrats held the balance of power with twenty-five. That set the stage for the Liberals and the NDP to topple Miller. Peterson and Rae forged a two-year deal that included enacting a number of NDP policies. In return, the NDP voted non-confidence in Miller's government, and Peterson assumed the premier's post.

Once the two-year accord ended, in 1987, Peterson led the Liberals to a huge majority and the NDP became the official Opposition in the legislature. In 1990, with his party's popularity soaring, Peterson expected to claim another majority. Many thought the premier was gambling too much in the high-stakes game of politics, and, indeed, the plan backfired badly. Rae led the NDP to a stunning majority in one of the biggest election upsets in Ontario history. After the election I phoned Peterson to offer condolences, and he didn't sound too good. I believe he had been crying all night long.

I remember Bob Rae stating that Trudeau said MPs off Parliament Hill were nobodies, so I reminded him, "You are the premier, but I'm the lieutenant-governor. In short, I'm your boss." Rae still doesn't understand how he became premier with 37 percent of the vote.

The timing of the election immediately sparked other problems, and I was in the middle of them. Peterson had been scheduled to travel to Japan to help promote Toronto's bid to hold the 1996 Olympics. Now, however, he wasn't interested in going. Since the trip was only days after the NDP took office, Rae was also reluctant to go, so he turned to me as his replacement. His decision to send me was widely criticized since it was felt that, as a figurehead, my participation would not carry much weight with the International Olympic Committee. Rae would not bend to the pressure, so I went to Tokyo in the fall of 1990 to anchor Toronto's bid for the Summer Games.

Being involved in the Olympics bid taught me how the Americans played hardball. We didn't have the resources of the Coca-Cola boys from Atlanta. Our delegation gave out pencils; Atlanta was giving out scholarships. Members of the Olympic committee told us how good Toronto's bid was, how Toronto was an ideal choice — clean, safe, and so cosmopolitan — and then they gave the Games to Atlanta. I won't say the Americans bought their way to the Olympics, but …

Before the intrusiveness of television, the Olympics provided a grand amateur athletic spectacle. TV's influence has made them too commercial, with competing cities putting big money on the line in bids to host the Games. I felt strongly that holding the Olympics would be good for the entire community, but we were also hampered immensely by the Bread Not Circuses coalition of groups opposed to Toronto's bid. I think we were pretty confident we could be successful, but we couldn't match the Americans' money, and too many opponents poisoned our bid.

When we lost the Olympic bid, it was one of my saddest moments in public life. Our liaison on the Olympic committee came out from where they were deliberating and gave us a signal and we knew we had lost. The letdown was indescribable. I felt sick when I thought about all those people, particularly the younger people, who had worked so hard for that bid, only to fall victim to the questionable practices of the IOC. We were the front-runners until those last days when the group from Atlanta started buying votes. You could say we lost because we were typically Canadian. That is, we believed in playing by the rules. It cost us, but at least we lost knowing we had played fairly. At least we could walk away with our heads held high.

As I neared completion of my term as lieutenant-governor in 1991, it was a period of great reflection for me. Ascending to that role was a great milestone, an unforgettable experience. I told the members of the legislature I had aimed to put a human face on the office, and it was an approach that suited my character, as far as I am concerned. I feel I was able to do that.

Although one could contend that the role is largely ceremonial, there is more pressure than meets the eye, both personal and public. In public, I was responsible for protecting the Crown's good name. As well, the public honours — such as having schools, other buildings, and highways named after me — were gratifying and humbling, but they left me with lingering concerns. I felt I had to be perfect at all times. I couldn't let my guard down and let mortal weaknesses get the better of me. I had to walk a pretty fine line, because I knew a lot of people were depending on my principles and integrity. I feel a similar sense of responsibility today toward organizations I work with, such as the Ontario Heritage Trust and the Toronto Raptors Foundation, and toward my role as a university chancellor. People depend on me. I can't let them down.

I'm sure it's impossible to go through life without regrets, but one of my greatest disappointments is that my mother never witnessed any of my accomplishments. I felt that disappointment most acutely at times such as when I was stepping down from a successful run as lieutenant-governor. She died before I even finished college, and yet, as the title of this book suggests, it was her philosophical gem — "Go to school, you're a little black boy" — that powered me toward all I've achieved.

As I look back at my time as the Queen's representative in Ontario, I think I enhanced the image of the province and country by my deeds and thoughts, though there always remains so much to do. I wish I had the power to fully change the world, for if I did I would make people learn to respect one another. It's as simple as that. We have to understand that we are all seeking the same thing and that we have a lot in common. We want to be loved, we want to raise and protect our children, we want to make good lives for ourselves. Rather than focus on differences that tear us apart, we need to sit down, talk, and explore our similarities. Too many people don't know their neighbours — the ones across the backyard fence or the ones across the border. We have lost a lot of wonderful people because we have not recognized them because of their race, religion, or sex — all superficial reasons for not seeing a person's true potential.

It all begins with respect, whether it's among friends or strangers. Respect is everything. I remember telling a young couple who had just become engaged that love is a great thing, but respect transcends love. It holds everything together. If you respect people, you won't hurt them.

I've always striven to do my best, whether at McMaster or Osgoode, where I finished in the top quarter of the class. It was the same with the practice of law. I wanted to find my niche and do well in it, but I always insisted it be had to be in a fair and honest manner, not showy. So when I became lieutenant-governor, I wanted to do as good a job as possible, but at the same time I was still the grandfather who would go over to visit his son's family for Sunday dinner. You could still find my wife out in front of our house, touching up the yard, sweeping the sidewalk, and chatting with neighbours. There should be no airs for the Queen's representative and his or her family, and there weren't.

I think that was reflected well by Keith when he was interviewed once. He talked about Yvonne and me visiting him, and how I'd be playing with the girls, and he said he would look up and just sit there and stare at me, almost in disbelief, because this was the lieutenant-governor of Ontario, the representative of the Queen in the province. Similarly, when I was asked at that time what I intended to do now that I would have more spare time, my answer was to spend time with my wife, son, daughter-in-law, and two grandchildren. The lieutenant-governor's role is a glamorous one, but the sacrifices my family made so I could serve in that office were huge. My parents separated and both died very young, and that is a huge part of why my family is so important to me.

We all know the expression that behind every good man is a good (or better) woman, and that was certainly the case in our marriage. My drive not to fail was fuelled by my love for Yvonne. I couldn't have lived with myself if I'd let her down. I've touched on this several times, but I don't tire of it: her wisdom, beauty, courage, and strength always left me in awe and motivated me intensely.

With about one month left in my mandate as lieutenant-governor, I recall telling people I was looking forward to a more relaxed lifestyle and more family life. But I knew I would miss the job, for it was such a wonderful experience. I mean, how many people nearing their retirement meet and host Prince Charles and Princess Diana, who were on an official visit to Ontario? That was a thrilling experience, and I'm sure it is easy to understand why I found it difficult to step down. Perhaps it's somewhat related to the notion of stardom, but when I was out and about with Prince Charles and Princess Diana, it was clear there was a strong and sincere affection for them. I doubt many of those throngs of people from Sudbury to Toronto would want to see the monarchy disappear. Quite the opposite, actually.

I don't want this to sound like a tired cliché, because it isn't. I am a people person and always have been. I love people, and to me that is an absolute prerequisite for a post such as lieutenant-governor. It's demanding, and the volume of activity will invariably wear on you if you are not comfortable with the requirements of the post. Near the end of my term, my staff compiled a list of the activities in which I had participated, and I looked at it and thought, *If someone had told me six years earlier all this was going to happen, I wouldn't have believed it.* I had met 290 dignitaries, received 78,283 guests, visited 704 communities of all sizes, held 715 receptions in the lieutenant-governor's suite, visited 235 schools, shaken 240,000 hands, signed 60,000 orders-in-council and cabinet documents, and given royal assent to 551 bills. Told you I liked to work hard. Of course, many of those figures overlap, but it was gratifying to me to see those numbers, which told me I had been busy, active, and committed to my job.

One of the outcomes that I am most pleased about is the extent to which my term as lieutenant-governor reinforced my belief in the great strength of this country and the province of Ontario. As I was stepping down, I told the alumni magazine at my alma mater: "This is one of the few admitting countries in the world, and of those [countries] that people have the opportunity to go to, they all want to come to Canada, regardless of race, creed, colour, sex or religion. People are able to find justice and freedom from oppression. Canadians like to complain. But that's the right you have, living in a democracy — you can complain all you want and nobody's going to bother you, nobody's going to hit you, nobody's going to put you in jail." Or shoot you, for that matter. Those were not new observations for me, but six years as lieutenant-governor enhanced those views immensely. All you have to do is look at the TV news, read the newspapers, listen to the radio, and compare. There are some horror stories around the world — deprivation, hunger, starvation, brutality, terrorism, dictatorships. Walk your thoughts through circumstances like that and realize how fortunate we are. That was illustrated constantly for me as I travelled this province.

I enjoyed the pomp and ceremony of the vice-regal job. It gave me a chance to meet people all over the province, and I loved the respect they had for the role and the admiration they showed me. But all things have to come to an end. Bob Rae, premier after the 1990 election, wanted me to stay, and so did Prime Minister Mulroney. I told them I was tired.

CHAPTER 13

The Next Challenge — Chancellor, University of Guelph

Shortly after I stepped down as lieutenant-governor, I got a call from the University of Guelph inviting me to become the school's chancellor. It was an honour to be asked by then president Brian Segal, and I happily accepted. By coincidence, just a few days later I was offered the same job by the University of Toronto. I had to tell them it was too late. I know the University of Toronto is a prestigious and widely respected institution, but at the University of Guelph I have had the opportunity to witness and share in the remarkable development of a school that has dramatically ascended to academic heights. Guelph is recognized internationally for its research and teaching, while at home it is consistently at the top in the rankings of Canada's comprehensive universities.

There had been overtures from the university about the chancellor's position while I was still lieutenant-governor, so when I stepped down and the phone rang, I was ready to commit myself. By that point, I really didn't have to give a lot of thought to the decision. Given my educational beliefs, it was a natural fit. It also gave me a platform to continue my advocacy on behalf of young people. The chancellor's job meant I would still get to talk and meet with young people, only these were at the older end of the spectrum, university students ready to face the world. I started out trying to inspire these young adults in 1991, and I continue to do that to this day; 2006 found me in my fifth term as chancellor.

Of the three presidents at Guelph with whom I have worked — Brian Segal, Mordechai Rozanski, and Alastair Summerlee — I had the longest connection with Dr. Rozanski (whom I knew as Mort), who served as president from 1993 to 2003. Understandably, our friendship is strong, and it's based on more than just time spent together. While our cultural backgrounds couldn't be more different, our cultural experiences have a great deal in common. Mort's early life, like mine, was not easy. Indeed, I should even say that his background was fraught with more danger and risk than mine. That he even saw life at all was in many ways against the odds, for his parents were Polish survivors of the Holocaust. They eventually made their way to Montreal in 1953, after stops in Israel and France.

Similar to mine, Mort's parents were deprived of an education. While my mother never had the opportunity for an education, her belief in the power of learning never wavered. Mort's parents held the same firm belief, and this underlying and unifying ideal was a bond we already shared when we met formally for the first time at his installation as president of the University of Guelph. During our time together, we made quite a pair, me at six-foot-three and Mort at five-foot-four. The visual disparity masked our visceral rapport, and we wasted little time putting it into practice at the installation in 1993. We were on the front porch of the president's house and, naturally, we were both wearing University of Guelph ties. In an effort to break the ice, I'm sure, he looked up at me and pointed out that his tie had just one emblem on it while mine was covered with them.

"How does one get all those emblems?" he asked.

"Young man," I replied in feigned gruffness, "you have to earn them." The ice was broken, and the first steps of a lasting partnership and friendship had been taken.

Mort often sought out and seemed to welcome my counsel, beginning on that first day of his presidency. He asked if I had any advice for a rookie. My response — and I would give it again today and always — was suitable for anyone, not just rookie university presidents. You have to listen to people, and the effort has to be sincere. You can't fool people with token listening. You have to engage them, smile at them, and set the stage for relationships. Don't be looking over their shoulders for the next best person to talk to. That's Lincoln MacCauley Alexander Sr. talking, Big Alex, through the body of his son, seventy years later.

When I talk about the importance of engaging people, a large component in making that effort successful is paying attention — listening, as I explained to Mort. One summer not too long ago, we were at a Hamilton Philharmonic performance, and there were perhaps four or five University of Guelph students in attendance. I'd met them at convocation a couple of months earlier and I remembered their names, so I was able to greet them personally. Bill Kelly, the Hamilton councillor I mentioned earlier, was flabbergasted and just stood there smiling and shaking his head, surprised I could remember. To me, though, it's pretty simple: Listen to people and give them the respect they deserve. I try to fix my eyes on you.

Rob McLaughlin, now an associate vice-president of the university, put it this way when I was first appointed chancellor in 1991: "When you meet him and when he looks at you and shakes your hand, you think that he has waited his whole life to meet you. You have his undivided attention." There you are. Mort grasped that, I think, and he and I were able to accomplish a great deal as a pair when we were in public.

We'd have plenty of fun during convocation, and I have to admit I'm a bit of a scamp sometimes because I liked to see if I could get him off his game. One of his functions as students came across the stage to get their degrees was to pass on any tidbit of information about the new grad. It might be that her name was Yvonne, same as my wife, or Erika, same as my granddaughter. The idea was that it would help me engage the grad, because I always like to have a brief, personal chat with each one.

One time a big, strapping, blond young man from rural Ontario was heading across the stage, and Mort leaned over and said, "His last name's Alexander." I smiled and winked at Mort, as if to say, "Watch this."

"So-and-so Alexander," it was announced.

"Alexander," I said. "Hmm. Alexander. Do you think we're related?"

Mort choked back a snort, and the poor kid, who I think was already somewhat awestruck at the whole affair — graduation doesn't happen every day — was fumbling for some sort of response before we all had a bit of a chuckle. But that's the importance of communication. Mort told me those kids were more interested in what message I had for each of

I had the privilege of celebrating Dr. Jane Goodall's honorary degree from the University of Guelph in 1998.

them as they crossed the stage than the message of the president or speakers receiving an honorary degree. Since I've handed out degrees to more than twenty thousand students, that's a lot of messages!

Many times Mort has pointed out the similarities in our backgrounds that led to our shared belief in the value of education. He refers to it as the transformational power of education, and we're both evidence of that, despite obstacles such as racism, which refuses to be beaten out of existence, even at institutions of higher learning.

One time we were at a dinner hosted by Mort. As I recall, the gathering was related to one of our fundraising drives at the university, so there were a lot of what I refer to as heavy hitters and movers and shakers among the guests. Mort had me seated strategically at one table in the hope that I could encourage some potential donors.

Mort stood up at one point to address the guests, and one of the high-end people at my table made reference to the "little Jew." Well, that was like hearing my law dean refer to the "nigger in the woodpile." While some people might think it wise to bite their tongues, my response once again was the opposite. I took that individual to task and said he had a grave responsibility to lead the fight to eradicate such attitudes, rather than repeat them. Maybe it cost the university a donation, but as far as I'm concerned, it's more important to take on those attitudes, especially among those who have the power and influence to know and act better.

The fight against racism is seldom pleasurable, but in 1992 it was particularly gratifying when Premier Bob Rae established the Lincoln M. Alexander Award, given annually to two young Ontarians between the ages of sixteen and twenty-five for service and leadership in eliminating racial discrimination. To me, the establishment of the award indicated that we had come a long way on race issues, but it was also a reminder there was much more work to do. That is one benefit of the award — it provides an incentive for people to be active in bringing about a better environment for race relations. In certain respects, the award complemented my role as chancellor at the University of Guelph, since it aims to encourage and develop young adults.

When each of my three-year terms as chancellor began to wind down, Mort would approach me and ask if I would consider another term. I'd toss up the odd obstacle or so and ask if there was really anything more I could offer, but in the end he knew how honoured I was to hold the post and to be chosen regularly with full senate support. At one point he got down on one knee, as if to propose, though we both knew I was going to return for another term.

In 2003, Mort moved on to become president of Rider University in New Jersey. In his ten years as president, Guelph was named Canada's top-rated comprehensive university on three occasions. It has seen academic and research excellence by faculty, students, and staff, as well as two successful capital campaigns, increasing Guelph's endowment by 300 percent.

As Mort's second term as president neared its end, we were in the midst of hunting for his replacement. One of the central issues was whether we could or even should fill the position from within the university. There are different schools of thought on the issue. Those who argue for external hirings contend that vibrant academic institutions require the churn of new blood. On the other hand, there are those who insist internal hirings, if the appropriate candidate exists, benefit the university greatly by providing continuity and stability. Eventually we decided the answer to our search was right in front of us when we chose Alastair Summerlee, who was then vice-president academic and provost.

Of course, I knew him pretty well and had come to appreciate his style and his sense of humour, and I was impressed by his remarkable intelligence. I'm not saying that because he's my boss, either, because I'm his boss. What I soon recognized was that he was widely admired throughout the campus. His humanity is evident to everyone, and it's shared with everyone from deans to the janitors. And he is thoroughly committed to his institution, as any good president must be. Not surprisingly, he's highly regarded in university circles across Canada and around the world.

Alastair has been a busy globetrotter for the university, covering our country and beyond to raise the profile of the school while at the same time trying to bolster its coffers. Fundraising is a critical part of a Canadian university's success and future, and he works at it in earnest. I must say, though, that he causes me concern over his volume of work — he's not just handling his president's duties, he also does research and some teaching. His job is extremely onerous, but he enjoys it.

As was the case when I did it with Mort, convocation continued to deliver its share of fun. One time, both Alastair and I were caught off guard after an attractive young female graduate visited us on stage. She asked, after she'd met with me, if she could give me a kiss — totally innocent, of course. I was dumbfounded, and before I could mumble out a reply, she just went ahead and did it. The place erupted after that daring act. That doesn't happen every day to the chancellor, I can tell you, and the president and I were reduced to a state of amused shock.

I probably make a mess out of scheduling plans at convocation because I do like to say something to each graduate. And if they respond, well then we just have to have a little chat. I imagine the extended visits might drive Alastair and organizers crazy, but he recognizes how much the students are enjoying it.

Every once in a while, I'll say to a grad, "Hey, where's the party tonight?"

I like it best if they say, "It's at my place."

"And you haven't invited me?" I reply. "Why not? I'm hurt."

"Oh, oh, you wanna come? Of course, yeah, sure," they often say.

Other times, I'll point to a piece of clothing or jewelry. "Hey, I like the look of that. Where did you get it?" or, "Hey, you're too young to be getting a degree."

Usually they get a good chuckle out of our little repartee. I think it relaxes them, then they can really have fun and appreciate the significance of their important day.

I won't say I have a photographic memory. I don't think I do. But I have a definite aptitude for remembering certain details, and names and faces are good examples. In one of the more memorable instances, I told a young woman at convocation that I knew her.

"Oh, you must be thinking of someone else," she said. "Although you did come to my high school once."

I then proceeded to tell her the name of the school, the town, and when I visited.

Later, Alastair told me, "That was magical. You just added to the legend."

In the course of my years, I can report that I have had the thrill of seeing more and more people of colour cross that stage. I'll tell you this with 100-percent certainty: It is possible to physically feel your pride soar. It happens to me, and I know it happens to these graduates. When I encounter young blacks at graduation, I have to admit I'm inclined to be somewhat solemn with them. I look them square in the eye and deliver one short sentence — "I'm relying on you." Alastair says he finds these among the most compelling, powerful moments at convocation. Those may be the only words we exchange, but in them are centuries of pain, decades of sacrifice, and generations of suffering, but also the promise of the future. They have a responsibility to those who went before, and they know it. They have become champions.

Anyone who knows me even remotely will know how exciting I find it to be surrounded by our students. That's why I love events such as convocation. I feed off their energy and enthusiasm. The edge of anticipation is contagious. Many of them have told me I've inspired them, but I can assure you such inspiration is a two-way street. They have invigorated me by giving me the privilege to serve them, work with them, and, dare I say, dream with them. When I attend convocation, I feel as though I am sitting there as witness to the future of our country, even our planet. These young graduates — and I am referring to all the bright young college and university graduates across Canada, with a bias for ours, to be sure — are brimming with promise, so I am very proud to be involved in such a meaningful way, sending them off to take on the challenges of the world.

As university graduates, there comes a certain responsibility to advocate for a better world, one of equality and freedom from intolerance. In a note to graduates of 1993–1994, I wrote: "The value of your education can never be calculated. Your degree or diploma will empower you and enrich your country. At the same time, it places on you the obligation to keep the faith with previous generations who built and fought for your nation, to strive for a society free of intolerance and violence, to protect educational opportunities for others and to use the skills you have developed for the betterment of society." When I speak publicly like this, they are never empty words for me. At every one of these events, from convocation to casual meetings with students, I am freshly reminded of what education has meant to me, and I firmly believe I have taken that great gift of learning and used it to make a difference in our world.

I do try hard to have a meaningful impact on my university in all the things I do. I counsel the president, and generally my contributions are welcomed. In fact, Alastair says he always knows marching orders are coming down when I preface my observations with, "Look here, my boy, this is what you need to know."

Regardless, one of the kindest compliments I've received was from Alastair, who told me that he credits me in large part with his ability to do his job. It all traces its way back to Big Alex. The president doesn't consider himself especially strong socially, or at least he didn't in the early part of his mandate. I'd dispute that, but that's his assessment. In any case, it all has to do with recognizing and putting into practice the power of communication. You have to work the room, and I have the luxury of being able to draw on several election campaigns' worth of training in capturing people's attention and engaging them. But Alastair says it as if it were a revelation: "Watch Linc. He just goes and talks to people." Yes, that pretty much nails it. It all flows from there. And for that, Alastair has described me as his role model. You hear that, Dad? I was listening.

Alastair laughs when he calls me the most anti-conservative Conservative he's ever met, though he admits to perhaps having a certain bias when it comes to assessing the sensibilities of people with my political leaning. Yet in the course of my work and political career, I have been exposed to some of the most caring people imaginable, from John Diefenbaker (apartheid) to Joe Clark (women's and gay rights) to Brian Mulroney (environmental issues). Sorry, but social consciences are not handed out solely to socialists … or Liberals, if that happens to be the side of the fence they're sitting on that day. We may have different notions of how to achieve goals, but that doesn't detract from the fact that we aim for honourable outcomes.

In 1992, as the exciting years at the University of Guelph were just getting rolling, my world was dealt a horrible blow when, after decades of dedicated friendship, my former law partner Jack Millar died of cancer. Words alone cannot describe my feelings about him, though I will try. He was an incomparable individual, courageous and strong in his beliefs, a person who judged people the proper way, by what's in their heads and hearts. It was a devastating loss for me, so I can't imagine the pain it dealt to his wife, Marge, his two sons, and his daughter. I drew strength at the time from the realization, as I'd known right from our early days at Mac, that I'd been privileged and blessed to share a significant part of my life with a rare and great person.

That same year, I had a serious health scare. Shortly after I left the lieutenant-governor's office, doctors discovered a growth on my lung, which explains the scar I now have on my back. Doctors at Toronto General Hospital removed the cancerous upper lobe of my right lung, and the entire process scared the hell out of me. The growth was discovered when I went for a regular checkup for my prostate gland, which involved a blood test. The doctor said there was something wrong with me, because my blood was cloudy, but I told him I hadn't been feeling out of sorts at all.

Most people who have cancer put on a good face. If you don't, you're defeated, and then cancer can be the kiss of death. A lot of people don't want to go to the doctor — older men in particular, because they don't like that finger up their anus during the prostate examination. Most men think they're immortal. I did. I tried to keep my cancer diagnosis private to insulate me and my family, but word got out. The media reported that I was recovering very well from lung cancer surgery. I told reporters I was "very lucky and very blessed," adding that Yvonne and the family were pleased at the positive outcome of such a major operation.

While I was busy developing my role as university chancellor, another pressing engagement also captured my attention — national unity. Reporting from Charlottetown, where I was serving as an honorary chair of Ontario's "yes" committee in negotiations for the Charlottetown Accord, the *Toronto Star* quoted me as saying that a rejection of the accord was a sign of troubled times ahead. "With a 'no,' there was nothing but uncertainty. I know there will be problems during the coming years. I feel it in my bones. You have the expectations of the French, the Native peoples.... You'll never get that kind of agreement again in a heck of a long time. If you don't like [Prime Minister] Brian Mulroney or [Ontario Premier] Bob Rae, you don't take it out on the country." I felt so strongly about that.

I believed it was important for Ontarians to support the constitutional amendments proposed in the accord because I saw it clearly as a blueprint for Canada's survival. The accord was reasonable, made sense, and was workable. Two other former lieutenant-governors, my immediate predecessor, John Black Aird, and Pauline McGibbon, were also honorary chairs of the committee.

"This is a great country, but the adhesive that was keeping it together isn't any good any more. And someone had to come up with a new adhesive, and this is it," I told the *Toronto Star*. "The 'no' vote — with all due respect, this is a democracy and I must listen to them — but what they want me to do is to accept the status quo and all the uncertainties that go with it. I want more than that."

I told Ontarians and Quebecois that this was a crisis and they must vote "yes," and Ontario did vote yes, but by the narrowest of margins. In the end, the accord was defeated after only Newfoundland, New Brunswick, Prince Edward Island, and the Northwest Territories gave it strong support.

CANADA

PRIME MINISTER · PREMIER MINISTRE

Ottawa, Ontario
K1A 0A2

April 13, 1994

Dear Mr. Alexander:

I would like to offer my belated thanks for the letter of congratulations that you sent on the occasion of our election victory.

Your very kind words were warmly appreciated. I count myself most fortunate to have been born in a nation that allows all its people - even those from small mill towns in Quebec - an opportunity to realize their greatest dreams.

Please accept my warmest regards.

Sincerely,

Jean Chrétien

The Honourable Lincoln M. Alexander
30 Proctor Boulevard
Hamilton, Ontario
L8M 2M3

Letter from Prime Minister Jean Chrétien after I wrote to congratulate him on his election victory.

A couple of years after I stepped down as lieutenant-governor, I accepted a job with the Government Business Consulting Group, run by Fred Doucet, a close friend of Brian Mulroney and his chief of staff after the 1984 election. It was a large Ottawa lobbying firm, and accepting the offer brought me a lot of heat from the media. To the critics, I said all the other lieutenant-governors were wealthy and I was the poor one. I argued that it was perfectly legal to be a consultant or lobbyist in Canada and that I should be entitled to make a living. Even though I was in my early seventies, I made it clear I wasn't ready to retire. Hell, I'm eighty-four now and I'm still not ready to retire. In the end, it was a brewing storm that never materialized. I quit because the consulting group was sold; the new owners brought in their own slate of people and I was out.

That, of course, was long before Prime Minister Stephen Harper's notion of a five-year waiting period before former ministers or senior bureaucrats could take lobbying jobs. Even then, I had been out of politics for thirteen years, while the lieutenant-governor's post gave me limited political leverage, at least in theory. I didn't see the consulting role as one of being an apologist for any business but rather one in which I could represent certain companies whose outlooks I supported.

Another objection was that the lobbying position could be considered partisan, but that was nonsense since the job would require that I work with MPs and government officials representing all political stripes. Goodness, I didn't need those headlines at my age, especially when I had not done anything illegal.

I disagreed with the political analysts and opposition MPs who contended there was a difference between my situation and that of former governor general Ed Schreyer, who became Canada's high commissioner to Australia after leaving Rideau Hall. They said that given the low-key nature of the posting to Australia, it could be considered an appropriate transition. But, to me, an ambassadorial or high commissioner's post is the biggest lobbyist job of all — for Canada's interests.

It's always nice to be recognized as a candidate with potential for an important post, even if it's not in the cards.

A case in point was the offer, in 1997, to become Ontario's integrity commissioner. I was seventy-five at the time, and I simply decided that, even though the post would have been interesting and challenging, I was past the point of needing challenges on that scale. The job involves ruling on MPPs' conflict of interest issues. After former judge Gregory Evans, who had served in the job since it was created in 1988, announced he was stepping down, a storm of controversy erupted when the government contemplated naming a civil servant to the post. That would have been a rather compromised individual, judging the people he or she worked for, wouldn't you say? The government turned to me, I passed, and I've never regretted the decision.

Notwithstanding my age, I was busy, serving the University of Guelph and sitting on several corporate and volunteer boards. Then, in 1999, a *Windsor Star* editorial suggested me as a possible successor to Roméo LeBlanc as governor general of Canada. "Alexander has the dignity, the presence and the deep working-class roots venerated by Canadians. In Alexander, we can see the kind of inspirational qualities that would serve the position and Canadians well." The kind words were appreciated, but I was seventy-seven at the time and I knew my age would be a concern. At any rate, it didn't happen. Adrienne Clarkson succeeded LeBlanc. My name had been put forward in the late 1980s for the post as well, but it went to Ray Hnatyshyn after I expressed concern due to my lack of French. Barbara McDougall, who lobbied on my behalf for that appointment, still looks at me in disbelief that I didn't pursue it.

Toronto Sun columnist Peter Worthington also pointed to me as an ideal candidate for governor general. It was hardly the grandest endorsement, especially after he had denounced the suggestion that the eminently qualified Bob Rae would be a good choice for the post. Still, he argued that I was a role model for "any citizen," not just blacks, which I considered a compliment. The comment indicated that cultural or racial barriers can be overcome to permit success and opportunity for all individuals — which is what Canada at its core strives to do. It's about merit, not superficial distinctions. In that column, Worthington expressed admiration for the fact I was a "100-percent unhyphenated Canadian" and quoted me as saying once during a lunch with him at a posh place years ago, "Who'd have thought, way back when, that I'd someday be eating in the same room as all the big shots I see around me. Come to think of it, as lieutenant-governor, I guess I'm the biggest shot in the room."

Throughout my years at the University of Guelph, I continued to receive recognition in areas outside the university. In 1995, I was honoured to be one of twenty-five people named by Premier Bob Rae and Minister of Trade Frances Lankin as the Ontario government's special envoys for trade. While not onerous, the role was a nice link back to my lieutenant-governor days and an opportunity to advance the interests of Ontario.

In 1997, I was awarded the Churchill Society Award for Excellence in the Cause of Parliamentary Democracy. The organizers described me as a "great bridge builder: between nations, as witness his work for the Inter-Parliamentary Union and the Commonwealth Parliamentary Associations; between economic interest groups, as witness his work for Workers' Compensation and for the Canadian School of Management; and, not least, between races, as witness his many awards from the Armenian, Black and Jewish communities." In particular, the "bridge builder" reference reflects my approach to issues and people.

Then, in 1998, I was one of four Canadians inducted into the Terry Fox Hall of Fame. The honour is for those who have a tradition of service to the disabled. As lieutenant-governor, I was patron for the annual Lieutenant Governor's Games for children with disabilities at Variety Village. I was always so impressed by the optimism and determination of those competing in the games. My contention when speaking at or about these events was that they serve an important role in demonstrating the scope of talent in the disabled community and that we have to make it easier for the disabled to share and use their skills and wisdom.

I have received numerous honours, for which I am truly grateful, but I have chosen to mention these in particular because I think you can trace their roots to pursuing education and drawing out all of our talents and intelligence. As chancellor, I have explained in various interviews how fortunate I was to be born in Canada to parents — in particular my mother — who were wise enough to advise me to embrace the educational system. As a black, education represented my best chance for success. I think I've proven that. Aside from lack of money, nothing could block the son of a maid and a railway porter from going to university and law school. Education was empowerment. We hold a responsibility to all the generations of Canadians who came before. We have to meet that responsibility with an iron will to recognize, develop, and strengthen education's role as central to our economic prosperity.

One of our initiatives at the University of Guelph, Project Go, neatly brought together my thoughts about education and opportunity for the underprivileged. Launched in 1995, Project Go forged a bond with one of Canada's most multicultural schools, L'Amoreaux Collegiate in

Scarborough, to help tear down barriers to higher education and diversify our student population. The concept is an outstanding illustration of what I call active advocacy.

When I was reappointed to a second term as chancellor, it was an unprecedented unanimous vote. At the time, a botany professor named Roger Horton pointed to my "commitment of time and care" to the university and said that my work extended far beyond the ceremonial and public. To me, that observation really affirmed what I'd always believed. If I were going to take something on, it would be full bore with no half measures. Anything less, as far as I'm concerned, would diminish all my previous work and that of those who had served in similar roles before me.

I have relished the role of chancellor, and I think I have been a great advocate. I am not afraid to speak up for the university, even if I happen to be in less than welcoming circumstances. At one event — the retirement of the chancellor of York University, I believe — there was all this flattering stuff being thrown around: blah blah university this and blah blah university that. Finally, I stood up and said, "I'm the chancellor of the University of Guelph, the greatest comprehensive university in the country."

I'm not going to apologize for any boosterism I engage in for the University of Guelph. Of course, people say all the good things they're required to when they talk about the institution they represent. But my university — I call it that — has been a great source of pride for me, and I have always been sincere in my advocacy for it.

Over the years, while I've talked about myself as circumstances demanded, it's not necessarily like me to stand up and thump my chest and tell you I am the greatest MP, or the greatest lieutenant-governor, or the greatest university chancellor. But I will tell you I think I am one great university chancellor because I believe in education and my university. Yes, I'd tell you that.

CHAPTER 14

The Loss of My Beloved Yvonne

When I tell people that Yvonne was my rock, I mean it in every imaginable sense of the word. She anchored me emotionally and intellectually. She was balance and stability, the one who could be counted on for anything, no matter what. Here is what I would consider a prime example. Throughout my law career, years in Ottawa, and term as lieutenant-governor, I always left my phone number listed in the phone book, and it still is. As a public person, I felt that was essential. Yet for great periods of time, I would be away from home, leaving Yvonne to manage the callers. You can imagine the range of calls I got, from supportive constituents to angry, belligerent voters, from friends to hate-spewing racists. Although she had every right to object to being put in that position, she recognized the importance I placed on providing public access and so she handled it diligently, with her usual tact, grace, and dignity.

When Yvonne died after a lengthy battle with Alzheimer's disease on May 15, 1999, I was devastated. I had met Sister Teresa Carmel on one of her many visits to the hospital during the time Yvonne was at death's door. I told the sister that I didn't know why this was happening to Yvonne and that God was letting me down. I was so angry. I said I had tried to be good, and Yvonne was just so completely good. There could be no justification for Him taking her from me, I reasoned. I told the sister I didn't think I could adjust to life without Yvonne. I couldn't go on.

Calmly, Sister Teresa told me my anger was understandable and that I should tell God I was mad. She said He wanted to hear the source of my concerns and my anguish. I said I couldn't confront Him because in my anger I would use foul language and strike out. I didn't want to do that, because I worried that if I did it, He would take me as well. She said, "He is an understanding God. Trust me. Don't worry." So I did tell God in no uncertain terms, using foul language at its worst, that I was angry and that He had let me down. I asked Him what the hell was going on, Him taking my wife. I poured out all my anxious emotions over the loss of Yvonne.

I now recognize that this was an important step in my grieving process, for within two days, I had settled down and I was thankful He had taken her. I had needed to unburden my soul, and I was able to come to the conclusion that dying was the best thing for Yvonne, despite my personal pain. In fact, I tell people now to do just that — confront God — in their time of grief. That is not to say the gaping hole that was left in my world had been filled, for that is impossible and always will be. But I was able to gain perspective, and that enabled me to set about dealing with being without her. Otherwise, I'm certain I would have forever remained cemented in despair.

I always thought I would die before Yvonne, so when she died, it was as if my legs were cut off. You're sort of walking on the nubs trying to stand up straight, but you can't. Then, eventually, you get the legs back and you can walk tall. Yvonne was also my friend and drinking buddy, so to speak, even though she didn't drink much. My life revolved around her, though when she was gone, Keith, his wife, Joyce, and my granddaughters, Erika and Marissa, helped fill the void. Indeed, among the many instances of good fortune in my life is the fact that my son chose well when he made Joyce his life partner. Aside from giving us wonderful granddaughters, she has provided boundless support and care to me in these later years.

For more than fifty years Yvonne was the one who moulded me, counselled me, and had confidence in me. I relied on her. The lessons I've learned, the advice I give — so much of it has been derived from the insight and strength of Yvonne. She was a wise, proud, and determined woman, and she had to be very strong to allow me the scope I had to pursue the political and various other occupations and appointments

I think my devastation over Yvonne's death is abundantly evident from this photo, in which my son Keith guides me compassionately, while Hilary Weston (right) watches. The photo was taken following the funeral service for Yvonne at Dodsworth and Brown Funeral Home in Hamilton.

I've filled. Yvonne was focused on me. If people didn't like me, it didn't matter, because I always knew she loved me. Without her backing, enthusiasm, and love, I'm not sure what I would have accomplished.

Marrying Yvonne was the smartest thing I ever did. Our relationship, from the first time we met, endured for almost sixty years before death took her away from me. She did so much for me that I couldn't fail her, and as a result I always tried to excel and to make her proud of me. I lived in fear of proving unworthy of her and of losing her love, but I could never contemplate actually losing her. A friend of Yvonne's, Pamela Bragoli, once called her "the woman behind the man. She supported Linc so well when he was lieutenant-governor." She noted Yvonne's humble origins, but also her dignity, and said she "was a lady in every sense of the word"; that was so true.

The Provincial Council of Women, the Canadian Women's Breast Cancer Foundation, the Women's Canadian Club of Hamilton, and the

Order of the Eastern Star were among the organizations with which Yvonne was involved. She had passion for the sick, the poor, and the elderly, and she was devoted to helping in her quiet, dignified manner.

Yvonne was proud of me, and you could see it in her deeds and actions. Some women are funny, they don't want to tell you they love you, and she was like that. I'd have to force it out of her by saying to her many times, "Say 'Linc, I love you.'" She would eventually.

Yvonne never complained. She never asked for anything. Instead, she inspired me to accomplish significant goals, and she encouraged and supported me. About the time of our fiftieth anniversary, a reporter asked me the secret to a long marriage, and I said, "Never let disagreements last more than a day." If you do, it can fester and grow to an issue way beyond what it deserves to be because you've lost control. There were times when she and I fought like cats and dogs, but we never dragged the disagreements out for days. Then again, I was smart enough to realize she was never wrong.

Marge Millar used to tease me that Yvonne had to be one very special person to put up with me because I had such a strong presence and personality. Part of that I trace back to my love of people, which leads me to be the outgoing person I am. I relish the fact, as Marge points out, that I can't go a block in Hamilton (and a lot of other places, I dare say) without people calling out to me. Then I'd rather stop and talk than just wave and keep going. That's me. And that's what made Yvonne so special. Her lack of selfishness was astonishing, and I was the main beneficiary. She let Linc be Linc. She made it all possible.

CHAPTER 15

Two Parties, One Birthday

D r. and Mrs. Leo and Ines Freitag moved to a home on Proctor Boulevard in 1957, one year before the Alexander family moved in. Along with becoming fast friends, we also became associated professionally. Leo was my physician; I was his lawyer. Leo died in 1996, and in the course of time, after Yvonne died in 1999, Ines and I began sharing outings together. She is a very beautiful, elegant, and cultured woman and so much of our time together is spent attending concerts and the theatre. She is very knowledgeable and loves chamber music, opera, and operatic soloists, many of whom she knows.

She described me as a jazz and blues man when we first started sharing outings to concerts and the theatre. However, with her knowledge and experience, Ines has vastly enhanced my understanding of the arts. This has been a wonderful thing for us to share, and I can now say that chamber music and opera are particular favourites of mine, though I am not an expert. I can thank her for that.

While we meshed nicely on issues like the arts, we do have a few points of disagreement, such as our taste in political leaders. She's an admirer, for instance, of Bill Clinton, while I think the resoluteness of George W. Bush is ideal, much to her chagrin and that of many of my other friends. She says she's inclined toward intellectual leadership, which is why Clinton appeals to her. Suffice to say that in her mind Bush is far removed from that category of leadership.

Our friendly disagreement over U.S. politics, our dinners, and the concerts are among the many wonderful rewards of having companionship at this point in my life. It is nice to have someone close with whom to share events, and in recent years I have had the good fortune to be the subject of a few such special occasions.

In 2001, Senator Don Oliver and Galen Weston wanted to stage a grand celebration leading up to my eightieth birthday. While I acquiesced eventually — you have to put up a bit of a fight — I wanted to ensure that the proceeds would be used in a way that reflected my goals. The tribute served as a fundraiser for a pair of scholarships to enable visible minorities, Native Canadians, and disabled students to attend the University of Guelph. I was pleasantly surprised when university vice-president Rob McLaughlin reported the event had raised about $600,000. The two Lincoln Alexander Chancellor's Scholarships, aimed at encouraging diversity and developing young leaders, each provided $20,000 over eight semesters.

In the end, this old populist managed to scare up more than six hundred people to squeeze into the Canadian Room at Toronto's Royal York, my home away from home when I was lieutenant-governor. While the party was billed as black-tie optional, it was anything but stodgy. As an advocate for the arts and as a member of the board of Shaw Festival, as well as close friends with impresarios Ed, Anne, and David Mirvish, I had actors, opera singers, and jazz musicians also attend. Equally gratifying, besides entertainment celebrities and political stars, were former staff members from my days in the lieutenant-governor's office, university students, pupils from schools named after me, and even human rights activists. Adding the scholarship component tied in nicely with my own philosophy of the importance of education to advancing in today's society. I have touched a few bases, I realized.

I told the *Hamilton Spectator*: "This is my kind of party. Movers and shakers and heavy hitters, beautiful women, handsome men all dressed to the nines and here for a good cause." Hilary and Galen Weston, as co-chairs, did a fantastic job.

My political career was represented by former premiers and cabinet members, as well as by MPs and MPPs. With my membership on the boards of several companies, there was a tidy sprinkling of chief executives. Among an astonishing number of personal tributes were ones from Hilary Weston, former premier Bob Rae, former lieutenant-governor Hal Jackman, contralto Maureen Forrester, television journalist Knowlton Nash, and Senator Anne Cools. Videotaped messages came from several people, including former Ontario premiers David Peterson and Mike Harris, former prime ministers Joe Clark and Brian Mulroney, and Prime Minister Jean Chrétien.

Hilary Weston said that I had changed the vice-regal role in Ontario by bringing "dignity, fun, and an intangible spirit" to the job. She added, "With your warmth and generous spirit, you have won our respect, admiration, and love. Equally at home in the political arena and amongst people of all walks of life, you have become an inspiring role model and have shown us what it is to be a good man."

In his videotaped message, Chrétien said, "The career of Lincoln Alexander has been long and distinguished, spanning both the public and private realms. This event is a wonderful testimony to his many outstanding achievements and dedicated service to community and country." Mike Harris's message said, "You remind us that determination, hard work, and compassion are what make Canada great. Our province and our country are much richer for your presence."

I had by this time become the chairman of the Toronto Raptors Foundation, which over the years has raised more than $15 million for Ontario charities that support youth programs and sports for at-risk children. In light of this role, I received a pair of basketball shoes autographed by former Raptors star Vince Carter (now with the New Jersey Nets). Even with my size-fourteen feet, I couldn't fill those shoes.

My involvement with the Toronto Raptors Foundation was brought about by my good friend Steve Stavro. Steve had considered me for the board of Maple Leaf Sports and Entertainment, of which he was chairman at the time, but instead asked me to head the foundation. Sadly, as I was completing this memoir, Steve died. I had actually spoken and shared some laughs with him earlier that day, and I was shocked to be told by his wife, Sally, that he had died later the same day. I sobbed like a baby, uncontrolled.

Usually, a person celebrates a birthday only once with a major bash. But for my eightieth, a second party was being organized. Like the Toronto party in December, the second party was for a good cause too. On the actual date of my eightieth birthday, January 21, 2002, I was feted by eight hundred guests at Carmen's banquet hall in Hamilton, this time at a fundraiser for St. Joseph's Healthcare in Hamilton. A group of Hamilton's best-known citizens, including philanthropist Morgan Firestone, Liberal MP Stan Keyes, my close friend Ines Freitag, and Craig Dowhaniuk, executive director of the Morgan Firestone Foundation, planned the party. I told the *Hamilton Spectator* I was "thrilled and honoured," and that it was the first real birthday party I had had since about 1937, when I was in my teens. That one, all those years ago, didn't turn out so well, I explained. "Everyone was joking and one guy started laughing and he laughed so hard that he spit all over the cake. I don't think anybody ate the cake." That birthday party was in Toronto, just before I went to New York. Thankfully, there was no spitting on the cake at my galas in Hamilton and Toronto.

For my birthday, Yvonne usually gave me a card and a bottle of men's cologne. This one would be a little different. There were so many close friends and Hamilton people. Craig Dowhaniuk chaired the party committee, along with David Braley of Orlick Industries, Ron Foxcroft of Fluke Transport, and Ron Joyce of Tim Hortons. I wanted the party to be fun but affordable for average Hamiltonians. The Toronto dinner cost $1,000 a person; in Hamilton it was $125 a ticket.

I was flattered that Morgan Firestone was involved. He had spearheaded other fundraisers featuring global celebrities such as Bill Clinton, Margaret Thatcher, George Bush, Shimon Peres, and Sophia Loren. "They were big shots; I'm just a small shot," I told the *Spectator*. At the fundraiser featuring Sophia Loren, in 1999, I got to meet her and fell in love with her, "but she's too young for me," I joked.

They called the Hamilton dinner "To Linc with Love." Dowhaniuk told the *Spectator* he thought something should be done to honour Hamilton's "most distinguished citizen. He is a local Hamilton treasure and he's got complete class. But he never forgets that Hamilton is his home town and what better thing to do than give a hometown party for Linc." I was flattered.

I was also pleased that the proceeds were going to St. Joe's. Aside from being a top-notch institution, there were some nuns at St. Joe's who would have me over for dinner once in a while; I had to thank them, too. In acknowledging the guests and organizers I reiterated the values I adhere to and follow in my life: work hard, try your best, be fair and honest, and look after the less fortunate. These are good things, and it's good that people are prepared to honour someone for those beliefs.

Organizers prepared a commemorative program for the event, along with a video of my life. The event raised more than $100,000 for the Yvonne Alexander Memorial Fund, with the money going to the Firestone Institute of Respiratory Health at St. Joseph's. It was not the first time Yvonne's memory had been honoured. In June, a month after she died, the Yvonne Alexander Award for commitment to the Easter Seal Society was given for the first time. "I've never been so moved, and I've been around a while," I told people at the St. Joe's fundraiser that night.

"You know, I prayed for the past month that I would make eighty," I said before the banquet began. "When I got up this morning I said, 'Goodness gracious, I've made it.'" I acknowledged to the guests that I had been blessed with a wonderful life, that I had had my ups and downs but had come out ahead in the long run. I said that our hometown university, McMaster, had been important to me because it provided the base on which I could grow. It was my launch pad. I also paid tribute to the great riding of Hamilton West, which I had served so long in Parliament and to which I could always look for enthusiastic support.

Premier Mike Harris, along with civic leaders and Hamilton citizens, again toasted me. "You've done what everybody else dreams of, you've made a difference," Harris said. He added, kindly, that Hamilton's finest had become Ontario's finest and Canada's finest.

By 2002, I had been appointed to an unprecedented fifth term as chancellor of the University of Guelph and had presided over the convocation of thousands of graduates, an emotionally gratifying experience. At fall convocation, I was given a tribute book signed by friends and colleagues in honour of my eightieth birthday. The school also awarded the first Lincoln Alexander Chancellor's Scholarships, generated by the Toronto gala. The scholarship program has been particularly gratifying to me because without an education my path in life would have been very different. It was great to recognize now that others would get to benefit from pursuing post-secondary studies who otherwise might not have had the chance.

In the summer of 2006 I was continuing as chancellor, and the flexibility of the role has thankfully allowed me to pursue other interests, such as the Toronto Raptors Foundation, Shaw Festival board, Ontario Press Council, Quebecor-Ontario Media Advisory Board, and Canadian Race Relations Foundation, to mention but a few. There's no slowing down this guy.

CHAPTER 16

~

A Lifetime Fighting for Racial Equality

From the streets of Toronto and Harlem as a child, to the roadblocks in finding employment after graduating from McMaster, even to getting established as a lawyer, throughout my life racial issues have been in the forefront for me. Of course, racial problems go far beyond workplace discrimination. The tensions between the black community and the Metro Toronto police are a case in point.

It must be said that the vast majority of our police officers work hard in an often unenviable situation. They serve and protect us with admirable tact, skill, and good faith, and for that they deserve our respect and our trust. But it's also a fact that members of the black community have legitimate concerns about treatment they've received from police. There has been insufficient sensitivity on the part of some officers. A disturbing example was the raid on a Scarborough church in the middle of a service, during which the police arrested, and subsequently released, five youths wrongly identified as robbery suspects.

Toronto is not Los Angeles or New York, and we all know the United Nations has said the Ontario capital is one of the best places in the world to live. I don't disagree, although I acknowledge it has some warts. I was particularly disturbed by the riots in Toronto on May 4, 1992, when an angry mob rampaged on Yonge Street. The demonstrators were protesting against the fatal police shooting of a young black man in Toronto just days after the acquittal on assault charges of Los Angeles police officers videotaped brutally beating Rodney King. In a report on the riot, commissioned by Premier Bob Rae, Stephen Lewis wrote: "What we are dealing with, at root, and fundamentally, is anti-black racism. It is blacks who are being shot, it is black youth that is unemployed in excessive numbers, it is black students who are being inappropriately streamed in schools, it is black kids who are disproportionately dropping out."

Yet, despite those frustrations, I felt the black community should look internally as well as externally to find the answers to its problems. What bothered me was that most public comment had come from black activists — especially the head of the Black Action Defence Committee, Dudley Laws — and not from the rest of the community. I knew it wouldn't be popular, but I had to say what I was thinking. "People are saying Dudley Laws does not speak for me," I told reporters. "They're saying he's not my leader, and, in fairness to Dudley, he probably doesn't claim to represent anybody. I don't blame Dudley, but his viewpoint probably doesn't represent as many people out there as you might think," I added.

"I've never heard anyone say that it's my fault as a black person, that it could be our parental upbringing, our education, our lack of confidence, or whatever that is contributing to the situation," I said. "There is definitely a perception by some blacks that the police are there only to serve and protect white people. The police aren't perfect, and I'm not perfect, and I can understand why some people feel this way. But we can't get carried away with inflammatory rhetoric. It just causes polarization."

I don't deny that the police force has had some bad apples in its ranks, but I think the majority are doing a good job and always have. "The chief [Julian Fantino] has been trying to make the most from the demands of a multicultural city. But the police shouldn't be used as the scapegoat ... The problems lie in loss of job opportunities, economic deprivation and myths and attitudes that exist by whites regarding people of colour. That's the problem," I said.

In 2002, the day after the *Toronto Star* published an extensive and very controversial report on racial profiling by police in Toronto, I called for a summit on policing, race relations, and racial profiling. I didn't want to embarrass the police. Instead, I thought the best way to address the concerns raised by the *Star* was to meet them head-on. I felt the summit should be seen as an attempt to identify and eradicate a serious problem while shoring up the credibility of the police. All parties involved in the issue participated in the meeting, and while I knew change wouldn't happen overnight, it was a start.

Former police chief Fantino strenuously insisted Toronto police do not engage in racial profiling and do not condone it. He said the *Star* story had caused "much distress in the black community, the community-at-large and with our police officers." His statement also noted that a recent poll had given Toronto police a 94 percent approval rating from the community. Fantino said police treat all citizens alike, while former mayor Mel Lastman said that they only catch "bad guys" and that racial profiling is not an issue with Toronto police.

I wasn't the only one who found Fantino's reaction troubling. Among others, Valerie Steele, president of the Jamaican-Canadian Association, said she received dozens of calls a week from people complaining about police treatment, and she suggested the chief's denial was the same as calling all the city's blacks liars.

In retrospect, Fantino's initial response was perhaps not all that different from that of any leader whose people have been attacked. You get defensive and you strive to protect them. But genuine leaders ultimately seek the truth, because there can be no greater safety net, no greater means for establishing and maintaining your integrity, than truth and honesty. At the conclusion of the summit, which I called historic, I announced I had commitments from all levels of police and government to end racial profiling and restore confidence in the system through which public complaints are heard.

Chief Fantino, Mayor Lastman, Toronto Police Services Board Chairman Norm Gardner, Solicitor General Bob Runciman, and other police officers and politicians joined with me when I made a statement on the summit's work. We came up with three recommendations to ease racial tensions:

Making the police complaint system more independent and accessible for members of the public who have objections about the conduct of police. Related to this, Bill 103, the Independent Police Review Act, received first reading in April 2006. Bill 103 was intended to establish a new public complaints process through amendments to the Police Services Act.

Improving training for police recruits in race relations (Keith Forde, a black, is now deputy chief in charge of hiring and firing).

Approaching senior levels of government for funding to enable cities to address issues that involve race and police work.

The *Hamilton Spectator* picked up the Toronto story, reporting that Chief Ken Robertson had vowed not to tolerate racial profiling by the Hamilton police. Robertson conceded that his force was not perfect but said that he would encourage dialogue with the community. I said I was happy with the chief and "95 percent" of his officers and that a summit similar to the one in Toronto was not needed in Hamilton.

Racial profiling by police had come home to me years before, when I was still practising law. Once Yvonne was followed by a police cruiser, apparently merely because she was driving a new car. I called Hamilton's chief of police at the time and told him I was mad as hell. I said, "There's somebody following my wife. Now, you know my wife. She's not a whore, she's not a crook, she's just a hard-working housewife, and your people are following her. Why the hell are they following her?" It never happened again, but that's how far profiling goes. I have first-hand experience of what it means, and it disturbs me a lot.

It is simply, sadly the case that black parents in Hamilton and throughout the country warn their children about the high risk of being stopped by police because of the colour of their skin. They know what it is like growing up black, regardless of their socio-economic status. I was visiting a friend in Toronto some time before this latest controversy on race and policing hit the news. He told me he advised his teenage son that it was fine to hang around with a group of white teens, but to be aware that when trouble comes, he will be the first one police come to see.

Knowing their sons are more likely to be stopped, many black parents provide pointers on how to respond to the police. One mother told me she taught her son always to comply with police, even if he thinks he is being unfairly targeted. She said once her son could drive, she was unable to sleep until he returned home at night because she worried he would be stopped for the infamous DWB (driving while black). In fact, as I wrote this memoir I had a call from the daughter of Morley Weaver, with whom I went to Africa, who said her daughter, who is white, was with a black male friend in Ottawa on the weekend when they were unjustifiably stopped by police. I advised her to take it to the top — the police board or the chief.

Fortunately, we were able to get top-level support in the Ontario legislature. Bob Runciman, the solicitor general, said he was taking concerns about unfair treatment of blacks by police seriously and was willing to meet community leaders to discuss it. He told the legislature he had no knowledge police are targeting blacks, but if the accusations prove to be true he would address them. Runciman also said he trusted my judgment. "If Mr. Alexander believes there is some substance to the suggestions that have been released to the public [in the *Star* report], I'm quite prepared, and this government's quite prepared, to sit down with not only Mr. Alexander but other people who have an interest in this subject to discuss it, to see if there is a real problem here. I understand there is a real concern, but to ensure that if indeed there is a real problem here, that it's eradicated."

The issue had been also raised in the legislature by Liberal MPP Alvin Curling, who was Ontario's only black MPP at the time. "Let me assure the minister there is a problem … Those problems go beyond the police and beyond the city limits," Curling said.

None of this should be construed as a lack of respect for the police. There is no bigger supporter of our men and women in blue than me. I am an honorary chief of several police services, and the honorary commissioner of the Ontario Provincial Police, whose headquarters in Orillia is named after me. It was in 1994 that David Christopherson, who was Ontario's solicitor general at the time, visited Hamilton council to announce that the new four-storey OPP headquarters in Orillia would be named after me. OPP Commissioner Thomas O'Grady also spoke at the announcement event, and they presented me with a framed artist's drawing of the headquarters. I was wearing my honorary OPP uniform, and I remember praising the police officials for "standing up to be counted." The *Hamilton Spectator*, which covered the session, also noted that I paid tribute to Yvonne. "Forty-six years of marriage, she is the one who should receive the plaques, she should get the uniform and she should get the plugs."

Although I have never shied away from pointing to serious problems that have arisen in our police services, I have immense respect for the women and men who protect us. In my capacity as honorary commissioner, there was no real job description, and much of the work was ceremonial, but it was important to me that I behaved in a way that would enhance pride in and respect for the OPP among the general public. And adding a little levity from time to time doesn't hurt either.

I was able to elicit a few chuckles in 1995 at the opening of the new headquarters when I said, "It's so nice to receive such an honour while I'm still alive. Usually, they only give it to you after you're dead." That line also works when they name a school or parkway after you, by the way.

Of course, there are events with racial overtones in a wide variety of locations that have nothing to do with the police. One example was the minstrel show the Simcoe Lions Club had put on for four decades as a fundraiser for community projects. Denounced as racist by some, it featured white performers made up as blacks in straw hats. One year, it attracted an audience of nearly 2,800 and raised $10,000. Great to raise the money, but the method of doing it was terrible.

"Why don't they just paint their faces white, put on red wigs, and run around like the clowns they are?" I said in a news story. "The shows are stupid, obnoxious, and not in keeping with today's multicultural society." I called the Simcoe Lions Club president, Ed Collins, to challenge him about the show, and he suggested I might feel differently if I attended a performance. Of course, I wouldn't be caught dead at such a travesty.

I also called James Earl, Simcoe's mayor, to tell him that if he were worth his salt he would put the matter before town council and pass a resolution banning the minstrel show. Earl told a reporter that I "went up and down [his] back about sixteen times about the show and he wouldn't let me get a word in edgewise."

I wasn't the only one to find fault with the minstrel show. It also drew fire from officials of the Ontario Human Rights Commission and Hamilton's Race Relations Committee, as well as ordinary, thinking Canadians. Finally, appropriately, it was abandoned in the early 1990s. Even Lions Clubs International asked the Simcoe club to put a stop to it. "In this day and age, it's not an appropriate kind of thing," Pat

Cannon, a media relations officer for the Chicago-based organization, told the *Toronto Star*.

Collins acknowledged that the Simcoe Lions Club local district governor had also been contacted by the Chicago office. "I'm sure that there will be some changes made for next year's show," he told the *Star*.

When the arts address racial issues, context and theme are crucial. Each case must be addressed on its own merits. There should be room for literary licence if the overall objective is to create awareness of discrimination. One example is the controversy that arose about teaching Harper Lee's novel *To Kill a Mockingbird* in English classes. Objections centred on the word *nigger*. I acknowledged that I too objected to that derogatory term, but it was important to look beyond it to the book's objective. I argued that novels such as Lee's can be effective in fighting racism if teachers show sensitivity in presenting them to their classes. Similarly, I regard *Uncle Tom's Cabin*, by Harriet Beecher Stowe, as a piece of history. I once said in an interview with the *Hamilton Spectator* that I couldn't remember how old I was when I first read it, and though knew some people might find it offensive, "nevertheless, you learn what the past was and it should not happen in the future." I was delighted to have the opportunity as chairman of the Ontario Heritage Trust to declare that this world-renowned cabin would be protected. We are fortunate to have the opportunity to save this valuable resource and to remind people from around the world of the plight of Uncle Tom and those who used the Underground Railroad.

In 1993, when the United Way and the Canadian National Institute for the Blind presented a revival of the musical *Show Boat* as a fundraiser, it prompted different reactions from blacks, some of whom charged that it portrayed racist stereotypes that were best left buried. Ruth Grant, the United Way chairwoman, acknowledged the "heartfelt concerns and the issues that have been raised by members of the black community" but contended that shutting down *Show Boat* was not the answer.

I argued that, whatever its evils or merits, the show should not be boycotted. "How can I judge something if I don't go and see it?" I asked. At a meeting at the Toronto offices of Livent, producer Garth Drabinsky's company, I asked Drabinsky and the show's director, Hal Prince, to listen carefully to the black community's concerns. I determined that I would get involved in the debate of whether the show should go on. And it did. It later played on Broadway without any protest from New York's black community.

In 1996, Prime Minister Jean Chrétien appointed me chairman of the newly formed Canadian Race Relations Foundation. The challenge facing the foundation was to identify racism and determine how to combat it. While I was proud to take on the role of founding chairman, I think it's tragic that, in this day and age of so-called enlightenment, such an organization is needed. Regardless, I had to look at it as an essential step in the process to get us where we need to go to battle discrimination. I knew we could not be complacent.

The foundation, based in Toronto, was established with a $24-million government endowment. It came about as a provision in the Japanese Canadian Redress Agreement, which the Mulroney government had signed in 1988 to compensate Japanese Canadians for the seizure of their property and internment during the Second World War. The National Association of Japanese Canadians saw the foundation as a significant step toward preventing such mistreatment from being repeated.

I insisted that the foundation should become the first national organization to focus on gathering information about racism. Its operating budget was to come from fundraising, investments, and donations. My position had a salary, but I wasn't about to break the bank. A condition of my MP pension was that I could not earn more than $5,000 a year from this job, and it was taxable. But it gave me a stage on which to continue to advocate against racism, so the money was obviously of little consequence.

Given the abundance of ethnic groups in this country, along with our reputation as an inclusive and tolerant society, it's easy to be complacent and believe such an anti-racism campaign was overkill. It was not. I simply had to point to race issues in the news at the time to make my case. Read the papers and the evidence is regularly there: The desecration of a Jewish cemetery with anti-Semitic slurs, the attack in Toronto on two elderly Jewish men, and youth violence in British Columbia when skinheads were sentenced for killing an elderly Sikh man.

When my term as the first chairman of the Race Relations Foundation ended, I was honoured to receive its inaugural Lifetime

Achievement Award at a tribute to mark my contributions to the organization. The incoming chairman, Patrick Case, director of the University of Guelph's Human Rights and Equity Office, called me a role model and added, "It's an incredible honour for me to be replacing an icon." The foundation's executive director, Dr. Karen Mock, said I epitomized the organization's role in providing independent leadership in the struggle against racism.

While this struggle continued, in December 1998, Isabel Bassett, Ontario's citizenship, culture, and recreation minister, presented me with the Award for Outstanding Achievement in Human Rights. The award was to mark the fiftieth anniversary of the signing of the United Nations Universal Declaration of Human Rights. I was particularly honoured because the award recognizes outstanding Ontarians for advancing human rights and fostering a climate of improved understanding and mutual respect.

I take every opportunity to speak out on racism, including my eightieth birthday, when the *Hamilton Spectator* reported my lament about how much it has cost this country. I also waded into the controversy over the suggestion by some academics that it was time to think about experimenting with alternative — that is, separate — schools for black students. "If you don't have a black boss in the police department, does that mean you can't be a policeman?" I asked. "If you don't have a black person as head of the law society, does that mean that you can't get a law degree? These university professors ought to get out of their classrooms and see what's going on." I am totally and vehemently against separating black kids so they can learn black English, which is unacceptable and will affect them later on in the work force. The U.S. used to have black schools that were supposedly equal, but they had to be abandoned because they were not effective and isolated people.

In July 2002, at a Prince Edward Island meeting on race relations, I said Canadians must remain vigilant about racism, not only in others but also in ourselves. I told those at the meeting that it is important to keep talking about racism because it has not gone away; it is a part of our history of which we should not be proud. Despite our reputation for supporting freedom and human rights, we still have to acknowledge our past shortcomings.

In December 2003, I gave an address on relations between the black community and police. "In our discussions this morning, there are a couple of things that we should bear in mind. One is that there isn't one unified black community. Just as with most communities, there is not an elected overall leadership to speak with one voice. It should therefore not be surprising to see different reactions from different factions," I said. "The second thing is this. Even though reactions and approaches may differ, there is an amazing sense of unity in what is being demanded of the police, of the different levels of government and of themselves — ourselves."

I'm also acutely aware that blacks are not the only victims of prejudice. In the two months that followed the terrorist attacks on New York's World Trade Center and the Pentagon on September 11, 2001, Hamilton police investigated eighty-two hate crimes — double the amount they normally deal with in an entire year. Similar crimes were committed across the country. Mayor Bob Wade rose to the challenge, and the Strengthening Hamilton's Community Initiative (SHCI) was the result. I said the SHCI could make a difference in addressing what our chief of police had called a crisis. But I remained positive. "I was here when things were really tough. I mean you couldn't go anywhere. You couldn't get a job. You were spat on. You were discarded like an old shoe," I told the *Spectator*. "But I see it now … people with zero tolerance. I don't look back. I look to the future because the future starts with us. I'm very optimistic."

Racism must be battled on many levels. In November 2001, I wrote to the federal Minister of Justice to applaud the government for the "inclusion of stricter provisions for hate crime and hate on the internet" in its proposed Anti-Terrorism Act. I commended Prime Minister Chrétien for his initiative to reassure Canada's Muslim communities in the aftermath of the terrorist attacks on September 11, 2001. But I also said the definition of terrorism in the legislation was too broad and I was concerned about "the risk of increased racial profiling at borders and in policing and security work."

On a personal front, I've always believed that I was first class, never second. As I told the *Ontarion*, the independent student newspaper at the University of Guelph, in 2003: "I don't believe in second-class citizenship, and that's why I'm always speaking out when I find that men, women, and children — white, black, yellow, and brown — are being picked on because of their colour and aren't being given the opportunity to make a substantial contribution to the economic, social and political development of this country." I hate the way the word *tolerant* is used. It is not the proper way of accepting other races — being tolerant. That means putting up with someone, and that is not acceptable. You tolerate dogs peeing on the grass, bee stings, and ants ruining your picnic, but not other people. Tolerance is not respect. You don't have to love me, but you have to respect me.

Once, while campaigning in Halifax on behalf of Bob Stanfield, I noticed that the white people were on one side of the room and the black people were on the other side. I said to myself, *This is not right,* and I told them all to get out there and integrate and dance together. I will do things like that. I think that's why God put me on Earth. It wasn't a popular idea, and disturbing at the time for some people, but it worked.

Racism is, simply, a product of ignorance, but I am an optimist and have seen great strides taken toward eradicating that evil. I think it is a product of the Canadian character that we are far more inclined than so many other countries to judge people on the quality of their minds and thinking, the quality of their character, than in any superficial factor such as colour. We can't disenfranchise people for such meaningless reasons. We all need to work together to make certain Canada is the great nation it can be, and in many ways already is.

We need to look to the future, while we pick up the torch from those who went before us. In that respect, the death of Coretta Scott King on January 30, 2006, was a watershed moment. The loss of Mrs. King reminded us that the era of the black leaders of the 1960s was over and that others would have to take their place. There is still a lot of work to be done.

When Mrs. King died, Thane Burnett of the *Toronto Sun* wrote a story about my trail-blazing role for Canadian blacks. I was honoured to be thought of at the time of the death of such a great woman. I was saddened by her death and praised her courage in continuing the fight for racial equality in the United States after the assassination in 1968 of her husband, Martin Luther King Jr. Burnett traced my life from my roots as the son of a railway porter and maid in Toronto to serving as Ontario's first black lieutenant-governor. "How many black kids in Toronto today really believe that can happen to them?" he wrote. "Perhaps more than we're led to believe."

I said that while I still think Canadian streets are kinder to blacks than those in U.S. cities, the new challenge is to convince young people that there's a better way to earn $1,000 than selling dope. That is the same on both sides of the border, and it comes from the work of the Kings. But the evolution of race relations will be stalled if only minorities understand its importance: it's a societal problem, not a black or white one. While I was encouraged that politicians were ready to address the root causes of urban violence, I was concerned by the conspiracy of silence when trouble strikes. Community members need to speak up during police investigations.

Worse still is the unfair image such incidents give the entire community. A gunshot is heard and "every person of colour is blamed, though the vast majority are taxpayers, working and meeting the bills and raising up good families," I told Burnett. But I believe in being positive, and I pointed out that many young people, such as my grandchildren and thousands of others, are attending university or college and advancing their career opportunities.

They are people like Bassel Ali, a nineteen-year-old McMaster student who won an award in my name for his work in eliminating racial discrimination. These are the stories that are often left out of the headlines. This is the new generation that is ready to take up the torch. The fact they are prepared to meet the challenge is, I think, a fitting tribute to the memories of Coretta and Martin Luther King.

It's not idle chatter to point out that there is still too much deep-seated racism among us. To illustrate, I'll end this chapter with a letter I received a few years ago. I hesitated to run it out of concern that it might somehow embolden the letter writer and other bigots like him. However, I decided to include it because it so clearly illustrated the pathetic, narrow "thinking" of a small contingent of people. Keep in mind this was sent to a seventy-one-year-old man who had served his country in wartime and served publicly in Parliament. This letter followed me being named, along with a couple of dozen others, as special trade envoy for the Province of Ontario by Bob Rae.

[Received Feb. 8, 1993]

Taking a job as agent the Gov't. Fucking lovely. You can't get by on Pensions? Greedy? You NIGGER piece of shit. Your Prostituting your position. They Probably only gave Lt. Govrs' job because you were a Smart Ass Nigger. Well, your proving Tax-Payers Right! Greedy — More Big Bucks? Wife like to shop? Is she White or Black. Probably white eh? NO Black Woman Good Enough For You? You + Wife Are Trash — Rich Trash eh! I seen you on TV. Respected you at times. Your Still a Slave Being Bought AGAIN! Hope you have a "STROKE". Wind up in a Wheelchair! Will Look Good on You. God Punishes Those Who are Greedy! What you gunna do with extra money — "Open up a chain of CAR-WASHES? FUCK YOU!

Unsigned of course, the blank mark of a coward.

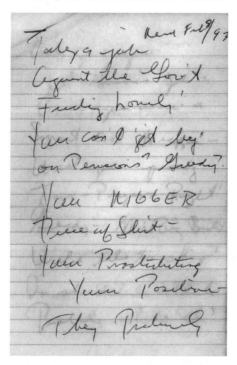

The racist letter I received in 1993.

CHAPTER 17

Diversions — The Arts and Sports

The perks of public activity include exposure to many facets of life, from the wide spectrum of issues before Parliament to the diversions of the arts and sports. I've enjoyed them all. The arts and sports have played a special part in my life. They have provided not just entertainment but also contact with people who have become special to me.

When it comes to the arts, I've had the honour of serving on the board of such a revered organization as the Shaw Festival in Niagara-on-the-Lake, but my interest and involvement goes deeper. We have outstanding performing arts activities in Hamilton, and Toronto offers more still. Indeed, in our part of the province — and I am looking west to Stratford as well — we have a dynamic and extensive arts community that may well be unparalleled in the world.

It's through the arts that I've met and made great friends, and it's through sharing such joys that our relationships continue to thrive. For instance, there are Michael and Mary Romeo, whom I met at the opera in Hamilton in the mid-1980s when I was lieutenant-governor. Michael was president of Opera Hamilton's board of directors at the time, and they were hosting me at that evening's performance of Gaetano Donizetti's *Lucia di Lammermoor*. I was still relatively new to opera, and at one point I leaned over to Mary and told her I'd always loved the piece but had had no idea what it was. I think that honest observation opened the door to our friendship.

Later that evening, the Romeos escorted me backstage to meet the performers, but they were caught a little off guard when I stopped and chatted as much with members of the stage crew as with the stars of the performance. I thanked all the people who were involved in making the performance a success. That was a lesson in my thinking that I think captured the Romeos' respect: Everybody matters.

The value of the arts cannot be calculated, but governments routinely have to make decisions on arts funding and sometimes tend to favour one form over another. It isn't an easy call. The arts are complex, and they all want government help. Without music and theatre, our lives would be diminished. Experiencing them both, live in a theatre, is a special treat. The arts bring people together, and the main thing is that the shared experience opens doors of communication.

Whether it's opera, chamber music, jazz, the Shaw Festival, or the Stratford Festival, I love to attend such performances. But we must remember the talent before us is achieved only after years of hard work and hardship. Performers have to love their craft and find it fulfilling because for many of them the monetary rewards are merely enough to scratch out an existence. Yet they are rich in other ways. The satisfaction of doing what you love is priceless. So many people who want happiness find that it eludes them because they choose employment based on compensation, not fulfillment. High-powered jobs often bring stress and frustration. People beat their brains out for the bottom line. A lot of people have realized that and are much happier doing what they want. I like to watch people performing their trade, doing the thing they love. And I'd say I'm not picky about these things. I'm not a critic.

Another great friendship in my life that was forged through exposure to the arts is the one I share with Ed, Anne, and David Mirvish. I've known that remarkable family for a couple of decades now; I first met them in my role as lieutenant-governor, when I attended many of their theatre premieres.

I got to know Anne especially well because I sat for her so she could sculpt my bust in clay. She said it was such an honour to be sculpting me (she said she was "proud and privileged"), but the honour for me was equal, since Anne chose only people who truly interested her. She didn't need to crank out pieces to keep food on the table.

Her approach is to draw out her subjects and engage their thoughts so the art can best capture the person. She was brilliant at that. She would tease me sometimes because I would close my eyes for a brief rest, and then she'd be right back at me, asking questions and pushing me. We talked about everything. She used to say she really didn't have an interest in politics and didn't understand all the ins and outs of that game, but of course she did. She is a very intelligent woman who loves a good conversation.

Anne and Ed were very fond of Yvonne. When she died, I was in a deep state of despair and worried about whether I could carry on. Among other things, it made me acutely aware of my age. I remember one time complaining to Anne that I was getting old. She set me straight. She said, "We're not old, we're just getting older." There's a beautiful, subtle distinction there. The former suggests an end; the latter says there's more to come.

On more than one occasion, Anne told me I had done great things for the black community in our country. Coming from her, a comment like that carried a deeper significance. I know that she faced anti-Semitism growing up in Hamilton during her teen years. She was once turned down for a job at a music store because she was Jewish. Another time, she won a singing contest at which the audience chose the winner, but the bandleader refused to let her sing with them. Anne told me she ran home crying. Imagine doing that to a teenage girl! Yet she was bigger than all that and distinguished between the evil people and the decent ones. In the end, in Hamilton, she had more non-Jewish friends than Jewish.

I understand she was great singer — and I must say she still is beautiful — though Ed didn't want her singing in public after they were married. How good was she? In one contest, Anne was chosen as the most promising singer from among sixty other contestants — by none other than Percy Faith.

As for Ed, I can't help but respect a person who worked so hard for his well-earned success. His father died when Ed was just fifteen, and Ed went on to built a successful business with no formal training. He and Anne started their first store with $377. As Anne likes to say, Ed's business acumen was learned on the job, and you always learn more from what goes wrong than from what goes right.

As a good friend of the Mirvishes, I continue to attend major theatre openings in Toronto, thanks in large part to their son, David. In March 2006, I saw the world premiere of *The Lord of the Rings* and was very impressed. Perhaps I'm soft because I love the theatre, but the critics weren't so kind to the play and it did close after a rather short run. But then, they were wrong about productions such as *The Phantom of the Opera* and *Les Misérables*, so I take them with a grain of salt.

One trait I have tried to maintain throughout my life — whether I was a student, lawyer, politician, the Queen's representative, or university chancellor — is that I would not let healthy debate or challenges linger in my mind. Nothing productive comes from that, only debilitating grudges. If you were to canvass my friends, I expect you would discover I've had disagreements or verbal dustups with a tidy number of them. In Parliament, we'd engage in some pretty energetic jousting with those on the other side of the House ... then we would go out to dinner.

A more recent example of this came about in my role as a member of the board of Shaw Festival at Niagara-on-the-Lake. Another board member at the time, Greg Aziz, wasn't showing up at board meetings, and his participation was valuable for the success of the operation. He was busy, I was certain, although I hadn't met him yet. Nevertheless, I picked up the phone one evening and introduced myself, then proceeded to chide him over his lack of attendance. Now, Greg is chairman, chief executive officer, and president of National Steel Car, so I wasn't chastising some schoolboy. (Actually, Greg says I "busted his ass.") It wasn't a confrontation, but rather a challenge; strong people like Greg respond to such things, and he did. The issue discussed and resolved, we went on to become very good friends. I often have dinner with him and his wife, Irene, and we also go to the theatre from time to time. On my ability to twist arms, Greg once remarked that if I called from Halifax and asked him to drive out and get me, he would. But I only twist arms for a good cause, or if I need a ride.

My involvement in both the arts and sports is not a contradiction. Quite the contrary; they have a common link. They both provide, among other things, entertainment, an important diversion from the stresses of daily life, and a valuable means to expand our scope as human beings. Over the last few years, one of the real joys I've had has been chairing the Toronto Raptors Foundation and working with people such as executive director Bev Deeth and her team. During that time, basketball has become my favourite sport, aided by the fact my granddaughters, Erika and Marissa, both played the game well, and they and their mother, Joyce, love to watch it. Beyond that, however, the foundation allows me to continue to do good work in the community. I know cynics might choose to look askance at the efforts of such organizations, but the Raptors and the Toronto Maple Leafs gave more than $2 million back to the community in 2005, with special emphasis on kids in distress. Why shouldn't successful organizations make such efforts?

My role with the Raptors organization serves a wider social and cultural purpose, I believe. As Maple Leaf Sports and Entertainment president Richard Peddie has adroitly pointed out, pro basketball, while having a preponderance of young black men on the courts, is becoming more and more multicultural as players from Europe, Canada, and South America begin to make it in the NBA. The Raptors have also been leaders in getting blacks into management. A good example is Wayne Embry, senior adviser to the Raptors president, who served as interim general manager after Rob Babcock was fired. In fact, the Raptors' first general manager, former Detroit Pistons star Isiah Thomas, is black, as is the club's current head coach, Sam Mitchell.

From time to time I'll visit the Raptors dressing room, generally to say hello and perhaps cheer up the players if they've lost a game. Oh yes, and for another reason — to see what it feels like to be the shortest person in the room. That hasn't happened too many times in my life. My relationship with the team is somewhat arm's-length, and I wouldn't say I get to know the players intimately, but I garner a certain amount of respect, I think, as "that distinguished-looking old man who comes in here from time to time."

When the Raptors invited me to chair the foundation, I let it be known that if I felt strongly about something, I would speak my mind, no matter what team executives or others thought. I haven't turned away from confrontation over my beliefs in a long, long time, and I wasn't about to change. As far as I can tell, they embraced my approach. As a matter of fact, when Larry Tannenbaum and his group took over from Steve Stavro, I told Larry I was ready to submit my resignation. Larry said, "Linc, you have our confidence and you have the job for as long as you want it." That was nice to hear and comforting, since often the new broom sweeps clean.

I have to admit the pleasure I derive from this position is far greater than what's expected of me in my official capacity. We meet formally four times a year to review our fundraising priorities. I do occasional speaking engagements or accompany players on things like visits to hospitals. Bev, the executive director of the Raptors Foundation and director of community development for the Raptors and the Toronto Maple Leafs, helps me manage my time for the foundation. We figure my formal appearances now average one or two a month. That's hardly daunting. And then I get to go to basketball games.

I wouldn't say I'm a student of the game, but it is good entertainment and a remarkable experience watching these great athletes from my courtside seat. Back when I was in full voice and my granddaughters were playing basketball, I would have quite a time at their games. I didn't hesitate to holler, or maybe jump up and applaud; hopefully I didn't embarrass them too much. I can't jump around anymore, but I put my cane to good use by waving it in approval of good plays or using it to threaten the opposition.

One gratifying experience I had as a result of this role came in February 2004. February is Black History Month, and in recognition of that the team invited Reuben "Hurricane" Carter and me to address the Raptors players. We wanted to send the message that, as high-profile individuals, they could lead and make a difference in their communities. Judging by the success of the foundation, which generates a great deal of its income from golf tournaments, bowling competitions, and similar events in which players participate, I know our message is getting through.

Sports has such potential for stimulating and uniting our communities, whether through professional initiatives such as the Raptors Foundation or with kids at the local arena, ball field, gym, or soccer pitch. During my tenure as lieutenant-governor, I met and became instant friends with sports columnist George Gross. I can't recall the event George was attending at Queen's Park, but it is safe to say our interest in the province's youth and athletics dovetailed nicely.

I was determined to focus on youth and education during my term, while George had been committed for years to disabled kids and Variety Village. For decades, Variety Village has offered programming and services for individuals with special needs. It's a world-class sports training and fitness operation and a wonderful fit with George's sports writing. For more than twenty years, through his column in the *Toronto Sun*, he has led the annual fundraising drive, which has generated more than $1 million for Variety Village. I've found great rewards in my regular visits to the Village, and I have George to thank for that in many ways.

George's interest in young people knew no limits. One of the people he became close friends with was Canadian sprinter Ben Johnson, who electrified the world. Johnson was eventually caught in a doping scandal during the 1988 Olympics in Seoul, South Korea. Before that, though, I

I was on hand to congratulate Ben Johnson when he won Canada's outstanding athlete award in 1987. I had offered to mentor Ben at the behest of good friend George Gross, but unfortunately he was not interested in the offer.

think George's well-honed journalist's instinct told him this was a troubled young man who needed guidance. George asked me if I would help, and naturally I said I would. George, I think, felt that getting guidance from another black person, one who could be regarded as successful and accomplished, might perhaps draw out the notoriously quiet and shy Johnson. From a personal standpoint, and in no way condoning drugging by athletes, I think he was singled out from among a cast of other competitors doing precisely the same thing.

Sadly, and I think to George's profound disappointment, Johnson simply wasn't interested. I'm not sure what I would have said to him, nor am I saying I could have helped him avoid the difficulties he later faced. But when there are willing, helping hands, it is sad when they're turned down and sadder still when the outcome isn't favourable.

CHAPTER 18

On the Issues of the Day

Same-sex marriage has been a controversial issue in Canada and Parliament in recent years, but it doesn't bother me one bit. The opponents say you've got to believe in the Bible. Well, they used to use the Bible to justify lynching, too, so there goes that argument. You've got to change with the times. Besides, women don't need men anymore. Life goes on without having to get into bed with the other sex. In matters such as this, we have to remind ourselves that God is a forgiving God and not a mean old man.

As a fighter for fairness and equal rights for so long in my life, I believe fervently in the equality of the sexes. Women had been getting shut out for years and now they're big shots in corporations, professions, the arts, and all walks of life, which is the way it should be. Look at our university, the University of Guelph. Its student population used to be 40 percent women, 60 percent men, and now that ratio has been more than reversed. Now what is needed is for the gap to be eliminated in the area of equal pay for work of equal value.

As well, if you don't accept equality of the sexes, then you are a dying breed. Women today can say, "I'll live with you, but I don't need you." Some people have a problem with people living together, but if you live together it is not a sin as far as I am concerned … just make sure you've got the legal stuff looked after.

Politics is changing. We need more common sense, more thinking along the lines of Mike Harris's Common Sense Revolution. I say that as a pragmatist, so I won't say that Harris was right with all his policies, but the idea of common sense was one people could relate to. Sometimes you have the courage to ask yourself, "Is this the right thing to do?"

When it comes to religion, for one thing, you can't live in the seventh century or seventeenth century and apply it to the twenty-first century. I would have gone to Martin Luther King's church every Sunday. I think churches have to smarten up. You can't have that right-wing religion or you won't get young people. And you must have music. You go to church to get inspired, and when you don't get inspired you don't keep coming.

That was not the case with Rev. Dr. Francis Chisholm. When he arrived in 1967 as minister of Stewart Memorial Church in Hamilton, Yvonne and I developed a close friendship with him. He helped shape our spiritual lives, and, because churches serve this function so often, he influenced our social lives as well.

This was a year or so before my first election to Parliament, so my time was soon to become more and more in demand. Nevertheless, whenever I could, I continued to sing with the choir at Stewart, where I'm sure my deep, booming voice was appreciated. From time to time, I'd be called upon to do solos at Rev. Chisholm's beckoning, so I imagine I turned in an acceptable performance. I also served as clerk at Stewart Memorial. This meant handling records and legal matters, so I was able to draw on my profession. Rev. Chisholm and the church community appreciated this. I also felt it was important to reach out and engage our parishioners, particularly our younger ones, since they are critical to the future of the church.

Rev. Chisholm's calling has brought him in close contact with our family. He married Keith and Joyce (their wedding reception was held at the officers' mess in Hamilton in the James Street Armouries) and he baptized my granddaughters. He also handled Yvonne's funeral and was a tower of strength at the time of her death.

I would have been a good minister. I find it easy to speak, or at least I found it easier and easier as I moved through my political and professional lives. I haven't flaunted that, but I do want people to respect me. I'm a communicator, and that's why I won five elections. I'd ask people who heard me speak what I had said, and they would know. They had heard. To be heard because you have to touch people with your emotions.

But now people don't have time for church. They're not inspired. The reason I have fallen away from formal religion is that I have not been inspired. But I have a good relationship with God, especially after my wife died and I got my anger out. The older I got, the more I realized I was mortal, so I tried to lead an exemplary, clean life. I had to. You can't mess up as a role model.

I was on hand in 1987 to help Stewart Memorial celebrate fifty years as a non-denominational congregation. I said, "When I listen to a summary of this church's history, I think of words like *leadership, courage, conviction,* and *hard work.*" These are traits I clearly regard as the underpinnings of greatness and success, and they are the ones I have valued throughout my life, whether it involved politics, fighting racism, or even faith.

I still pray every day, three or four times. I pray and talk to my wife. I pray and thank God for allowing me to reach eighty-four. As for other faiths, I believe in live and let live. I don't condemn any other religion. I am a Christian, but I am not saying mine is best.

As for news issues, I continue to follow events and keep up on the issues of the day. I read several newspapers and keep an eye on television news as well. One of the more interesting events occurred in the aftermath of Hurricane Katrina and its devastation of the Gulf Coast, especially New Orleans.

With such a large black community in the area being displaced by the flooding Katrina caused, some people linked the federal and local governments' poor handling of the situation to racism. I think most blacks in that area think it was racism. But look at Andrew Young, former U.S. ambassador to the United Nations and mayor of Atlanta. He said boldly and bravely at the time that you can't say it was racism; what the cameras were showing were all blacks, but there were a lot of poor white people in the same predicament, and they were desperate, too, you just didn't see them. So I question the TV tactics.

I find it hard to believe the government didn't come to the aid of people because they were black, notwithstanding their poor track record. I don't think it would have been done in fifteen minutes if they were all white either. Yes, as for equality, we're not there yet, but I can't see saying that racism existed in this case. I don't forget that that country is actually two countries, black and white, but my view in this case is that it was incompetence at its best. However, you can't tell that to the blacks down there because they like to play the race card. Furthermore, President George W. Bush would have been smarter to hire some high-ranking black official to lead the recovery and inquiry.

Still, Bush has appointed a lot of black people to positions of power. Look at Condoleezza Rice and Colin Powell. They've succeeded in a white world. I identify more with Powell; he is talented, and people want him to run for president, but it never gets very far due to the fact that there are states that don't believe in equal rights, at least in terms of voting for a black president. I'm a politician, and I know a lot about politics. Outsiders will take advantage of the race card. My issue is whether people are prepared to back him, and he is right to be skeptical in that regard.

I'd rather go out a winner than a loser, and I believe Powell thinks the same way. Go out on top. What does he need politics for? I have a lot of respect for him. He has Jamaican roots, like me. I admire him because I can imagine and understand the pressure he was under. A lot of people wanted him to be a gunslinger, but he wasn't prepared to behave in a way that was unacceptable to him or that could not be justified by the facts. I'd like to know how deep that rift is within the Bush administration.

The changing attitudes that brought Colin Powell to prominence in the U.S. are at play in Canada as well. We are a nation of people of many origins, not just from British and European stock. I was pleasantly surprised when Prime Minister Paul Martin chose Michaelle Jean, who was born in Haiti, to succeed Adrienne Clarkson as governor general. I didn't think I would see something like that for quite some time. I think she was a perfect choice. She's black, beautiful, and intelligent and will make her mark. Diversity is working in Canada, and Paul Martin showed wisdom in making his choice.

Proportional representation in Parliament is another issue gaining more attention in Canada. Its purpose is to more closely align the percentage of seats a party wins in the House of Commons with its percentage of the popular vote. That is not the case in the current first-past-the-post system, where smaller parties such as the Greens and even the New Democrats are often under-represented in terms of the popular vote. For instance, in the 2004 federal election, the Green Party received more than five hundred thousand votes yet did not elect a single MP.

Meanwhile, fewer Liberal voters in Atlantic Canada alone elected twenty-two Liberal MPs.

While the two major parties, the Conservatives and the Liberals, almost always gain more seats from first-past-the-post than the popular vote would justify, they, too, are under-represented in some regions. For instance, the Liberals are under-represented in Western Canada, while the Conservatives suffer the same fate in major cities such as Toronto, Montreal, and Vancouver. Proportional representation or a combination of it and the traditional constituency races, which the Law Commission of Canada is advocating, can help balance out those inequities.

Let's face it, with few exceptions most voters cast their ballots for a party or its leader. Local candidates are most often viewed as the embodiment of national party policy (unless, of course, you are Lincoln M. Alexander in Hamilton West). There's nothing wrong with casting your ballot for the party rather than the candidate. The problem is with our electoral system.

A party that receives 25 percent of the national vote should occupy 25 percent of the seats in Parliament. It's a proven system that has been in use in European nations and others around the globe for decades. New Zealand switched to mixed-member proportional representation in 1993. The idea is being promoted by groups across Canada, including Fair Vote Canada, a multi-partisan citizens' campaign for voting system reform. I'm among a group of people that backs Fair Vote Canada's call for the government to initiate a public consultation process on election reform and hold a referendum so Canadians can decide which voting system they prefer.

CHAPTER 19

Facing the Future

A few days after my eighty-fourth birthday in January 2006, the provincial government announced it was going ahead with the construction of the Alexander Pavilion — named after Yvonne — at the St. Peter's Hospital site on Maplewood Avenue in Hamilton. A $1.3-million grant would get the job started, and more funds were on the way for the $21.9-million state-of-the art facility. It was the culmination, as the *Hamilton Spectator* reported, of a "20-year mission to upgrade a weathered hospital wing that houses fifty of Hamilton's most complex Alzheimer patients." Yvonne had been a patient at St. Peter's, so it was an emotional time when I attended the announcement ceremony. I called it "one of the most wonderful institutions there is" and said I was proud that it would be named after Yvonne and me. It was a wonderful belated birthday gift. With the year starting off with great news like that, how can I help but be optimistic about the future?

At eighty-four, I still don't plan to slow down, even though my legs haven't made it easy for me in the last few years. In the fall of 2005, on top of meeting my commitments as chancellor of the University of Guelph, I still found time and energy for a train trip on my own to Halifax, a trip by bus to Niagara Falls for a day of gambling, regular day trips to places such as Port Dover for a perch dinner, and a vacation in Cuba.

The five-day Halifax trip was a good chance to get away from the fax machine, the phone, and other things. I wanted a break. It was nostalgic, too, in a way, because I used to campaign there, beginning with the federal election of 1968. There is a long black history in the Halifax area, and Nova Scotia was always an important place to promote racial harmony. I loved the trip, except for the pain. From Montreal to Halifax, it's eighteen hours by train. The problem was that my compartment was so tiny. By the time I arrived, I felt as if I were near death.

Now that my life is in its later stages, it gives me a good feeling to see what people think of me and what I've done. Lots of people on the train recognized me and wanted to have their pictures taken with me. Some people are always in a rush, but I have to stop and talk. I tell my friends that, and they're always trying to pull me away. The people on the train were saying to their kids, "This is a famous man. He has a highway named after him. He's a former governor general." I'd correct them and tell them I was a former lieutenant-governor. Then they'd want pictures with their families. I just wish my mom and dad could see that.

On the day trip to Port Dover with a couple of pals to sample the famous perch, we saw two bishops and an auxiliary bishop from Hamilton. I quipped to my friends and others in the restaurant, "We are very blessed today because we have three bishops here with us."

My interest in the trip to Cuba arose when my close friends Austin and Herta Murray began talking about how they'd like to go and see Havana's renowned architecture. Herta had last visited there in the pre-Castro days when Batista was in power. The Canadian ambassador to Cuba, Alexandra Bugailiskis, heard about my interest and invited me to visit. Five of us went on the trip — me, my daughter-in-law, Joyce, my granddaughter Erika, and the Murrays. I found the Cuban people to be warm, gracious, and kind. They greet you with a smile, and it is genuine, not a façade. They're willing to share with you what they have. I've never been treated so magnificently.

Lieutenant-Governor James Bartleman, a former Canadian ambassador to Cuba, gave me a hand-carved rosewood box engraved with the words *Ontario* and *Canada* to present to Fidel Castro, but Castro was too sick to meet me. Apparently he was admitted to hospital the night of a reception at the Canadian embassy. Instead, I met his brother, Ramon, who is eighty-two and still likes flirting with the girls. I also enjoyed a reunion with Tony Vigoa, an old friend who was Cuban consul general during my lieutenant-governor days. He had invited me many times to visit Cuba, but every time I suggested it to the federal government, which grants approval for out-of-country trips, I'd be told I shouldn't go, as federal officials were worried about upsetting the Americans. I spoke at the University of Havana about multiculturalism and racism in Canada and the rights we have in our constitution relating to freedom, justice, and tolerance. About twenty-five Canadian students were on hand to hear my speech.

I love Niagara Falls and take the bus there a couple of times a year to visit the casino, although on one of my last trips I got on the wrong bus and ended up doing a lot of walking, which was hard on my legs. I like the atmosphere in the casino. People are screaming and yelling. It's the ambiance of the place and the good food. I have the buffet and I meet a lot of people, and a lot of people know who I am. It's nice not to be forgotten. I also go to Flamboro Downs, but there aren't as many gambling attractions there. As for the gambling issue, I think you have to build casinos. Governments take money from tobacco and alcohol, but they're not supposed to take it from gambling? It can be good for the economy if properly managed.

I've worked hard through my life to get and maintain something very fundamental and everyone's right — respect. In my way of thinking, a primary way to draw respect for oneself is to be prepared to return it in kind. It generates loyalty, commitment, and productivity. My friend Mary Romeo jokes that people who have worked with me in my various roles have shown a huge loyalty to me. But that, like respect, is a two-way street. I'll give you an example. These days, my drivers are like a lifeline. Late one night one of my drivers went off the road several times and onto the curb of the highway, where they have put those ridges in the pavement to make a noise to alert drivers — bumpity, bumpity, bumpity. The driver admitted he had been nodding off. The people who were with me expressed concern about our safety, the story got out, and more friends and acquaintances urged me to let the driver go. Well, for one thing, this had never happened before, so I saw it as an isolated incident. But more importantly, that industrious guy was working two other jobs to better his and his family's prospects. To me such a person deserved support and understanding, not dismissal. I would not let him go.

I continue to keep busy with my duties as chancellor. Our university has forged an academic relationship with Humber College that has expanded the scope of the University of Guelph and delivered some unanticipated pleasures to me. As my friends know and as has been related here, I am a jazz lover, and it just so happens that Humber turns out some of the best jazz musicians in our country today. While I was somewhat aware of the music component at Humber, this old brain still gets a huge volume of information to process, so when Alastair invited me to a performance at Humber one evening, I was expecting to sit somewhat agonizingly through a modest performance by admirably earnest students. Was I wrong. I was transported completely by the skill and depth of talent of these young musicians. It was positively invigorating. Indeed, they would have been wise to have me check my cane because when I'm in the midst of such a musical transportation it tends to become like a conductor's baton, though far more dangerous. To the best of my knowledge, I didn't put anyone's eye out, fortunately. It was such fun, and I can tell you with certainty that the future of jazz music in this country could not be brighter.

I have more evidence of that, too, and it just so happens it's another example of the great things at my university. For my eighty-fourth birthday, Alastair hosted a small dinner at the president's house at the University of Guelph. (By the way, there's another thing, our chef is the former chief chef at the Vatican, Domenico Ranalli, so I take great pains not to miss a dinner at the university!) For this birthday dinner, one of the school's physics professors was engaged to sing. If you haven't heard it already, remember this name: Diane Nalini. Not only does this lovely woman, a Rhodes scholar, have a beautiful voice, she was kind enough to share the mike with yours truly throughout her performance. We cooked, though I might be biased in saying that, but it was nice to dust off the old pipes and belt out a few favourites. I had had some polyps removed from my throat in the fall of 2005, so it was nice to put the old voice to the test. It may not be strong enough now to draw crowds the size of those in Africa in 1960, but I was able to manoeuvre my way through the tunes fairly stylishly. My president tells me I was right on key. In fact, I think Diane and I should lay down a few cool duets on her next album. Gimme a call.

When I'm home in Hamilton, I manage to keep busy and entertained. One day I went to big-time wrestling in Toronto, and I had my picture taken with Hulk Hogan. We had box seats. Those wrestling people sure know how to market, and their wrestlers are great athletes. It was great entertainment.

While I'm Canadian to the core, I must say these days I appreciate the milder weather if only because it adds an element of freedom in my daily life. In particular, I can hop — well, lumber — onto my motorized scooter and head out on the town. I love working my way up Main and King Streets in Hamilton and chatting with folks on the street. One of my favourite destinations is Denninger's Foods of the World. Along with the food and camaraderie I find there, I've also been privileged to become close friends with the business's owners, the Murrays, my co-travellers to Cuba.

Denninger's is a busy place and I meet lots of people there, from students and business people to politicians such as Hamilton Mayor Larry DiIanni and former mayor Bob Morrow. And I love the food: I'll tell you my favourites, in hopes my doctor isn't reading — bacon, steaks, sausages, cakes, tortes, and cinnamon Danish. Oh, yes, and cocoa made by my sweethearts on the lunch counter.

These days, I have help around home — someone to cut the grass and a housekeeper — but I do all my own cooking. I love steak, but I take cholesterol pills among a lengthy collection of other medications. I take pills for gout, for my bladder, and for memory (I have been particularly vigilant with these while working on this book). In total, I take six or seven pills morning and night. That's important, with the busy agenda I still maintain. In the early part of 2006, I was still averaging had twenty engagements a month, ranging from business meetings to the opera, from chamber concerts to gala dinners. I stay busy because it keeps me going. I want to be active. If I had nothing to do when I got up in the morning, I think I'd drop dead.

Family life has always been important to me, and it continues to be in retirement. I have loved watching my granddaughters compete in sports, at which they excel. They've been active from an early age, and I think that is important. You start to develop concepts of participation and teamwork. I'm not sure my granddaughters have always liked me being at games because I like to yell a lot. But it is a great source of pride for me to see them playing and enjoying it.

My granddaughters and I are very tight and they are always around here. I was out on my scooter one beautiful spring day in 2006 — I love my scooter and the freedom of movement it gives me — and I was stopped by these two beautiful young women who were out shopping for sunglasses. It was my granddaughters, and it's so exciting to meet up with them by accident. So we did lunch. They are good girls and have good grades, and I'm so lucky to have them in my life. For Yvonne, they were the loves of her life. She was a very happy grandmother, and they loved her too. I see both of them trying to be like her — graceful and honourable. Fortunately, they both were able to get to know her well before she died.

At eighty-four, I'm still enthusiastically looking to the future, but I also fondly remember the past, particularly the family members and friends whom I have cherished, from Yvonne and our family to John and Marge Millar and so many more, many of them chronicled in these pages. So if, after reading these pages, you conclude all of these personal relationships are important to me, it's because they are. These friends and family have enriched my life. They have helped make me become the person I am. They have helped me make a difference. What might that difference be? Well, three or four years ago, a feature story on me in the *Hamilton Spectator* analyzed the short form of my name that people often use — Linc. The article compared it to the word *link* and said its definition was "a connecting structure" and "a torch used to light a darkened street."

I liked that. I intend to continue to be that torch, right up to the moment I take my last breath, for there is such fulfillment in doing the right thing. And then it will be okay, because when I get to heaven — and I don't think that's hoping too much — there will be two special people to meet me. I await a glorious reunion with Yvonne, the love of my life. And there will be my mother, who I know will meet me, and she'll tell me I've done well. Because I went to school, this little black boy.

EPILOGUE

~

As I was going through the final stages of preparing this book, I received one of the most interesting honours I've received, and one I'm particularly proud of because of how it came to be. In June 2006 I was named the greatest Hamiltonian of all time.

The search for the greatest Hamiltonian was a component in a *Hamilton Spectator* feature series called the Hamilton Memory Project. Now, I'm a pretty smart fellow, and I make a point of not automatically taking things at face value. Indeed, if one were so inclined, one could raise an eyebrow and perhaps minimize the importance of the award. I myself had some concerns with respect to assessing individuals by way of a contest, but the community genuinely seemed keen on the project.

I know why newspapers run contests and produce special series. They need readers: readers mean advertising, and advertising means profits. So newspapers are always on the lookout for fresh and different content to offer readers, along with delivering their regular and hopefully reliable diet of news and features.

All that said, what made this special was that the winner was determined by a vote of readers, mainly fellow Hamiltonians. For about sixty years these people have been so much more than co-habitants of an urban centre. They have been colleagues, acquaintances, constituents, and friends. They have, in fact, been an extended family that opened its collective arms and embraced me, transforming me quickly from being an outsider to being one of the clan.

The contest involved several rounds of elimination, based primarily on names suggested by the *Spectator*. After the first introduction of nominees, readers were invited to add to the list, and they did. It was an impressive list of fine people who had done so much for our community, and it was gratifying to be among them. Eventually the list was down to five — Arthur Weisz, medical pioneer Elizabeth Bagshaw, maestro Boris Brott, influential community leader Thomas McQuesten, and me. Eventually along with me in the final was Weisz, a remarkable man who is a Holocaust survivor and who came to Canada with little more than a suitcase before becoming one of Ontario's largest landlords. While his business acumen certainly set him apart, I believe it is how he quietly and effectively used his success to contribute vastly to the betterment of Hamilton through charitable efforts. It is a testament to the city of Hamilton that the finalists in this project were a Holocaust survivor and a black man. Does that not, in a nutshell, capture the essence of Canada, Canadians, and what we aspire to?

When I wrote near the end of this book that Hamilton was my city and that I was never going to leave it, the greatest Hamiltonian contest was just getting started. Now, of course, I express those sentiments stronger than ever, if that's possible.

APPENDIX

Curriculum Vitae

Colonel the Honourable Lincoln M. Alexander
P.C., C.C., K.St.J., O.Ont., C.D., Q.C.,
B.A., LL.B. LL.D. (Hon), D.S. Litt. (Hon)

Chancellor, University of Guelph, 1991–present

Served as Chairman of the Canadian Race Relations Foundation, 1996–2003

Lieutenant Governor of Ontario, 1985–1991

Born Toronto, Ontario, January 21, 1922, son of the late Lincoln MacCauley Alexander of St. Vincent and the Grenadines, and the late Mae Rose Alexander (née Royale) of Jamaica.

Served with Royal Canadian Air Force (Corporal) 1942–1945. Honorary Colonel 2 Tactical Aviation Wing, 1985–1991.

Educated at McMaster University, B.A. 1949. Graduated Osgoode Hall Law School, 1953. Appointed Queen's Counsel, 1965. Former partner in firm of Millar, Alexander, Tokiwa and Isaacs, 1963–1979.

Elected to House of Commons as the Member of Parliament for Hamilton West (Progressive Conservative), June 25, 1968. Re-elected 1972, 1974, 1979, 1980. Served as Federal Minister of Labour, 1979.

Observer to the United Nations 1976 and 1978. Former member of Inter-Parliamentary Union (Canadian Group); former member of Commonwealth Parliamentary Association (Canadian Branch); former member of Canadian NATO Parliamentary Association; former member of Canada-United States Parliamentary Delegation.

Served as Chairman of the Workers' Compensation Board (Ontario), June 1, 1980–September 19, 1985.

Honours and Awards

- St. Ursula Award, 1969

- Appointed to The Most Venerable Order of the Hospital of St. John of Jerusalem: Officer, 1981; Commander (Brother), 1983; Knight of Grace, 1985

- Man of the Year Award by Ethnic Press Council of Canada Inc., 1982

- Inducted into McMaster University Distinguished Alumni Gallery, 1982

- Caribana Cultural Committee, Cultural Achievement Award, 1984

- House of Commons, Certificate of Service Award, 1984

- Honorary Counsel, Stewart Memorial Church, Hamilton, September 20, 1985

- John G. Diefenbaker Memorial Foundation Award, November 1985

- Designated a Paul Harris Fellow, The Rotary Foundation of Rotary International, 1986

- Received the 36th Annual Humanitarian Award of Beth Sholom Brotherhood, May 1986

- Honouree of the Year, 1986 Hamilton Negev Dinner, Jewish National Fund of Canada

- Received the degree of Doctor of Laws (*honoris causa*) from each of the following universities:

    University of Toronto, June 1986
    McMaster University, November 1987
    University of Western Ontario, October 1988
    York University, November 1990
    Royal Military College, May 1991
    Queen's University, October 1992

- Awarded Boy Scout of Canada Silver Acorn by the Governor General of Canada, November 1988

- Government of Ontario Provincial Sport Citation in the Humanities Category, 1988

- Kiwanis Foundation Outstanding Citizen Award and Kiwanis Foundation Mel Osborne Fellow, August 1989

- Honorary Senior Fellow, Renison College, University of Waterloo, 1989

- Thornhill Secondary School 1st Canadian Unity Award Recipient, 1989

- Human Relations Award Recipient, Canadian Council of Christians and Jews, 1989

- Honorary Chief of Police, Metropolitan Toronto Police, November 1989

- Honorary Fellow of the Canadian School of Management, 1989

- Lincoln M. Alexander Public School, Hamilton, 1989

- Armenian Community Centre of Toronto, Outstanding Canadian Award, June 1990

- Knight of the Military and Hospitaller Order of Saint Lazarus of Jerusalem, 1990

- As an Osgoode Hall graduate between the years 1889 and 1960, awarded LL.B. degree by the Senate of York University, June 1991

- Appointed to the honorary office of Commissioner of the Ontario Provincial Police, June 1, 1991

- Invested as Honorary Commander of the Ordo Sancti Constantini Magni, June 1991

- Installed as Chancellor of the University of Guelph, October 4, 1991

- Lincoln M. Alexander Public School, Ajax, 1992

- Appointed Officer of the Order of Ontario, March 1992

- Invested by President of Senegal as an Officer of National Order of the Lion, 1992

- Elected Honorary Bencher of the Law Society of Upper Canada, June 10, 1992

- Appointed Companion of the Order of Canada by His Excellency the Right Honourable R.J. Hnatyshyn, June 25, 1992

- Awarded Canada 125 Medal, November 1992

- Inducted into the Hamilton Gallery of Distinction, November 5, 1992

- Granted the Award of Merit by the City of Toronto, March 1993

- Received the Degree of Doctor of Sacred Letters from Trinity College, May 1993

- Elected Honorary Member of the Ontario Association of Chiefs of Police, June 1993

- Presented with the Sertoma Club of Hamilton Lester B. Pearson Award, May 10, 1994

- Appointed to the Most Venerable Order of the Hospital of St. John of Jerusalem, Knight of Justice, June 4, 1994

- Received Canadian Forces Decoration (CD), December 1994

- Appointed Honorary Chief of the York Regional Police, April 27, 1995

- Award of Excellence by Osgoode Hall Law School Alumni Association, 1996

- Recipient of the Toronto Onyx Lions Club 1996 Award

- Appointed Chairman of the Canadian Race Relations Foundation by the Prime Minister of Canada, the Right Honourable Jean Chrétien, 1996–2003

- Awarded Lifetime Achievement Award by Canadian Association of Black Lawyers, 1997

- Lincoln M. Alexander Parkway ("The Linc"), Hamilton, 1997

- Recipient of the Black History Month J. C. Holland Award, 1998

- Inducted to the Terry Fox Hall of Fame, 1998

- Recipient of the Government of Ontario Award for Outstanding Achievement in Human Rights, 1998

- Appointed Honorary Chief of Hamilton Wentworth Regional Police, May 10, 1999

- Presented with the Vice-Regal Badge of Service by the lieutenant-governor, January 1, 2000

- Lincoln M. Alexander Secondary School, Mississauga, 2000

- Received the Harry Jerome Award for Lifetime Achievement, 2001

- Appointed Honorary Fire Chief of Toronto Fire Services, June 2002

- Presented with the Golden Jubilee Medal by the governor general, August 28, 2002

- Presented with the Law Society Medal by the Law Society of Upper Canada, 2002

- Awarded a Fellow of Upper Canada College by Upper Canada College, September 2002

- Received Great Canadian National Leadership Award on National Flag Day, from Our Lady of Lourdes High School, February 14, 2003

- Canadian Race Relations Foundation Award for Lifetime Achievement, March 2003

- Appointed Chair, Ontario Heritage Foundation, April 1, 2004

- Former Honorary Ambassador for the 2010 Commonwealth Games bid

- Voted greatest Hamiltonian ever in survey conducted by the *Hamilton Spectator*, June 2006

Clubs and Associations

- Honorary Director of the Air Cadet League of Ontario (Ontario Committee)

- Honorary Director of the Ontario League of the Royal Canadian Army Cadets

- Honorary life member, the Navy League of Canada

- Honorary life member of the Ontario Chamber of Commerce

- Member and past president of Hamilton Optimist Club

- Member of Hamilton Lawyers Club

- Member of Wentworth County Law Association

- Member Canadian Bar Association

- Member of Scottish Rite, Hadji Temple Shrine, 33rd (PHA)

- Past president of International Association of Industrial Accident Boards and Commissions

- Former chair Canadian Race Relations Foundation

Currently

Serves on the Board of Governors and the Board of Trustees of the University of Guelph and is in fifth term as chancellor.

Serves on the board of the Doctor's Hospital, the Shaw Festival, the Royal Agricultural Winter Fair, the Chamber Works Ensemble of Hamilton, the Raptors Foundation, and the Ontario Heritage Trust. Also serves as a consultant to the board of George Weston Limited as a member of the Quebecor Ontario Advisory Board and as patron or honorary officer of several charitable organizations.

Married Yvonne Phyllis Harrison (deceased May 15, 1999) daughter of the late Robert Harrison and the late Edythe (née Lewis) Harrison, on September 10, 1948, in Hamilton. Has one son, Keith, and daughter-in-law, Joyce. Has two granddaughters, Erika and Marissa. Religious affiliation is Baptist. Hobbies include music and gardening.

INDEX